THE BRITISH INFANTRY

THE BRITISH INFANTRY 1660–1945

THE EVOLUTION OF A FIGHTING FORCE

by Frederick Myatt

BLANDFORD PRESS
POOLE · DORSET

First published in the U.K. 1983 by Blandford Press,
Link House, West Street, Poole, Dorset BH15 1LL

Distributed in the United States by
Sterling Publishing Co., Inc.
2 Park Avenue, New York, N.Y. 10016

British Library Cataloguing in Publication Data

ISBN 0 7137 1392 5

British Library Cataloguing in Publication Data

Myatt, Frederick
  The British infantry 1660-1945.
  1. Great Britain. *Army*—Infantry—History
  I. Title
  356'.11'0941   UA650

Typeset by Inforum Ltd, Portsmouth, U.K.
Printed in U.K. by Biddles Ltd, Guildford

CONTENTS

FOREWORD

BY MAJOR-GENERAL P.F.A. SIBBALD C.B., O.B.E.
DIRECTOR OF INFANTRY

The author is well known as a military historian and I am glad to be able to write a foreword to his latest interesting and much needed book. Most of the literature of my arm of the service has been written from a purely regimental point of view, so that it is refreshing to find a work which considers the British Infantry as an arm.

It deals primarily with progress, and in it the writer records the collective evolution of the Infantry mainly in terms of organization, fire power and tactics, although the vital human factor is not neglected. He uses the various battles and campaigns of our proud history to show how lessons have been learnt (if sometimes belatedly) and applied to meet the challenges of the future. The various reforms and reorganizations almost invariably met with fierce opposition from the traditionalists, yet in spite of this it is true to say that in virtually every case a better structure emerged.

The question of what motivates the infantry soldier in battle is discussed in the Introduction, and I am glad to say that the author, himself an infantryman of much experience, attributes a great deal to our regimental system, a sentiment with which I agree wholeheartedly. Although, like many British institutions, the system developed largely by chance, it has proved itself over the years to be the greatest strength of our arm of the service. Inevitably it is sometimes criticized, most often perhaps on the grounds that it is 'divisive', but this I feel is due to a misunderstanding of its purpose; certainly it is not a belief likely to be entertained for a moment by anyone who has actually seen a brigade of British Infantry in action.

I am now nearing the end of my service, which has spanned most of the post-war operations from Korea to Ulster and I look back on my career from private soldier to my present appointment, with pride and affection. It has been a great privilege and honour to serve all over the world with loyal and steadfast infantryman of high professional calibre, and I doubt if I could have had a more rewarding or happier life in any other profession. In particular I would like to pay tribute to the warrant officers, staff-sergeants and sergeants who form the backbone of the Army.

I commend this perceptive and informative book to all British infantrymen – and also to many others who would like a better understanding of the arm of the service in which I have been proud to serve.

Warminster 1983   Peter Sibbald

ACKNOWLEDGEMENTS

In assembling material, particularly for the last two chapters, it has been necessary to pick the brains of a number of friends, all infantrymen and all fighting soldiers with a wealth of experience, and I must take this opportunity of thanking them collectively. I am also grateful, as ever, to the Librarian and staff of the Ministry of Defence Library (Army & Central) for a great deal of help with this and other books in the last 20 years, and to successive commandants of the School of Infantry for the use of the library there. I must also thank Major-General P.F.A. Sibbald, C.B., O.B.E., Director of Infantry, for so kindly contributing the Foreword.

Certain of the books quoted in the text are still subject to copyright, and I must acknowledge my indebtedness to the following for their kind permission to quote from their works:

Michael Joseph (Clifford, H. *Letters and Sketches from the Crimea*)

Methuen & Co. Ltd. (Fuller, J.F.C. *Armament and History*)

Curtis Brown, London, on behalf of the estate of Major-General J.F.C. Fuller (Fuller, J.F.C. *British Light Infantry in the Eighteenth Century*)

INTRODUCTION

The British Infantry, considered as a force to be seriously reckoned with, was a relatively late arrival on the world military scene. It is true that the archers of the Hundred Years War made a notable contribution to the art of employing effective missile action on foot, but after them there was a long period when Britain virtually turned her back on Europe. During this time her interests were almost exclusively nautical and her land forces languished.

The Civil Wars of the mid seventeenth century saw the emergence of a formidable body of infantry culminating in the New Model Army, and it was their sons and grandsons who first established (or perhaps it would be more correct to say re-established) a European reputation during the War of the Spanish Succession.

It so happened that this national rise to prominence coincided very closely with a universal increase in the importance of infantry. This change, which resulted from improved fire power and more flexible systems of tactical manoeuvre, was to a great extent completed by the middle of the eighteenth century so that by the end of the Seven Years War it is true to say that dominance on the battlefield had largely passed to the previously humble foot soldiers, amongst whom those of Britain were pre-eminent.

Although this pre-eminence was undeniable it is perhaps difficult to say why it should have occurred, although doubtless the strange and wholly fortuitous mixture of blood must have had much to do with it. The wild blend of stolid Saxon axemen with active, intelligent Normans and fierce Norsemen, especially when reinforced by the fiery, older, native strain, certainly produced a superb natural infantry.

The British Infantry, although historically the largest and most important fighting element in the British Army, has never really regarded itself as an homogeneous arm, having from its earliest days been splintered into a collection of highly individual regi-

1

ments. One has but to go into any good military library to be conscious of this, for there will inevitably be row upon row of books on regimental history but very few indeed on the Infantry as a body. This regimental system, which has served the British Infantry well, inevitably depends to some extent on distinctions and differences which are essential to establish the sort of 'family' pride on which the whole thing is based. These however, although important in their sphere, are largely on the surface, and below them there is an essential uniformity of armament, organization, tactical doctrine, and purpose, without which individual battalions could not act together effectively. It is with this aspect of the British Infantry that this book is largely concerned.

Having said this, it must also be admitted that inevitably it also deals with the regimental system for the good reason that in spite of certain limitations it has to a great extent been the cause of the success of the British Infantry in three centuries of almost continuous military operations. War is an odd, illogical occupation, in the course of which rational beings are called upon to expose themselves not only to hardship but to the risks of death or mutilation in a particularly unpleasant form, and it is difficult to decide quite why they do this. Not for financial gain certainly, for there are many easier and more lucrative ways of earning a living. Not, principally at least, from patriotism. Not even from fear of the consequences of refusal; it is fashionable in some quarters to deride military leadership as a myth based on the Army Act, but every experienced soldier will know that this is nonsense. If a man, or for that matter a unit, is going to break under fire it is certain that the fear of punishment will not stop it, for when death appears imminent the alternative of five years in jail may seem positively desirable by comparison.

War is essentially a corporate activity in which soldiers depend for their lives and safety upon the integrity of their fellows. Men are gregarious creatures who like to associate together in small, closed societies where everyone knows everyone else and wishes to stand well in the eyes of his fellows. This is why soldiers give unstinting allegiance to a unit, often to the extent that they would rather die than disgrace it, and it is this fact which forms the whole basis of the regimental system.

The system, being based on human nature and needs, is a remarkably strong one; it was for example noticeable that wartime soldiers, called up without reference to their own wishes and posted arbitrarily to regiments, quickly gave them the same allegiance as long term regular soldiers.

Although the history of the British Infantry is a relatively short one it is nevertheless very complex, so that it is impossible to cover every aspect of it in a single volume. In view of this it has been necessary to be rather strictly selective, and this book is primarily concerned with the aspects referred to earlier, to the unfortunate but inevitable exclusion of such fascinating subjects as uniform (a complete and complex subject on which hundreds of books have already been written) and many others.

1 DEVELOPMENTS BEFORE 1660

Several millions of years ago a breed of ape-like creatures more enterprising than most of their species left the relatively peaceful shelter of the forest and struck boldly into the plains. Individually they were puny specimens, at first sight remarkably ill-equipped physically to survive the appalling dangers which surrounded them, but appearances were to prove deceptive. Physically weak, they might be compared to the predators amongst whom they ventured, but they were to develop resources undreamt of by their enemies. They were intelligent, and soon grasped the concept of weapons to offset their own lack of natural fighting equipment; they were physically adaptable and soon learnt to run erect so as to leave their arms free to use these weapons; they learnt to communicate and so were enabled to act in concert; but above all they were aggressive and endowed with mental toughness and a fierce determination not to give in. No one really knows quite what strange mutation turned the erstwhile gentle vegetarians into ruthless and aggressive carnivores, but so it turned out. Their initial losses must have been enormous, yet in a short time (biologically speaking) the odd little bipeds were ruling the world and seem likely to continue to do so – unless indeed their sometimes irrational pugnacity induces them to destroy themselves with the hideous weapons which their highly developed brains have made available to them.

It may be human subconscious memories of these earlier wild days which gives the infantry its special regard, for it is certain that the qualities which raised the primitive apeman high above the other species are still the basic ones required by good infantry; it is for this reason that a book more concerned with military history than with genesis starts so early.

It is curious how little the role of the present-day infantryman differs from that of his primaeval forebears. His weapons are much

5

improved, as are his communications, yet he is still a relatively weak creature using skill, intelligence and determination to overcome his vastly more powerful adversaries. Nor are the primitive emotions far below the surface even now; those older readers who have fought as infantrymen, particularly perhaps in the Far East, Burma, or Korea, will remember the savagery of some of those desperate predawn hand-to-hand struggles in which civilized twentieth-century city dwellers wielded bayonet and sword, knife and club, with the same wild gusto shown by their savage predecessors thousands of years ago.

Almost nothing is known of the fighting methods of the earliest men. It is certain that once they had established themselves firmly, their natural pugnacity led them to do battle with each other for grazing rights, hunting grounds, waterholes and other likely sources of conflict. Battles between bands probably began with showers of stones and ended with hand-to-hand fighting with such primitive weapons as were available, thus demonstrating at a remarkably early date the basic rule that shock action should be preceded by fire.

Our earliest detailed military knowledge dates back to the rise of the first Mediterranean civilizations about 2000 BC. The days of the wandering herdsmen had gone, and static farmers had largely taken over. Palisaded villages gradually gave place to walled cities and subsistence economy developed into a much more complex system in which farmers, tradesmen and businesses all played their parts; most important of all, basic tribal rule was replaced by a new and much more sophisticated system of government.

It is probable that in the early days of wandering tribes conflicts were relatively few because the population was small and the natural resources large; but as the city-states grew up in relatively close proximity, causes of dispute increased and wars became frequent. When they occurred, fighting men were raised from amongst the ordinary citizens, for the concept of the professional soldier was still far in the future and the inhabitants of any state accepted as natural the fact that they had a duty to defend it by actual service in the field.

When these citizen levies were called out to fight there was no time to give them much training, so that tactical concepts and movements were necessarily of the simplest. All that could be hoped for was to maintain some sort of cohesion until the main head-on clash occurred, after which battle arrays tended to shiver into a multitude of individual combats. Fighting men provided their own arms and equipment, and as the richer ones amongst them could afford to outfit themselves well it was natural that they should fight in front. War was a matter of plain duty to the state and its logical end was triumph or defeat in single combat. The front rank was the position of honour and light troops, though occasionally used, were regarded with some disdain.

The arts of war, like those of peace, were given particular impetus by man's discovery of metal. Clubs, sharpened saplings, and primitive stone axes gave place to swords and spears, and defensive armour soon made its appearance; it was this need for special equipment which eventually gave rise to the professional fighting man.

By about 1000 BC the Greeks had become dominant; although never a single nation, the various states were closely linked by ties of blood, religion, and language, and were thus able to form formidable alliances when required. The basic military formation of the Greeks was the phalanx, a solid block of men with a frontage of 64 and a depth of 16 ranks, and this had certain obvious advantages. It was compact, it was easy to control, and – given well armoured spearmen in the first three or four ranks – well capable of breaking through an enemy battle line or beating off an attack. Its main disadvantage was that it was almost impossible to manoeuvre it except on a flat, level, plain. Broken ground, rocks, vegetation, and small water courses were all liable to throw it into confusion, and once gaps appeared a light, active enemy could force their way in and disrupt the whole array. Its inability to change front also made it particularly liable to sudden flank attacks; nevertheless its simplicity made it a suitable formation for citizen-soldiers and in one form or another it was to be with us well into the nineteenth century.

Alexander the Great saw the value of the phalanx, but he used it as a pivot for manoeuvre; when well screened by light, missile-armed infantry – slingers, archers, and javelin men – and flanked by cavalry it still proved a formidable basis for an army. Alexander used it with success in his wars in India, although its very solidity made it susceptible to attack by those fore-runners of modern armoured fighting vehicles, the war elephants of the Punjab.

In 146 BC the Greeks were finally defeated by the rising star of the Mediterranean, Rome. The basic fighting formation of the Roman army was the legion of some 4,000 infantry, and at first this was handled like a huge phalanx, eight men deep. The defects of this large and unwieldy formation were however soon apparent and the legion was then broken down into maniples; these were subunits usually of about 120 men and thus resembled the later company in size and manoeuvrability, although some, usually those used in reserve, were only about half that strength. The basic tactical formation was a triple line of maniples, the subunits being in small columns six ranks deep. Those in the second line covered the intervals in the first line, the third line, usually somewhat weaker than the others, being placed where it could best act as a reserve. The infantry wore armour and were equipped with javelins and swords, and a squadron of cavalry was usually attached to each legion to cover its flanks. This formation proved to be extremely effective and the Romans were soon masters of most of the known world.

In the early days of Rome, her soldiers were of the usual citizen militia, but by about 100 BC the Empire had grown to such a size that it could only be controlled by long-term professional soldiers, an interesting parallel with the British Army of the seventeenth century onwards.

These professional soldiers were usually enlisted from the proletariat, but had to be freemen. They enlisted for up to 25 years and long service enabled them to be highly trained. They were also extremely tough physically, and capable of performing long marches under heavy loads in spite of the fact that their sparse diet seems to have consisted mainly of coarse bread with a small protein supplement and a ration of wine. Their fighting qualities are too well known to need much repetition; their bravery, shadowed by a kind of arrogant brutality, was respected everywhere and carried their eagles to victory all over the known world.

At about this time the Romans introduced an intermediate unit, the cohort of three maniples. This increased the solidity of their battle order although it must have had some adverse effect on its flexibility. The reason for its adoption is not clear; possibly the wild barbarians were sufficiently aggressive to require close-order formations to oppose them, a fact which became well known to the British Infantry in its colonial wars of the second half of the nineteenth century.

By about AD 470 the Roman Empire had virtually collapsed under the steady pressure of the barbarians from the north and east. The Roman army had been on the defensive for some time – a sure indication of eventual disintegration – and cavalry had replaced infantry as the most important arm due to its superior mobility, an important consideration when too few troops are trying to guard a long frontier. The quality of the legions deteriorated rapidly; a few Romans remained as officers, but the rank and file were mostly barbarians or slaves, a sad contrast to the splendid citizen-soldiers of an earlier era.

The Roman army had always employed local levies, but these had usually been numerically insignificant and under strict control; however, as Roman citizens showed less and less desire to serve, whole bands of barbarians were taken into service under their own leaders. The Goths from the east were mostly horsemen who relied on the spear or the bow; they quickly copied the use of defensive armour from the Romans and their cavalry became formidable. This process was greatly accelerated by the general introduction in the fifth or sixth century of the stirrup, a device which made the horseman sufficiently firm in his saddle to fight serious battles hand-to-hand. Very soon Rome collapsed completely and these new and formidable horsemen took over control of much of Europe.

These new rulers were somewhat thinly spread in hostile territory and the various small bands tended to group themselves for purposes of security. Their main interest was war, which they considered to be a matter for the ruling classes, and in this they were right, since the type of down-trodden serf which emerged with the adoption of the feudal system was hardly likely to make a good soldier, even if he could be trusted with weapons, which was doubtful.

The concept of the mounted gentleman-soldier thus gained ground. Mobility became important at this time because of the extensive incursions of the Danes who landed from their ships, seized any horses available locally, and raided deeply into the European hinterland. It is an odd fact that almost the only country which did not resort to mobile mounted troops to counter the menace was England. This was partly due to the fact that Alfred chose to defend the country by means of a navy, and partly to his acceptance of Danish settlers within the Danelaw. This was a shrewd move, since there was room for everyone; the Danish settlers moreover soon became peaceful and prosperous but always remained ready to beat off the attacks of their erstwhile accomplices.

The chief military result of this was that the English continued to fight on foot with sword and axe, a method of warfare which seems to have been well-suited to the Saxon character.

Of this period Sir Charles Oman wrote in *A History of the Art of War; the Middle Ages* that:

> The true interest of the centuries of the early middle ages lies in the gradual evolution of new forms of warlike efficiency which end in the establishment of a military class as the chief factor in war and the decay among most peoples of the old system which made the tribe arrayed in arms the normal fighting force. Intimately connected with this change was an alteration in arms and equipment which transferred the outward appearance of war in a manner no less complete. The period of transition may be considered to end when, in the eleventh century, the feudal cavalier established his super-

iority over all the descriptions of troops which were pitted against him, from the Magyar horse-archers of the East to the Anglo-Danish axemen of the West. The fight at Hastings, the last attempt made for three centuries by infantry to withstand cavalry, serves to mark the termination of the epoch.

The spread of Christianity also played a significant role in military developments in Europe. The Church steadily increased its domination over the state, and of this phenomenon General Fuller wrote in his *Armaments and History* that:

Out of this search for dominance emerged the mediaeval concept of war as a trial by battle in which the Church refereed for God. War was not prohibited, nor were attempts made to abolish it because it was recognised as part of man's very nature, the fruits of original sin, which was the fulcrum of the Church's power. Therefore war could only be restricted and mitigated by Christianising – ennobling – the warrior and by limiting its duration.

Thus there came into being the idea of the Christian knight, a sort of saintly warrior devoting his life and fortune to the defence of his weaker brethren; traces of him may perhaps remain in the modern concept of gentility.

This almost universal acceptance that warfare was a matter for gentlemen lasted for several hundred years, primarily because it suited almost everyone. Wars were effectively limited in size and scope, and honest efforts were made to reduce the impact of them on non-combatants. It is possible to take a cynical view of this by asserting that such efforts were largely economic in intent, since extensive destruction of crops and towns at a time when agriculture was but little above subsistence level would have been disastrous for all, and there is possibly some truth in this. Even so the efforts, whatever inspired them, were worthy ones and did some good; one has but to look at the awful ravages wrought in the Thirty Years War to appreciate the relative humanity of earlier warfare.

Although at the time it was widely and understandably believed that feudal warfare represented the height of military efficiency, this was in fact a complete fallacy. There was no order, little discipline, and hardly any concept of even the most basic tactics. Armies were mere mobs and their leaders had little more skill than sufficed to hurl them head-on at each other; after the first clash the battle developed into hundreds of individual combats, these being considered the proper and honourable climax. There was no concept of scouting or reconnaissance. Maps hardly existed so that armies frequently lost each other completely; commanders anxious for glory sometimes found it desirable to despatch heralds to their adversaries bearing not only challenges but also the notification of some suitable rendezvous. Only in the art of fortification was any real progress made, and it was in this period that the castle became the highest manifestation of military art. Starting with simple timber or masonry towers on artificial mounds, the builders progressed to the huge and complex structures of the thirteenth and fourteenth centuries, many of which are still to be found in Europe and the Middle East.

Otherwise, the man-at-arms, fully armoured, well-mounted, and superbly trained in the individual use of sword, mace, or lance continued to dominate the battlefield. Apart from a highly honourable end in single combat with one of his peers, the only serious risk he ran was from missile weapons and these were in consequence frowned on. Infantry existed in fairly large numbers but continued to be a rabble, ill-armed, ill-organized, badly led, and generally thoroughly despised by the mounted men. Their only real military role came in sieges, otherwise they were regarded as little better than camp followers and treated accordingly.

The first slight break with tradition came in the Crusades, where the Christian knights found themselves harried by swarms of Turkish mounted archers who unsportingly felt no necessity to conform to the accepted Christian rules of warfare. As was usually the case with mounted archers their bows were weak and their arrows little more than irritating darts to fully armoured men, though they caused enough casualties amongst the horses to be a nuisance. Richard Coeur-de-Lion was sufficiently impressed with their potential to feel the need for an answer to it and found one ready to hand in the crossbow, a relatively new mechanical invention which needed no particular strength to use. Its missiles were more powerful, more accurate and longer ranging than the light arrows of the Turks, and a few companies of mercenaries equipped with this new, (and then terrible) missile arm, very soon restored the balance. So disturbed were the Christian nations by the potential of the crossbow that in 1139 the Lateran Council forbade its use against Christians. Little else was learnt from the Crusades; they seem to have been regarded as a sort of untypical colonial warfare hardly suited to gentlemen, and as soon as they were over Europe returned thankfully to its own well-established rules.

The longbow is a basic weapon, the origins of which are lost in antiquity. No single man can have invented it any more than one man can have invented the spear or the stone axe, for it has been

11

found in widely spaced communities which can have had no early contact with each other. It was used fairly extensively in Europe until well into the eleventh century, its employment at Hastings being well known, but thereafter all missile weapons fell into disuse except for sporting purposes. This, as we have seen, was partly due to feudal partiality for single combat, but there was also the consideration that bows were cheap and easy to make, so that no feudal ruler cared to see their use encouraged by his downtrodden peasantry.

The single exception to this came in Britain, where the feudal system was less strong. The British were not a perfect race, nor, perhaps surprisingly, have they yet become so. Nevertheless, once the suspicion or distrust of the original Saxon inhabitants for their Norman rulers had been overcome, a process which was largely complete 100 years after the conquest, a relatively liberal society came into being. There were of course great inequalities, much injustice, and a good deal of oppression, yet these in the main were no more than incidental in a well-ordered system where every man had not only his rights but his duties also. Serfdom in its true form hardly existed, the superior peasantry being represented by a strong class of sokemen, freemen and freeholders who were later to form the basis of a fine body of yeoman infantry. Even the villeins were being steadily emancipated, so that by the mid fourteenth century the bulk of the agricultural classes in the country were hired labourers, and if their lives were hard they at least had some freedom of action and a modicum of control over their own affairs.

The exact circumstances surrounding the reappearance of the bow are somewhat obscure. No mention was made of it in the Assize of Arms of 1181 from which it may be inferred that it was not then regarded as an important weapon of war. It must however have been in existence in some numbers and all the indications are that its country of survival was Wales. The Welsh were a warlike people who (perhaps like the Turks) saw no need to put themselves at a disadvantage in their almost continuous frontier warfare with the English by eschewing missile weapons.

These bows were stout, clumsy, cudgel-like elm poles, roughly whittled to shape and needing great skill and strength. Unlike the earlier European and Asiatic bows which were short and drawn to the chest only, these were long and drawn to the ear so that they produced a far more effective missile weapon than ever before, not even excluding the crossbow, which although powerful was slow in action and ineffective in bad weather.

King Henry I of England, a competent soldier, seems to have been the first to see the new potential of the bow and as early as

1135 his small company of archers played havoc with the French at Beaumont. After that its use spread rapidly throughout the country so that in a relatively few years it had become a national weapon and its use a popular national sport.

Its first use on a major scale was at Falkirk in 1298 where the Scottish schiltrons, solid wedge-like bodies of spearmen, were decimated by it. This decisive result may have led to overconfidence because at Bannockburn in 1314 Edward II brought forward his archers without support and had the mortification of seeing the Scottish horse ride through and over them, thus demonstrating the basic rule that any skirmish line needed an effective support behind it.

As soon as the basic tactical principles had been mastered it was time to employ them against the traditional enemies, the French, and they soon proved their worth at the great naval battles of Sluys in 1340. Previously sea fights had been a question of grappling and then engaging hand-to-hand, as though on dry land, but at Sluys the archers on the British ships slaughtered the soldiers and shipmen on their opponents' vessels before any close contact could be made. This success set the fashion for the Hundred Years War, in which British successes were largely attributed to the longbow.

The various British expeditions to France were always outnumbered, so that the main tactical expedient of their various commanders was to fight a defensive battle on ground of their own choosing. Provided that contact could be made, this was rarely very difficult to achieve because the gallant French men-at-arms, thirsting for the glory of single combat with their peers, were always anxious to attack on sight in the bull-at-a-gate way so characteristic of feudal chivalry.

British defensive tactics soon settled into an effective, well-tested pattern. The knights and their fully armoured retainers, known collectively as men-at-arms and almost invariably dismounted in battle, customarily formed the centre, with wings of archers on either flank. The ideal position was along the crest of a gentle slope and every advantage was made of obstacles – wet plough, vineyards, hedges, and the like – which might impede the slow, heavy French horses. The flanks of such positions had to be well-secured and this was usually achieved by resting them on a wood, a stream, a ravine, a village, or some other natural or man-made obstacle. On occasions where nothing suitable existed, as for example at Poitiers, a leaguer of wagons was formed and garrisoned with archers and spearmen. Improvised defences of this sort were to remain in use, at least against savage enemies not equipped with artillery, until the very end of the nineteenth century.

All that the British required thereafter was for the French to oblige with an attack, and this they never failed to do. They were met by a hail of arrows which pierced disconcertingly through armour and either killed the horses or so galled them that they were driven panic-stricken to the rear, shedding their riders and causing havoc in the rear echelons. Once this repulse was achieved the men-at-arms advanced and completed the victory; these attacks were often made in conjunction with the archers, who were always ready to cast aside their bows and set to with swords or war hammers on their exhausted and demoralized opponents.

The whole system constituted a major break with tradition, for the hitherto despised footman suddenly became a power to be reckoned with on the battlefield. Socially too it was something of a revolution, since knight and yeoman fought side by side in trust and mutual confidence. It also saw the beginning of professionalism, for although many young men were content to have served a campaign before returning to the plough, a good many soldiered on for year after year. Here perhaps we may discern the real beginnings of the British Infantry as we know it today.

The French on their side were outraged at what they considered to be a sad breach of chivalrous custom on the parts of the various English monarchs concerned. Fuller sums it up briefly in *Armament and History* by commenting that: 'This weapon did not fit their code of war. The Sword knew where it struck, the arrow did not, therefore it was a scoundrel's weapon.'

They tried various answers to the longbow, the first of which was the employment of companies of mercenary crossbowmen, but these despised foreigners with their clumsy weapons lacked the skill and spirit to bear down the confident British. Another experiment was to fight dismounted; this at least obviated the risk of serious falls from mortally wounded horses and also did away with the fearsome rushes of panicking chargers through their own ranks, but did not solve the problem of the long slow advance in the teeth of the arrows. Heavier armour seemed to offer one solution, but although it turned the arrows it so hampered its wearers that they fell relatively easy prey to their more lightly armed and so more active opponents.

As often happens the French were eventually saved by hitherto unperceived weaknesses on the part of their opponents; in the years after Agincourt there was a slow decline in leadership and discipline, and British aims were distracted by the threat of internal dissent. The French on the other hand rallied under the inspiration (if perhaps not the actual leadership) of Joan of Arc and developed a new and Fabian system of tactics based on raids and guerrilla warfare. When threatened with serious attack they retired to well-stocked fortresses leaving the invaders to starve or die of disease, and when the British made attempts to take these places they were met by the fire of hundreds of the new-fangled cannon which the French had seen fit to adopt as a missile answer to the arrow. In this they were right, for although guns were still relatively primitive they were nevertheless formidable weapons when used for static defence, where their weight and immobility were not disadvantages.

As far as England was concerned, much of the second half of the fifteenth century was taken up with the Wars of the Roses, a prolonged series of domestic struggles between two noble factions to decide who should rule the country. Although they stretched over some 30 years there was comparatively little fighting, and what there was produced little in the way of new tactical concepts. The main armies were of feudal-type levies, raised by commission of array and consisting, for the greater part, of the retainers of the various great landowners concerned. In general they contained the traditional mixture of men-at-arms and archers which had proved so successful in the Hundred Years War, although a few companies of handgunners, mainly Germans, were also employed.

Whoever was the de facto monarch at the time also controlled a considerable train of artillery, although the advantages of this were often more apparent than real. There had been great improvements in the manufacture and technical handling of cannon in the previous 100 years, but in spite of this they remained heavy and relatively immobile, and were thus best suited to siege warfare, whereas most of the fighting was of a mobile kind. On the European mainland every frontier was so heavily garnished with great fortified places that inevitably they dominated the warfare of the period, but this was not the case in England. The country had enjoyed domestic peace for a long period, and few except border towns had efficient fortifications. Even the nobility had in many cases abandoned their uncomfortable medieval castles (which, unlike their more modern counterparts, were in any case hardly proof against 'modern' artillery) and moved into comfortable houses. Major engagements thus tended to be what we should now call encounter battles, fought in the open without defences, and although usually quite brief they tended nevertheless to be bloody and thus decisive.

It seems clear that the bulk of the people of England had little enthusiasm for this prolonged and pointless struggle, and once it was over most of them were content to live in domestic peace under the strong hand of their new monarch, the Tudor Henry VII. It was perhaps because of this almost universal sentiment that for many years after the fighting was over the British people showed little

15

inclination towards land warfare. The period that followed was not, it is true, one of complete peace; apart from a good deal of irregular warfare along the border with Scotland (then of course a foreign country), and almost inevitable trouble in Ireland, the British saw a certain amount of further fighting against their old enemies, the French. It was perhaps the loss of Calais, their last bridgehead in France, in 1558, which gave them the final excuse to abandon further major adventures on the European mainland for many years.

Instead they took to their natural environment, the sea, as explorers, traders, and not infrequently as pirates, so that the light, fast warship became of paramount importance. This resulted in a serious decline of interest in military affairs and a corresponding increase in the status of the navy. The importance of this cannot be overemphasized for it set the whole pattern of development for the next 400 years. Nevertheless its short-term effects were unfortunate, for by turning their backs on Europe at this time the British virtually cut themselves off from participation in the considerable advances being made in the military art, due largely to the general adoption of gunpowder. The British of course made good use of this valuable commodity but their interests were naval and they concentrated on the development of naval gunnery, an art in which they were to lead the world for many years. As far as hand-held weapons were concerned they were content to retain their trust in the longbow which had served their forefathers so well, and herein they were wrong. It is true that a skilled archer could still outshoot a musketeer, but skilled archers were at a premium for it took years of patient training and practice to reach the standards of the men of Agincourt, and but few men in England could be bothered to make the sustained efforts necessary. Handguns were becoming common and any moderately intelligent young man could become proficient with one in a few months instead of the long years needed for the bow.

While the British had been experimenting with missile tactics to defeat the power of the armoured horseman, another small European country was busy developing its own highly individual answer to the problem. Switzerland was a small and relatively poor country surrounded by vastly more powerful neighbours and it was in order to curb their incursions that the Swiss developed their pike phalanx. The Swiss were poor but they were free men, active herdsmen, tough mountaineers, and all more than ready to defend their country to the last. They had few horses and little money to equip men-at-arms against the more numerous German knights; instead they resuscitated the phalanx, a solid block of footmen armed with a mixture of 18-foot (5.5-metre) pikes and halberds, together with a sprinkling of missile weapons – at first crossbows, but later handguns. No great new tactical principles were involved; the phalanx was simply a solid block of tough and fanatical fighters, and its real strength was in its discipline and training. The classical Greek phalanx had, as we have seen, a tendency to disintegrate on any but the most level ground, but the Swiss drilled themselves to the stage where they could cross moderately broken country, and they were probably the first army to march in step and to use drums and other music to achieve this. They had no commander-in-chief, indeed no senior officers of any kind, all operations apparently being decided on by a committee of captains, old and reliable soldiers, but little more than drill-masters.

The phalanx was divided into three columns, advancing in echelon with (usually) the right leading, and it was instant-aneously effective. Its fame spread rapidly and it was not long before the patriotic Swiss were offering themselves to the other nations of Europe as mercenaries. As soldiers, especially as mercenaries, they had certain disadvantages. They were fierce and brave and often brutal; for example they never took prisoners but slaughtered everyone who crossed their path, but they were also avaricious and quite unscrupulous. They fought for money, ready money at that, and if it was not forthcoming at the right time they either struck or went home, whatever the state of operations might be, a system which the princes of Europe, chronically short of ready cash, found disconcerting.

The eventual downfall of the Swiss phalanx was in its resistance to change and in some ways this was understandable, for it had a long history of success. European warfare of the fourteenth and fifteenth centuries was largely dominated by it and the Swiss saw no need to change a winning system. Herein they were wrong for the times were changing fast and other nations were developing new techniques and new weapons, particularly artillery. The phalanx was a moving fortress but with the grave disadvantage that unlike its static counterpart its walls were not made of stone but human bodies. If it could be stopped it could then be pounded to pieces by artillery, to which its relatively few missile weapons could make no effective reply, and in the event it proved relatively simple to stop. The Germans, always adaptable, trained lands-knechts, their own version of the Swiss pikemen. Though gener-ally slightly inferior to the genuine article, these men could usually bring the phalanx to a halt in a head-on collision, after which the guns took over. Partial charges by light cavalry against the flank of the leading column could also achieve the same end, for although the phalanx could beat off cavalry with ease it had to halt to do so, because even supermen could hardly be expected to make thrusts with a six-yard (5.5-metre) long pike to the flank while moving forward. Even if artillery was not available a new and effective enemy was found in the new Spanish infantry. Long years of fighting the Moors had created a light infantry, armed with sword and light shield and supported by musketeers, and it was quickly found that they were more than a match for their heavy adversaries. Thus, by the early years of the sixteenth century, the Swiss phalanx had lost much of its effectiveness, but in spite of this the pike was to play a significant role for a further 150 years, for the sword in the hands of a footman, although superior to the pike in combats of infantry only, could not contend on even terms with horsemen similarly armed.

The next formation therefore was a modified phalanx, a huge solid square of pikes with detachments of musketeers at the corners. This was developed by the Spaniards, then perhaps the foremost soldiers in Europe, but like similar formations it was to succumb in due course to improved missile power.

The invention of firearms caused enormous changes in military techniques. These however, did not occur overnight for developments and improvements in firearms were inevitably slow in a largely non-industrial era. Cannon of a sort had appeared on the battlefields of Europe by about the middle of the fourteenth century and were followed by handguns in the next 100 years, but it was probably not until the first half of the sixteenth century that they ceased to be auxiliaries and became principals.

The period of their development coincided so closely with the decline of the feudal system that it is tempting to say that the rise of one caused the downfall of the other. This, however, is no more than a half-truth. It is true that the development of effective cannon did much to hasten it because they strengthened the hands of monarchs against the previously semi-autonomous princes and barons on whom the system had been based. Their now old-fashioned castles, previously practically invulnerable to the primitive siege techniques available, could be battered down with comparative ease and although new defensive works, carefully designed to frustrate the cannonball, were soon developed, their construction was prohibitively expensive at anything less than national level, as indeed was the cost of garrisoning them. The old and lofty walled structures could be held by a mere handful of retainers but the new low-silhouette types could be taken by a *coup-de-main* unless adequately protected.

There were however other and perhaps more important factors. The world was progressing, particularly in the economic field, and the steady development of a money-based economy had begun to destroy the old agricultural one. Bankers and merchants, almost all concentrated in cities, had begun to assume a very considerable control over the financial resources of the state and this concentration of ready money made it relatively easy for rulers to lay their hands on it. The nobility could be invited to compound their feudal duties by cash payments, and rich industrialists could be taxed, all of which made it possible to raise and maintain larger armies than before. Freer institutions led to a wage-earning working class, so that armies came into direct economic competition with industry. Good pay – and perhaps the promise of loot and adventure – attracted men into these armies, and having regard to the steady rise in the use of firearms, a high proportion of these men became foot soldiers.

This was the dawn of professional armies. All over Europe the younger sons of the nobility and gentry, lacking land and scorning trade, soon began to form an officer class with its own code of honour. Their services were needed, for under the new system a good deal of laxity had begun to creep in. Moral standards were reduced, as was patriotism; war had become a business like any other except that by its very nature it attracted the wild and the shiftless, who needed to be kept under rigid discipline by the threat of savage punishment. Professional knowledge increased; ruses and deceptions of all kinds, which had been frowned on by the old feudal chivalry, now became accepted parts of the military art.

The cradle of these changes was perhaps the group of states we now call Italy, which at that time were the acknowledged leaders of the world as far as wealth and culture were concerned. They were the first countries to rely on professional soldiers, often not native-born Italians but true mercenaries who undertook to fight for states requiring their services on a strictly commercial basis. These condottieri set a fashion in mercenary service which was to endure for many years, and which provided a valuable source of income to some of the poorer countries of Europe whose chief export became fighting men. Many of these were not wholly influenced by purely financial reasons, particularly in the various wars of religion where Protestant tended to support Protestant and Catholic supported Catholic, even though a cash nexus was usually involved.

This increased professionalism had important results in the field of tactics. Previously it had only been possible to manoeuvre hastily raised levies by forming them into huge clumsy columns, but improvements in firearms had made these hideously expensive in terms of casualties. Improved mobile artillery could rake them through and through and modern cavalry, armed for the first time with the newly invented wheel-lock pistol, could gall them

19

unmercifully with fire. It was clear that newer and more flexible tactical systems were needed.

It was not until the last two decades of the sixteenth century that the British, after a long spell of maritime operations, re-entered the European scene when they intervened in the Netherlands in support of the Dutch Protestants. Their opponents there were the veteran soldiers of the army under the famous Spaniard, Parma, so that their reintroduction to modern land warfare was not initially a happy period for them. Hard experience however soon taught them their business and by the end of the century they had established a sound reputation as soldiers, having arrived in time to learn the latest military methods.

The basis of much of this new military theory was laid by Maurice of Nassau, but was finally brought to fruition by Gustavus Adolphus. He came to the Swedish throne in 1611, at the age of 18, and soon proved himself to be an exceptional soldier. Dash and courage, initiative and leadership are all common enough to good soldiers, and Gustavus Adolphus had them in full; but to them he added the less common attributes of original thought, great administrative and organizational ability, plus the driving energy to get things done. Much of his early fighting was against other Baltic states in an effort to maintain the balance of power in the area, but his great opportunity came in 1630 when he decided to take part in what was later to become known as the Thirty Years War. This was primarily a religious conflict and Gustavus Adolphus brought his country into it in the Protestant cause.

As Sweden was relatively poor and sparsely populated he had to make the best possible use of his manpower. This he did by an early form of conscription which his people appear to have accepted willingly, partly because of their patriotism, and partly because of their personal regard for him. In return he gave them good leadership and organization, and looked after them well as far as food, clothing, and other bodily wants were concerned; nor were their moral standards allowed to degenerate. Even the most careful use of manpower did not however give him the army he wanted, so almost half his force were foreigners. The bulk of these were Scots and Germans, and although they were paid professionals their attachment to the Protestant cause made them more than mere mercenaries.

His tactical concepts were based chiefly on fire power and mobility, and this he achieved by increasing the proportion of musketeers in his infantry, lightening their weapons, and introducing paper cartridges to speed their rate of fire. He similarly reduced the length and weight of the pike and largely abolished pikeman's armour. Having achieved this he then formed his infantry into small battalions of four companies; each of these consisted of 54 pikes and 72 muskets, although on occasion he withdrew up to 28 musketeers to skirmish or to act as artillery escorts, thus reducing the pike/musket ratio to about 50 per cent of each.

Until Gustavus Adolphus' day the only way of maintaining a steady fire of musketry had been the system invented by the Spaniard Pescara, in which the musketeers formed in 10 ranks, each firing and then filing away to the rear to reload, but the lighter musket and improved drill of the Swedes enabled a standard six-rank formation, with the pikes in the centre and the muskets on the flanks. On occasion the musketeers could close up into three ranks and fire simultaneously, although this was not normally resorted to since it left all the muskets empty together.

This extension of units at the expense of depth made it possible to cover a front with fewer soldiers than hitherto, so that Gustavus Adolphus usually had enough men available to fight in three lines; the units of the second covered the intervals of the first while the third, frequently numerically weaker than the other, acted as a reserve; exposed flanks could be covered by files of musketeers who could turn outwards if threatened.

The whole system, which was based very closely on that of the Roman legion at its best, gave a considerable degree of flexibility and a much greater relative degree of protection against artillery than had been possible in the old, thickly packed formations. In theory of course, cavalry could penetrate between the units, but in practice they would have been bold horsemen indeed who would have submitted themselves to a heavy and converging fire of musketry on front, flanks and rear. Each battalion had two mobile three-pounder guns which greatly increased their fire power without hampering them in any way.

There were also great administrative advantages. Almost for the first time an army had a logical system of units and subunits based on fixed establishments and this in its turn led to the setting up of a proper system of rank and thus automatically a proper chain of command.

The Swedish soldier-king was killed in action at the battle of Lutzen in 1632, but in his relatively short period of active command he had established a working system which was to be retained by the armies of Europe for many years after his death.

Britain was never officially involved in the Thirty Years War but a good many individuals served as volunteers on the side of the various Protestant contingents. Thus when the English Civil War started in 1642 it was natural that the training and tactics of the armies hastily improvised by both sides should have been based on continental teachings. The influence of the Swedish system was strong, though some preferred the older and somewhat simpler system of Maurice of Nassau as being easier and quicker to teach. This was an important consideration for there was little time to do more than instil the simplest rudiments of their business into the new levies. As the war progressed the armies on both sides gained experience the hard way and in the end a somewhat modified version of Gustavus Adolphus' methods seems to have held general sway.

One limiting factor was the initial scarcity of arms. As the Thirty Years War progressed the pike fell further and further out of fashion and the musket came into almost universal use, but at the beginning of the Civil War the scale on both sides was about half and half. It is difficult to say whether this was due to a natural conservatism or whether it was because pikes could be improvised locally whereas muskets could not.

In spite of the fact that the infantry was rising rapidly in importance the cavalry was still the dominant arm on the battlefield, and although the foot fought offensively it was largely regarded as a pivot of manoeuvre for the mounted arm. The real danger came when pikes and muskets were separated, for on open ground at least they were almost wholly dependant on each other for success – indeed for survival. The musketeers, once they had discharged their pieces, needed a safe refuge where they could go through the slow business of reloading, and in the absence of any natural obstacle they depended on the pikes to provide this. The pikes, while able to fend off cavalry, were extremely vulnerable to missile action, so that they in their turn needed fire support to keep enemy musketeers and guns at a safe distance, and in view of the short ranges of hand firearms this mutual support could only be ensured by close contact.

The ideal pattern for a battle was for the opening cavalry to fight on the wings while the infantry came to 'push of pike' in the centre. If the horsemen of one side could gain advantage over those of the other they could then strike the flanks of the enemy's infantry in the reasonable hopes that this extra shock would break them. In practice of course things tended to be somewhat less than ideal. Even in those days England was reasonably enclosed with hedges, ditches, walls, and plantations, to say nothing of natural obstacles in the form of streams, morasses, rabbit warrens and rocky outcrops. All these favoured the infantryman, and in particular the musketeer, since in effect they offered him the sort of support which he had otherwise to obtain from the pikes. As the war progressed the weapon ratio rose to about two to one in favour of the musket.

Both sides also made use of dragoons who in those days were infantrymen; their main distinction was that they rode to the battle rather than marched, but they dismounted to fight it. Troops of this nature were often employed in advance of the main army. They could, for example, be sent forward with the cavalry in order to seize an important defile, bridge, river crossing or similar feature of tactical importance.

The Civil War was won by Cromwell's New Model Army, which thereafter remained in existence as the national, although not of course a royal, army. A regiment of New Model infantry consisted of 10 companies of 120 men, one third pikes and two thirds muskets, and this was the standard organization at the time of the restoration of Charles II in 1660.

A unit of this sort naturally needed a small number of regimental officers of higher rank than captain. These were usually referred to as 'field' officers, presumably because it was originally in the field, i.e. on active service, that their chief duties lay, command and administration of individual companies being the business of their captains. It is interesting that the term has survived in the modern army.

2 1660–1713 FLINTLOCK AND BAYONET

On 1 January 1660 General Monck, a Royalist by conviction but a Parliamentarian after 1645 (perhaps as a matter of expediency), marched out of the border town of Coldstream with his regiment en route for London. His intention was to restore the monarchy and in this he was successful, for five months later King Charles II was riding through London amid the cheers of his subjects; ironically enough the cavalrymen who escorted him belonged to these same New Model regiments which had been responsible for the defeat of his father.

One of Charles's first acts was to make Monck a duke and appoint him lord-general, or as we should now class him, commander-in-chief. This no doubt was done largely through gratitude although it was also a matter of policy, for Monk, or Albemarle as we must now call him, was probably the only man in the kingdom capable of controlling the army.

The new king's original plan seems to have contemplated retaining at least some of the Commonwealth regiments and simply replacing their officers by royalist nominees of his own choice, but he quickly changed his mind. It was soon clear to him that the extreme republican sentiments which permeated the army would have made it very unreliable, so he decided on disbandment as the only practical alternative. The lord-general, who agreed with him, was responsible for putting the decision into operation and the tact and skill with which he handled his delicate task, allied to his own high reputation with the soldiery, enabled it to be completed without any trouble. A poll tax was imposed to defray the considerable cost of settling the arrears of pay, and arrangements were made to settle the discharged soldiers back into civil life with a minimum of friction. By the early months of 1661 the disbandment was virtually complete and at least 30,000 men had been disposed of.

Monck had taken the sensible precaution of keeping his own

regiment intact, and it was as well that he did so because very shortly they were called upon to suppress a small insurrection on the part of a fanatical sect calling itself the 'Fifth Monarchy Men'. This confirmed the necessity for a small permanent force to guard the king and ensure the security of the metropolis and, as the first steps in this direction had already been taken on 23 November 1660 by ordering the raising of a regiment to be known as the King's Royal Regiment of Guards, it did not take long to bring a nucleus into being.

This unit, which is still with us under the more familiar title of the Grenadier Guards, was raised by Colonel John Russell. He was a devoted Royalist, a member of the semi-secret organization the Sealed Knot, and had spent some time in the Tower after the abortive rising of 1658; thus his loyalty to Charles was absolute. There was no shortage of willing and acceptable volunteers and in a very short time the new regiment had been recruited to 12 companies, each 100 strong.

This was a start but more troops were clearly required and as Monck's regiment was ready to hand, and had proved reliable, it seemed eminently sensible to retain it. Therefore in February 1661 it laid down its arms briefly in token of disbandment, gave three cheers, and took them up again as the Lord-General's Regiment of Footguards. It is not clear what the men in the ranks thought of this; like most soldiers they were simple enough souls with a high reputation for discipline, and presumably they were ready enough to trust their general and follow where he led. The new regiment, proud of the part it had played in the Restoration, later adopted for its title the name of the remote border village whence it had set out for London, and is now better known as the Coldstream Guards.

Another problem now faced the king. During his exile in Flanders he had raised another small regiment of Guards which had given gallant service. These remained in garrison at Dunkirk (then a British possession) at the Restoration, but soon afterwards Charles sold that place back to the French and the regiment came home. Seniority vis-à-vis the new King's Royal Regiment of Guards then became a problem, since both had some claims to be regarded as the premier Guards regiment, and in 1665 Charles finally resolved the matter by amalgamating them. Twenty-four companies were however far too large a body to manoeuvre as one unit, so the king broke them down into two battalions, thus introducing into his infantry a system which is still in force in the British Army. The term battalion, which is of Italian origin, was not wholly new, but previously it had been used in a somewhat imprecise way, often to denote some unit formed for a particular task by the temporary grouping of a number of companies under one commander. After 1665 the term was used specifically to describe the standard infantry operational unit, and thereafter the regiment became almost wholly an administrative organization; for many years afterwards most regiments continued to be single-battalion in practice, and in these cases the distinction between the two terms inevitably tended to become blurred. It was not until the eventual establishment of all British Infantry regiments upon a basis of a minimum of two battalions that the distinction finally became clear. When Kipling referred in his poem *Route-Marching*, to 'a Regiment coming down the Grand Trunk Road' he really meant a battalion and he was by no means alone in his confusion of the two. It should also be mentioned here that most other armies continued to use regiments as operational formations where the British used brigades.

The next increase in establishment came with the withdrawal of a Scottish regiment in the French service. It had originally been raised in 1633 by a Colonel Hepburn, many of its original members having served under the great Gustavus Adolphus, and in 1661 Charles recalled it to England and incorporated it into the Royal Army. Once on the British establishment it was allowed to return to France where it remained until 1665 when it was recalled on the outbreak of war between Britain and Holland. It finally came back in 1678 and was given the title of the Royal Regiment by King Charles. It was however commonly known as Dumbarton's, after its colonel, George Douglas, who became the Earl of Dumbarton in the year of its final return; it is still the senior line regiment of the British Army under the title of the Royal Scots. In 1678 it had already reached a strength of 21 companies, but strangely enough it was not until 1686 that it was finally broken down into two permanent battalions.

Soon after his accession to the throne, Charles married the Portuguese princess Catherine of Braganza, who brought as part of her dowry the North African port of Tangier. The hinterland of the place was held by the Moors, a warlike race who maintained an almost constant state of hostilities against it, and although it was held by a garrison of Spanish and Portuguese troops it was evident that a British military presence would also be necessary. In October 1661 therefore the Earl of Peterborough raised a regiment for its defence and many veteran soldiers of the Commonwealth Army joined it. It was formed on an establishment of nine companies and by 1662 was in Tangier where it spent the next 22 years, much of it in active operations against the Moors. It took precedence immediately after Dumbarton's and will be better known to most people as the Queen's Regiment.

A third regiment came on to the British establishment in 1665, although it had then been in existence for nearly 100 years. In 1572 the London Guilds raised several bodies of troops to help the Dutch against the Spaniards, these various bodies being reduced to a single regiment in 1648. Although in the service of Holland, its members remained essentially loyal British subjects and particularly welcomed the restoration of Charles II. Then came the Anglo-Dutch war of 1664, when the Dutch began to have some reservations regarding the loyalty of the regiment; although this was unkind it was perhaps understandable in view of the regiment's uncompromising attachment to their country of origin. The Dutch demanded that its members should immediately renounce their allegiance to England with the alternative of being disbanded. The regiment unhesitatingly chose the latter course and its members were cast adrift, often in great distress and poverty. Most of them made their way home, many with the help of the British Ambassador, and these formed the basis of the new regiment which started as the Holland Regiment, and subsequently became the 3rd, but which is perhaps better known in British service as the Buffs. The regiment was originally raised for sea service and therefore had no pikes, but it reverted to normal infantry duties in 1667, and was rearmed accordingly.

A fourth regiment was raised in 1660, mainly in the West Country; it was initially intended as a reinforcement to Tangier and was at first known as the 2nd Tangier Regiment. After the evacuation of Tangier it returned to England and subsequently took its place as the 4th.

It may be as well at this stage to consider a typical infantry regiment of the Restoration period, which would in fact have differed very little from one of its predecessors of the New Model. At the head of a regiment was a colonel, often a member of the Royal Family or a distinguished general or nobleman, and he might not in fact have much to do with the day-to-day running of the regiment or even its command in action. This was left to the lieutenant-colonel who had a major as second-in-command, an adjutant, a chaplain, a surgeon and mate, a quartermaster, and a marshal or martial. All these are easily understood except the latter who appears to have performed the duties of a modern sergeant-major; at times, when the establishment was low, the quartermaster seems to have fulfilled this role in addition to his own. Then there were the companies, anything from eight to twelve and each consisting of a captain, two subalterns, an ensign, two sergeants, three corporals, two drummers, and 100 privates. The usual form was for the colonel, the lieutenant-colonel and the major also to hold the captaincies of three of the companies; the colonel's company was then commanded by a captain-lieutenant and the others by their senior subalterns, an odd system designed primarily to increase the emoluments of the three senior officers. When a regiment had two battalions it remained under a single colonel, the two battalions then each having its own lieutenant-colonel and staff.

These figures are typical but there were of course minor variations to them. Dumbarton's for example insisted on having a physician in addition to a surgeon and in 1679 also applied successfully for a pipe-major. The King's Regiment of Guards also added a drum-major, a sergeant and one piper in 1662 and fifers (one per company) in 1674. The Tangier Regiment carried a gunsmith on its headquarters establishments, due presumably to the fact that it was permanently in a remote garrison overseas where there were no other facilities for repairing weapons.

It must also be made clear that the figures given are for the higher or war establishment and were often drastically cut in peacetime. Sometimes whole units were disbanded but the general practice well into the nineteenth century was to reduce the number of companies, or the number of men in a company, or a combination of both. Units usually contrived to retain a minimum of seven or eight companies, although these were at times reduced to as few as 30 private soldiers. This system, though not wholly satisfactory, did at least retain a cadre on which to expand. When an emergency occurred the establishments were at once increased and it was then hoped that there would be plenty of men ready to return to the colours. It was in fact a primitive forerunner of the reserve system introduced some 200 years later. Before leaving this subject it should also be said that until the various unions occurred there were also Scottish and Irish establishments whose strengths, and even rates of pay, differed from those of England.

The weapons used in the period are dealt with in detail later in this chapter, so here it will be sufficient to repeat that they consisted of muskets and pikes in a ratio of about two to one.

James II, who succeeded his brother in 1685, was a competent soldier who had served several campaigns in Europe and who had an undoubted flair for organization. Unfortunately from the country's point of view he was also a devoted Catholic, which in the end was to prove his downfall. During his brother's reign he had been excluded by Parliament from holding any office because of his religion but once on the throne, being a narrow-minded, bigoted and vindictive individual, he was determined to have his own untrammelled way.

His first idea was to strengthen his army, which if all else failed he reckoned he could use as an instrument of oppression. Although

Parliament was, as ever, extremely chary of any proposal to increase the land forces it so happened that at that particular time the Duke of Monmouth, the illegitimate son of Charles II, landed in the West Country and raised his standard in the Protestant cause. This was flagrant rebellion, and although there were probably a good many members of Parliament who sympathized in secret, Monmouth's action could not be condoned. Thus James had the good fortune to get his own way without coming into conflict with the House of Commons, and was able to raise several regiments, four of which were to become the 12th, 13th, 14th and 15th.

One of his first actions was to bring onto the English establishment a regiment of foot Guards which his brother had caused to be raised in 1660 for garrison duties in Scotland, and so there came into official being a third or Scottish regiment of foot Guards which is also of course still with us. An historian of the regiment tells an amusing little story of how, when the regiment was first formed, the officer commanding it, though a Scot, disliked the pipes so much that he refused to allow pipers on the establishment, and insisted that if companies wanted pipers they were to be paid for privately by the captains concerned. It is an early example of the rugged individuality, combined with a strong sense of personal ownership, which was for many years to be the mark of colonels of British Infantry regiments.

James also recalled certain English and Scottish regiments from Holland and two of these were brought onto the English establishment and subsequently became the 5th and 6th Regiments. They returned to Holland almost immediately and it is perhaps ironical that their next appearance in England should have been under the banner of William.

An ordnance regiment was raised at the same time; it was designed to guard the military train and had no pikes, while for safety's sake all its muskets were flintlocks. It consisted of 12 companies of musketeers, but as the train then comprised both gunners and engineers (who were in fact virtually interchangeable) the new regiment, which in course of time became the 7th, also included a company of miners. It was followed in quick succession by four more regiments which subsequently became the 8th, 9th, 10th and 11th.

As soon as the Monmouth rebellion had been dealt with, Parliament attempted to reduce the army. Memories of Cromwell's military rule were still strong and they dreaded the thought of government by armed coercion. They considered (or at least found it convenient to consider) that the defence of the Kingdom could safely be left to the navy with a militia as second line. This latter, as they well knew, would be officered by the country magnates, many of whom had seats in the House, and thus by its nature could never be used to hold down the country. King James on the other hand argued (and with much truth) that the militia had proved useless in the recent campaign in the west, and when Parliament cut his military estimates by half he promptly prorogued it; nor was it recalled during his reign.

In order to ensure military support he then began to replace Protestant officers, particularly the more senior ones, by Catholics of his own choice. Simultaneously he established a considerable military camp at Hounslow, apparently with the object of over-awing London in general and Parliament in particular. This however did not prove successful, for anti-Catholic feeling in the country was strong and the soldiers as a whole proved to be no exception to the rule.

In 1688 the king imprisoned seven bishops in the Tower for refusing to read a notice ordering a relaxation of the penal laws against Catholics. They were promptly acquitted and the news provoked such immoderate joy amongst the soldiers that James became seriously alarmed and dispersed the camp, thinking pre-sumably that a spell of isolation might stop the spread of Protestant doctrine. After allowing a few weeks for this new idea to work he ordered Lichfield's regiment (later to be the 12th) to parade at Blackheath where he informed it that they might either take a pledge of indulgence to the Catholics or leave his service. To his fury almost every man at once grounded his arms, only two Catholic officers and three or four soldiers declining to do so. It was clear that his experiment had failed and he angrily bade them take up their arms, muttered that next time they would not be con-sulted, and so departed.

He next turned to his army in Ireland and began a wholesale and quite illegal cashiering and dismissing of Protestants on a variety of transparently flimsy pretexts, replacing them in all cases by Irish. This was madness, for the English regarded the Irish with contempt and it was this sort of conduct which had to a great extent caused the downfall of his father. The whole army in Ireland was in ferment; men refused to accept Catholic recruits, and officers were court-martialled and cashiered for protesting against their enlist-ment. At this moment the furious feeling against the Irish found vent in a remarkable doggerel ballad, *Lillibulero*, with a gay and catchy tune. It swept through the army and it was later said, probably with some justification, that it was one of the instru-ments which caused the king's downfall.

In Holland, King William of Orange, who had long waited the summons, was finally invited over with his wife Mary, a daughter of James but a confirmed Protestant. James took alarm and raised various new regiments, two of which later became the 16th and 17th, and summoned various other troops to him from Scotland. By then however, the die was cast and towards the end of the year William landed in England at Torbay. James marched west to meet him but by the time he reached Salisbury it was clear to him that his situation was hopeless. There were wholesale desertions, even by those he had regarded as his close friends and supporters, and James fled the country leaving the field open to William.

William III very soon found that he had serious problems in his newly acquired kingdom. The population as a whole were discontented and divided, and the army in particular was surly and angry, for in spite of its strong Protestant views it still felt, illogically perhaps but understandably, that it had allowed a foreign army to take over the country without firing a shot.

France declared war on Holland as a result of William's landing and the British, bound by treaty, at once despatched four battalions of Guards and six of the line to Holland. Amongst the latter was the Royal Scots who, feeling that they had been transferred from James' service to that of William, promptly mutinied. They set off for Scotland but were pursued and surrounded by a vastly superior Dutch force and very sensibly surrendered. William treated them leniently and they then went to Holland as ordered, but the episode was nevertheless unsettling. It led directly to the passing by Parliament of the Mutiny Act in 1689, a concession which as Fortescue truly says 'was wrung from it by the pressure of fear'.

In the same year that the Mutiny Act became law James II landed in Cork and William found himself faced with the reconquest of Ireland. This led to the raising of a number of new regiments; some of these were disbanded at the end of the war but six remained in existence to become in due course the 18th, 19th, 20th, 22nd, 23rd and 24th Regiments of foot. The missing number 21 fell to a Scots regiment which had been brought onto the British establishment the year before.

The British regiments in Flanders had in the meanwhile proved to be of poor quality and dubious discipline, and Marlborough was sent off to reorganize them, which he did with some success. Then came the Scottish rebellion and the disaster at Killiecrankie in 1689 when the Highlanders defeated the British troops present. These were represented by an English regiment, later the 13th, a Lowland regiment newly raised for the defence of Edinburgh which later became the 25th, and three Scottish regiments of the Dutch service.

The English regiment fought well and retained a good order; the Scots regrettably enough broke and ran. The battle is best known for the fact that the British could not plug their bayonets in after firing their volley before the Highlanders were upon them; this hastened, if it did not actually lead to, the invention of the socket bayonet.

This Scottish campaign gave rise to a regiment of Covenanters later to become the 26th (Cameronians). It should be added perhaps that they had no part in the Killiecrankie disaster.

The British troops in Ireland proved to be of very poor quality, being ill-led, ill-trained, ill-fed, and ill-clothed, so that although they improved perceptibly as the operations progressed, William put his main trust in his steady Dutch regiments. The Irish affair, which was over by 1691, led to the formation of a regiment of Irish Protestants from Enniskillen, later the 27th.

As soon as William had disposed of this problem he departed to Flanders. Parliament was surprisingly helpful and voted 50,000 British troops, so that taking his foreigners into consideration William had a large army. Unfortunately he was not up to coping with the French and although his troops fought well he suffered some reverses. His infantry did well at Steenkirk in 1692, where the 20-year-old Colonel Angus of the Cameronians fell at the head of his men, and again at Landen in 1693. The siege of Namur in 1695 gave the British Infantry a taste of siege work and earned the future 18th Regiment the title of Royal Irish, the first to be won on the actual field of battle. Then in 1697 the war ended with the Treaty of Rijswijk and the British came home, having learnt a good deal of practical soldiering in a hard school where, though not always successful, they had by no means disgraced themselves.

Parliament then announced that all regiments raised since 1680 were to be disbanded, and although William succeeded in modifying this somewhat, the reductions were nevertheless drastic. The army came down to 7,000 in England and 12,000 in Ireland; regiments were reduced to cadres, and as there was a shortage of money the thousands of men discharged were often cast off in great distress.

The next European trouble came about as the result of a large scale quarrel over the succession to the Spanish throne, from which the ensuing war took its name. In 1701 Britain, in accordance with its treaty with Holland, was required to send a force to that country and no one (except perhaps the House of Commons) was unduly surprised at the chaos which ensued in the scramble to raise new units and augment others. Perhaps fortunately, thousands of cast-off soldiers were in such dire distress that they were glad enough to return to the colours; amongst the new regiments raised were two which survived as the 35th and 36th.

In June 1701 Marlborough took 12 battalions to Flanders; in

September of the same year James II died, upon which the King of France recognized his son as King of England, a fact which caused great fury and greatly facilitated the raising of new units. Fifteen were formed in all, of which seven remained after the war to become the 28th, 29th, 33rd, 34th, 37th, 38th and 39th Regiments. The three missing numbers, 30th, 31st and 32nd, were all raised as marines in 1702 and did not become regiments of the line until 1715.

Then King William died, Anne took over, and the stage was set for the greatest conflict yet to be experienced by the British Army. Although a detailed account of the actual operations is outside the scope of the book, we must now consider the condition of the British Infantry when the war started and the lessons it learnt from it.

The organization of infantry battalions had altered very little since the Restoration and need not be reconsidered here. The real changes had come about in weapons; fire power had been increasing in importance for many years before 1660 so that by the time of the Restoration the most important infantry weapon was undoubtedly the musket. There was very little standardization in those days, particularly since many of the arms then in use may well have been the relics of those purchased hastily during the Civil War, but in spite of this it is possible to provide a reasonably accurate, if general, picture of the main type of musket then in use. Its barrel was at least 44 inches (112 centimetres) long and fired a loose-fitting spherical lead ball about 0.7 inches (18 millimetres) in diameter by means of a charge of black powder. At the breech end of the barrel, on the right side, was the pan, a shallow spoon-shaped projection from which a touchhole led into the bore. This pan held fine priming powder and was equipped with a swivel cover to keep out wind and rain. A hinged arm, equipped with screwjaws, was attached to the stock in such a way that pressure on the trigger caused the jaws to dip towards the pan. Into these jaws could be fitted the match, which gave the weapon its name; it consisted of a length of loose cotton cord soaked in a solution of saltpetre or some similar compound to make it burn steadily, and it could be so adjusted that pressure on the trigger lowered its glowing end into the priming. When this ignited, the flame passed into the main charge (which had been loaded from the muzzle end) and the shot was fired. Matchlocks were simple weapons in theory but complicated in practice, due chiefly to the need to remove the burning match from the jaws before the pan could be primed. This, together with the many other movements necessary to reload the piece reduced the rate of fire to about one round every three or four minutes. In the early days, when muskets had weighed 20 pounds (nine kilograms) or more, forked rests had been provided, and even

33

after the weapons had been reduced to a size where they could reasonably be fired from the shoulder without support, these rests had lingered on, presumably because they allowed the musketeer the use of both hands in reloading. They were however clumsy, awkward things and seem to have gone out of fashion for service purposes soon after the beginning of the Civil War in 1642. They lingered however for ceremonial purposes and it is possible that a few were still in use by sentries and the like as late as the Restoration.

The matchlock musket would probably kill in a purely random way up to 300 yards (275 metres), but was accurate under service conditions to little more than about 60 (55 metres). The lock functioned reasonably well in dry weather but rain could extinguish the match, or damp the priming, to the point where the piece would not fire. The burning match was also a constant source of danger in the presence of exposed powder and was also very liable to give away the position of musketeers at night. Its use also threw additional strain on the somewhat rudimentary supply services of the period, since armies in close contact were obliged to keep their matches burning and so got through vast quantities. Firth states as an example in *Cromwell's Army* that the garrison of Lyme, numbering 1,500 men, often got through five hundredweight (254 kilograms) of match in 24 hours.

There were at the time better ignition systems available for firearms. The wheel lock, which relied on the rotation of a clockwork-driven steel wheel against a piece of pyrites for sparks to ignite the priming, was expensive to manufacture, and its use thus confined almost entirely to mounted officers, but the snaphance, and its later development the true flintlock, were both rising in popularity. Both relied on the action of flint and steel, and both were simpler to use and a great deal more reliable than the matchlock; they were also safer in the presence of powder because they only made their fire at the moment required. Some weapons of this type had been used in the Civil Wars, particularly by troops guarding the artillery train, where accidental explosion was always a risk, and by dragoons; nevertheless the standard infantry firearm of the Restoration was the matchlock. Oddly enough Monck re-equipped his regiment with flintlocks on arrival in London in 1660, but these were replaced by the older type in 1665.

The flintlock was so obviously a superior weapon to the matchlock that it was bound to oust it in the long term; replacement seems to have begun by 1670 and by 1683 all the Guards regiments were fully equipped with flintlocks while the others had at least a percentage. It is likely that the changeover had been finally completed by 1700 at the latest. In 1684 each company of the Royal

Scots had 10 light fowling pieces, in addition to its normal muskets, for use by flankers, an early form of light-armed skirmishers.

Musketeers originally wore bandoliers, leather shoulder belts with 12 screw-topped cylindrical wooden containers, each containing a charge of powder, suspended from them; the equipment also included a flask of very fine powder for priming, and a bullet bag. In battle replenishment was by means of small 'budge' barrels of powder placed conveniently behind the firing line so that musketeers could refill their bandoliers when necessary. It is recorded that in one battle at Tangiers in 1680 the musketeers expended an average of three or four bandoliers in seven or eight hours which implies that they were in more or less continuous action.

Bandoliers were eventually replaced by cartridge boxes, worn on a belt over the left shoulder. Cartridges were made up in cylindrical screws of paper, each containing ball and charge, and were introduced with the flintlock.

The other principal weapon at the time of the Restoration was the pike, some 14 to 16 feet (4.3 to 4.9 metres) long. Unlike the musketeers, the pikemen wore part armour, usually a helmet and corselet, and this, combined with the weight and awkward size of their weapons, made it essential that they should be as large and strong as possible. The ratio of pikes to muskets had been decreasing for some years. In 1661 the King's Regiment of Guards had 500 pikes to 700 muskets, which was probably a fairly average proportion for the period. Regiments raised for sea service were armed entirely with muskets; in 1666 for example, the Holland Regiment had 13 flintlocks and 60 matchlocks in each company.

A new weapon which was to unify infantry tactics was the bayonet. Its earliest history is almost impossible to untangle since it seems to have come and gone and come back again in a most bewildering way. The Tangier Regiment had them in 1673, as did the dragoons, but it seems likely that they were not a general issue until about 1688. The earliest patterns had a tapered handle which jammed into the muzzle, so that once fixed they reduced the musket to a short pike only, with no missile capacity. This led to a disaster, and subsequently to the socket bayonet, which allowed the musket to be loaded and fired with the bayonet fixed. Bayonets of this type were probably in fairly general issue by the end of the century.

One of the lessons of the Thirty Years War had been the value of grenades in siege operations, and these were introduced into the British Army in 1677. They consisted of hollow iron spheres about three inches (76 millimetres) in diameter, filled with powder and equipped with a fuse which had to be lit by a match similar to that used in the matchlock musket. The whole thing weighed from three to four pounds (1.4 to 1.8 kilograms) and grenadiers were therefore selected from the biggest and most powerful men in the battalion. The original intention was that there should be a few in each company and in May 1677 Captain Lloyd of the King's Guards ran what would now be described as a cadre course. Two privates from each company of foot Guards, 54 men in all, attended, but by 1678 this concept had been abandoned and each battalion had its own grenadier company.

The grenadiers carried light flintlock muskets, commonly known as fusils, equipped with slings so that they could be slung across the back leaving both hands free. They were also equipped with bayonets, short swords or hangers, and hammer-hatchets, the latter designed to hack down palisades. Each man carried three or four grenades in a leather pouch, slung over his left shoulder and on the front of the shoulder strap was a perforated brass match case so that a burning match could be carried without risk of its being extinguished by rain. Although this book is not concerned with uniform it may be said here that at first the grenadiers wore loose bag-caps, rather like old fashioned nightcaps, so that their muskets could be slung without knocking them off. These were later stiffened and stylized into the more familiar mitre caps of the eighteenth century. Grenadiers usually carried their musket cartridges in a pouch worn on a narrow waistbelt in the centre of the body.

Soon after the introduction of the grenade, attempts were made to increase its efficiency by firing it from a discharger, usually a cup attachment to a musket. Some of these were extremely ingenious but they seem never to have become a general issue.

In 1682 the fire power of the infantry was further increased by the issue of two light brass three-pounder field pieces. These were normally moved by horses in the usual way, but on the battlefield they were drawn by detachments of soldiers using a special type of harness. They were handled and fired by selected infantrymen and not by the Royal Artillery.

The period 1660 to 1702 was a troubled one, and the extraordinary confusion of political events was matched by similar upheavals in the infantry, particularly in the matter of armament which naturally had an effect on tactics. As we have seen, the infantry during this period had matchlock muskets, flintlock muskets, and fusils; it had bandoliers and cartridge boxes; it had bayonets intermittently, some plug, some socket; it had pikes and swords; it had grenades; it even had light field pieces, and the problems of handling all these in some sort of tactical harmony were considerable and constantly changing.

The other arms were not affected to anything like the same degree; the cavalry had their swords and the artillery their guns, but the infantry was in a process of major transition. Fortunately this process was virtually complete by the outbreak of the War of the Spanish Succession so that the army which Marlborough took to Flanders had achieved a relatively uniform standard of arms and training.

The general introduction of the musket and bayonet had at least given the infantryman a standard weapon, equally well suited to shock or missile action, and had finally done away with the old and almost insoluble problem of handling pikemen and musketeers in close conjunction in the confusion of battle. It is sometimes asserted that there were still a few pikes remaining in the army which went to Flanders and this may possibly be so, but they had almost certainly been withdrawn before any serious fighting started. They had in fact been to some extent optional for several years; as early as 1689 the commanding officer of the regiment which later became the 10th had been offered muskets in lieu of those pikes he had left, and it is certain that before the end of the century some companies of foot Guards were wholly armed with muskets. The history of the Worcestershire Regiment (29th) quotes a Whitehall letter of 20 June 1702 instructing that the remaining pikes should be returned to store, and this may well have been their swan song.

The universal introduction of the flintlock in place of the earlier matchlock had naturally improved the fire power of infantry very considerably. Even under battle conditions well-trained soldiers could probably produce two rounds a minute, which made the fire of a battalion a very formidable proposition. The old six-deep formation was abandoned for one of half its depth, which allowed every man the free use of his musket, and this led in its turn to a considerable increase of the frontage of a battalion in line. The ranks were a pace apart, which having regard to the length of the musket barrel allowed every man to discharge his musket simultaneously if necessary. It must have been (like war itself) a very noisy, dirty and occasionally dangerous business, particularly for the front rank, and it is probable that the occasional soldier had his head blown off by an excited comrade behind him, but the thing was nevertheless not only possible, but normal practice.

The Duke of Marlborough was a great believer in infantry fire power. Any man not plying a musket was wasted in his view, which reduced still further the likelihood of any pikes lingering in his army. He abolished the old system of firing by successive ranks (which the French however continued until the end of the war) and in its place he substituted a system of fire by platoons. The word platoon, like many other military terms, has meant different things at different times, but in Marlborough's day it represented a fire unit half a company strong, or about 40 muskets. Assuming a normal battalion consisted of nine companies (including its grenadiers), this gave it 18 platoons, divided into three 'fires'. Although battalions varied the order somewhat, the broad principle was that six nominated platoons fired either together, all three ranks, or in rapid succession, followed by the second six and then by the third. Each 'fire' reloaded immediately, so that allowing for an interval of 15 seconds or so between volleys (which was often essential because of the smoke) a continuous fire could be kept up for a long period. As a minimum of one third of the muskets were always ready, the risk of a sudden successful dash at the line by hovering cavalry was also greatly reduced.

Marlborough took great interest in the swift and accurate performance of this drill, and on occasions was known to exercise the whole of the British Infantry under his own eye. Milner, in his *Journals, Battles, and Sieges*, describing a parade at Meldert in 1707, wrote that:

> The Duke of Marlborough reviewed all the British Corps who exercised and fired four rounds gradually before him, and that by the signal of the waving of a Pair of Colours for each Word of Command, performed by Colonel Wm Blakeney on the Top of one of our Pontoons, posted a little in the Front thereof; attended by each Drum-Major with a Drummer, in the Front of their respective Regiments, who at each wave of the Colours gave a tap on his Drum answerable to, and for each Word of Command, for which each Regiment observed to perform accordingly.

It is very likely that this was the drill originally invented by one Captain Barrell, sometime an adjutant of a battalion of the King's Guards, whom the historian of the regiment describes as 'rough in manner, but an excellent soldier.'

The development of linear tactics, although inevitable in view of the great increase in importance of musketry, had a certain deadening effect on mobility. In the old days of deep formations it was relatively easy to move them, but an extended three-deep line was almost impossible to move across country for more than a short distance – a fact which anyone with even basic experience of modern ceremonial drill on a level parade ground, will readily confirm. There seems however to have been little practical alternative except column of route, which was simply the six-deep line turned to a flank, and this was both slow and susceptible to cavalry, although a method of forming square from line did exist. There is no doubt that the concept of forming an open column of subunits by wheeling them right through 90 degrees from line was known, but it seems to have been little used. Bland, in his *Treatise of Military Discipline*, a book which sets out to systemize military procedures and tactics in the light of lessons learnt in the War of the Spanish Succession, certainly advocates the use of the column as a tactical formation, particularly by advance guards, and gives some general ideal of the system used, although he does not go into great detail. He also goes further and advocates a quick way of forming square by a battalion marching in a column consisting of four grand divisions each of four platoons, and gives the following details:

> As soon as the Word of Command 'Form the Square' is given, the first Grand Division halts and by that forms the Front Face.
> The second and third Grand-Divisions divide in the centre and wheel to the Right and Left outwards, and form the Right and Left faces thus: the two Platoons on the right of those Grand-Divisions wheel to the Right and form the Right Face; and the two Platoons on the Left of each wheel to the Left and form the Left Face.
> The fourth Grand Division marches on till they come to the Flanks of the Right and Left Faces, and then face to the Right-about on their Left Heels, which forms the Rear Face . . .

This detail is of particular interest because of its remarkable similarity to the famous 'quarter-distance square' of Peninsular days, to which reference is made in a later chapter. Colonel Fuller claims, in his *Sir John Moore's System of Training*, that this type of square was invented at Shorncliffe by the Light Brigade, but it seems at least possible that it was inspired by Bland's earlier version. Bland of course was writing after Marlborough's wars and there is certainly no indication that these systems were used in those wars, or even, very surprisingly, for half a century afterwards. It was indeed due to the relative inflexibility of infantry on the march that, when the ground permitted, Marlborough employed his cavalry as his mobile striking force, leaving to his infantry the more arduous duties of the static fire fight, varied with the storming of hills, earthworks, or palisaded villages – all situations in which even the best cavalry were comparatively helpless. The infantry also had some experience of sieges, which in general it did not greatly enjoy – a dislike which was still noticeable in Wellington's army 100 years later. The siege of Tournai in 1709 was particularly arduous due to the great amount of mining which went on. A report in the *Daily Courant* of 20 August 1709, clearly from a participant, describes how:

> Our miners and the enemy very often meet each other, when they have sharp combats till one side gives way. We have got into three or four of the enemies great galleries, which are thirty or forty feet underground and lead to several of their (mine) chambers, and there we fight in armour by lanthorn and candle, they disputing every inch of the gallery with us to hinder our finding their great mines. Yesternight we found one which was placed just under our Bomb batteries in which were 18 cwt of powder besides many bombs, and if we had not been so lucky as to find it, in a very few hours our batteries and some hundreds of men had taken a flight in the air!

One point of great interest is the actual marching powers of the infantry of Marlborough's army, for it was only by speed, by appearing unexpectedly, that he was able to achieve surprise. It is difficult to draw any accurate comparisons with modern times because of the very different circumstances prevailing in the early eighteenth century; most roads, even major highways, were of relatively poor quality while the lack of suitable parallel side roads increased the problem very considerably by making dispersion difficult. Thus it often happened that thousands of men were struggling down the same muddy track intermingled with clumsy wagons and almost equally clumsy guns. In such circumstances a jammed wheel, a broken axle, a damaged culvert, or a horse trapped in some particularly deep patch of mud, could cause appalling blockages for miles back. As anyone knows who has ever taken part in a long march the real requirement is for steady, unimpeded progress. Nothing is more irritating or more exhausting for heavily ladened infantry (or indeed for heavy draught horses) than the sort of stop-go progress which must have been all too common in those days.

There were other problems too. Thirty thousand men and a few wagons, even when well closed up on a good road, occupied about six miles (9.5 kilometres) of space, so that it was a good two hours march before the rear of the column reached the point of departure of the head. Nor did armies bivouac in this snake-like form if it was humanly possible to avoid it; they much preferred to get under cover in some town or village, often a little off the main route, where rations might be assembled, issued, and cooked.

A high standard of movement control was therefore necessary, although the small size of staffs, and in particular the complete absence of any faster means of communication than a galloping horse, must have made this very difficult to achieve.

On the march to the Danube in 1704, which was practically a peacetime operation, the infantry appear to have averaged about 10 miles (16 kilometres) a day, whereas when Napoleon's Grand Army marched to the Rhine 100 years later its average, according to Chandler, was over eighteen miles (30 kilometres) a day. The roads then were a good deal better and the existence of suitable secondary roads made it possible to allot a separate route for each corps which naturally reduced congestion.

3 1714–1762 THE '15 REBELLION TO THE SEVEN YEARS WAR

In spite of its many great victories, the British Army ended the War of the Spanish Succession in a state of low morale. Political intrigues, apparently approved if not actively encouraged by Queen Anne, led to the downfall and disgrace of Marlborough, the beloved 'Corporal John' of his soldiers, and with his departure the war tailed off in a welter of broken promises and deserted allies.

Hostilities were finally ended by the shameful Treaty of Utrecht, but long before the document had been signed Parliament was hard at work cutting the Army to the bone. Disbandments and reductions began almost at once, and in a comparatively short time upwards of 30,000 men had been turned adrift in circumstances of callous indifference. Within reason some reductions were of course inevitable, but those put in train in 1713 went far beyond either common sense or fair dealing. In the past, regimental seniority had provided the guidelines for disbandments and the principle of last raised, first reduced, had been rigorously adhered to, but now things were being done in a different and more sinister way. The strong Jacobite interest in Parliament saw and seized its chance to dispose of potential troublemakers and several regiments of considerable standing appear to have been marked down for disbandment chiefly because of their known strong sympathy to the Protestant cause, amongst them the 6th, 14th and 22nd. Other regiments selected for reduction were the 28th, 29th, 30th, 31st, 32nd, 33rd and 34th, and in these cases the objection was not on the grounds of seniority but on the scope of the operation, which bade fair to leave the country practically defenceless.

Then Queen Anne died, which was probably fortunate for the country and certainly a good thing for the British Infantry. She was succeeded by George of Hanover, a monarch with very different views on running the country's affairs, and a number of changes were quickly made. Marlborough returned from exile to a hero's welcome and a new ministry took over the running of the country. Even so, extensive disbandments would still have been essential had not the fall of the axe been halted by the Jacobite Rebellion of 1715, which not only saved the doomed regiments but also led to the raising of eight more.

The threat from the north, small scale though it was, threw the country into a panic and there was the familiar scramble to form an army capable of dealing with the wild Highlanders. Most regiments had been so severely reduced in numbers that they were mere cadres and the ranks of these had to be filled hastily. Nor was there any great enthusiasm for re-enlistment on the part of recently discharged veterans of Flanders and Spain, with the result that the job had to be done with hastily raised recruits.

The eight new regiments were all disbanded at the end of the emergency so that the next permanent addition to the standing army was a regiment formed in Nova Scotia by the grouping of a number of previously independent garrison companies. This later became the 40th and was the first permanent new infantry regiment to be raised by King George I. It was followed in 1719 by a regiment of Invalids formed from Chelsea pensioners who were recalled to the colours during the abortive Jacobite rebellion of that year. In spite of extensive Spanish support the attempt failed, but the new regiment, originally raised to undertake static duties in garrison, survived to become the 41st.

In 1722 the great Marlborough died and was buried in Westminster Abbey. A new funeral drill was invented for the occasion and so for the first time the regiments lining the route 'reversed arms' and then 'rested on their arms reversed'. Reversed arms (musket or rifle, for the drill is still in use) are carried under the left arm, butt forward, trigger guard uppermost, with the left hand at the small of the butt and the right reaching across the back to grasp the barrel and steady the piece. All marching in this position was, and is, done in slow time. A soldier rests on his arms reversed by lowering the muzzle of his piece to rest on his left toe, crossing his hands on the buttplate, and bowing his head. In passing it should be said that the three volleys fired over Marlborough's coffin were of much older origin, having, it is believed, been invented by the German landsknechts who fired them in honour of the Trinity.

In the years following the War of the Spanish Succession Britain became more and more of a world power, with colonies to garrison and treaties to honour, and all this led to a steady demand for more soldiers, particularly infantry. Few members of Parliament, whether Whigs or Tories, had much love for the idea of a standing army, for memories of Cromwell's rule were still strong. There was

43

in the House a strong and influential body of opinion which believed, or which at least professed to believe, that a militia was sufficient for the land defence of the country. Training, except of the most basic kind, was held to be quite unnecessary. In time of need, so the theory went, patriots of all classes would flock to the defence of the realm under the politically reliable leadership of the country magnates and would automatically defeat any enemy they met, it being well known that even untrained Englishmen were more than a match for the best-trained foreign soldiers; God had decreed it in his infinite wisdom and who were mere mortals to doubt it? Perhaps fortunately, a few mortals, many of them with practical experience of warfare, were prepared to doubt Holy Writ in this particular case, with the result that the regular army not only remained in being but continued to expand slowly. Financial stringency only made this possible by retaining home-based units at cadre strength, and this caused problems when reliefs were required for battalions overseas. One answer to this was by drafting from other regiments, a system which although universally detested in the Army appeared to have no practicable alternative. The situation in this respect became so difficult that battalions abroad, particularly those in unhealthy and thus unpopular stations, were simply left to rot away until disease, old age and neglect finally eliminated them.

Soldiers in England were not a great deal better off. There were few barracks available except in the great fortresses so that the usual custom was to billet soldiers in inns. As the innkeepers disliked this system, which was unprofitable, they took care to do things as cheaply as possible, crammed their unwelcomed guests into attics, leaky outhouses, or barns, and fed them as badly as they dared. Very naturally the soldiers got their own back when they could. John Shipp served somewhat later in the eighteenth century but circumstances had not changed much when he wrote:

> When we were treated in the scurvy way I have spoken of by landlords on our line of march, we never failed to leave some token of our displeasure behind us. Thus one day at Chelmsford we were compelled to submit to dreadful bad quarters . . . greasy puddings and fat stews made of the offal of his (i.e. the landlord's) house for the last month. The fat on the top of this heterogeneous mixture was an inch thick . . . my comrades, on quitting the house, evinced their disapprobation of the treatment they had met by writing with a lighted candle on the ceiling 'D. . .d bad quarters – how are you off for peasoup? Lead dumplings – lousy beds – dirty sheets . . . in addition to this it did not require any very aggravated treatment to induce us to

teach some of mine hosts ducks and geese to march part of the way on the road with us; to wit, until we could get them dressed!

This system of billetting was partly due to economy, but was also to some extent a matter of policy. Regiments in England were kept almost constantly on the move, partly to spread the burden amongst inns and partly to prevent their officers from getting together and hatching plots to seize power, for the memories of the Lord-Protector were still strong. The continued presence of ne'er-do-well, idle, drunken, and thieving soldiers amongst them was also calculated to bring home to the public the fearful way in which their taxes were squandered, and also to ensure that the men in red coats remained beyond the pale. It also encouraged soldiers to regard themselves as outcasts, for then they were less liable to resent being called out to quell riots, pursue smugglers, apprehend highwaymen, and generally keep the peace, all duties which in the absence of any regular force of civilian constabulary, fell to them all too regularly. The only part of the kingdom to have barracks was Ireland, where the lack of inns made them essential. Even so, in the troubled state of the country they were regarded more as police posts than anything else, with the result that regiments were often scattered in penny packets over several counties, with adverse effect on their discipline, training, and administration. Nevertheless the individual soldiers were probably more comfortable than in billets, for although the barracks were pretty stark they were at least permanent, and with a little interest on the part of the officers and work on the part of the men, might be rendered moderately comfortable, at least by the standards of the labouring class of the eighteenth century from which the soldiers in the ranks usually came. The scale of issue of utensils to a company of the period comprised, 'Two bellows, twelve wooden platters, twenty-four wooden dishes, four ladles, three dozen trenchers, six drinking horns, and twelve brown chamber pots.' Not luxurious, to be sure, but probably comparing favourably with the civilian standards of the troops concerned.

The garrison of the Highlands also presented a problem. The country was wild and remote, and the soldiers did not much like service there. One result of this was the raising of certain Highland companies to police their own people and this proved surprisingly successful. Service in them permitted Highlanders to wear the kilt and carry arms, privileges which were otherwise forbidden them, so that many men of good family were glad enough to serve in the ranks. The arms of these companies were formidable, since every man carried fusil and bayonet, broadsword, and steel pistol, the latter borne on the left side of the body by an arrangement of straps. These companies were subsequently formed into a regiment which eventually became the 42nd and which is still with us under its now more familiar title of the Black Watch.

The War of the Austrian Succession started in 1741 as a result of an international dispute over the succession of Maria Theresa, daughter of the late emperor, to the Austrian throne. The British sympathized with the claimant, whose accession had in fact been agreed by the principal powers. France took the other side, while Frederick of Prussia, who had recently come to the throne and who had inherited a large and well-trained army, thought only in terms of gains for himself and his country. The British Parliament, having agreed to support Maria Theresa, had no option but to grant the necessary funds to provide 12,000 men in her support, and at once the usual scramble to raise new regiments and fill the depleted ranks of the old ones began. Sixteen new infantry battalions were raised, of which six survived to become the 43rd to the 48th.

The first important battle of the campaign was Dettingen in 1743. The British Army was under the personal command of King George II, the last British monarch ever to lead his troops into action. On this occasion it found itself virtually trapped and therefore compelled to fight under unfavourable circumstances, and the victory was gained mainly as a result of the shattering effect of the musketry of the British regiments involved. The French cavalry in particular were rendered impotent by it, and suffered heavy casualties for no corresponding advantage. This was perhaps the first battle which marked the emergence of good infantry as the dominant arm on the battlefield.

The battle of Fontenoy in 1745 ended in defeat, yet in spite of this it raised the British Infantry to an even higher eminence in the eyes of the armies of Europe. The French, under the famous Marshal Saxe, were in a good defensive position on this occasion with their front protected by earthworks and their flanks secure, and they were thus able to await the arrival of the allied army with considerable confidence. The allies on the other hand, particularly the Dutch and the Austrians, showed little enthusiasm at the prospect of driving head-on against an obviously strong position, and common sense suggests that they were right. The Duke of Cumberland however, full of ardour, eventually overruled them and it was decided to attack. The plan was simple to the point of brutality; the allies would march against the French right, and the British against their left, in the hope that the line could be broken by sheer battering-ram action.

Reconnaissance had made it clear that the British attack would be seriously menaced by a strong redoubt on their right flank, and in order to neutralize it a brigade of three British battalions, the 12th, 13th, and 14th, was detailed to attack it in a preliminary operation while the main line advanced frontally across half a mile (0.8 kilometres) of open ground to the line of redoubts and earthworks which clearly indicated the French position.

Things soon went wrong; the allies hesitated so obviously that the French were able to move reserves to their left, on which the British were advancing alone, and to make things worse the attack on the redoubt never materialized. The reasons for this are still by no means clear, but the most obvious possibility is a language confusion. Certainly there was no question of lack of courage for when the main attack started Ingolsby, the brigadier concerned, at once formed his battalions on the right and took part in it. He survived and was subsequently court-martialled for his failure at the redoubt, but got away with nothing worse than a reprimand.

The main attack was in two waves, each of 10 battalions in line; all the battalions of the first line were British, but three of those on the left of the second were Hanoverians. In spite of the extreme difficulty of manoeuvring long lines across country, or even across a parade ground for that matter, the advance was made in good order, the troops moving at what was then the usual battle step of 75 paces a minute. This is what we now know as slow time, and was made necessary by the need for careful dressing.

It is not proposed to give a full description of the battle since these can be found in many of the standard works on the British Army. All that need be said is that in spite of heavy casualties caused by a murderous crossfire of artillery the attack continued unbroken until it halted within 30 yards (27.5 metres) of the French, received a scattered and not very effective fusillade from them, and replied with a thundering and devastating series of battalion volleys in succession. These shattered the French infantry which broke and ran, so that Saxe was forced to launch his cavalry in a diversionary attack to give them time to reform, and also to allow his reserves to come forward.

The British fell back a little and appear to have wheeled back a battalion on either flank, thus converting their array into a vast oblong, and against this the French horsemen rode in vain, an experience later described by one of the survivors as being like charging flaming fortresses. As soon as they were driven off the British, still torn by artillery, essayed another advance but by this time French reinforcements, including the Irish brigade, had reached the breast-works. Retreat became inevitable and this was in good order, several determined attacks on the rear by the indefatigable French cavalry being beaten off by battalions turning about in succession and firing volleys. Some regiments of British horse then came up and allowed the retreat to continue relatively unmolested. As was to be expected, casualties were enormous. The total strength of the infantry involved, including the Hanoverians, amounted to some 15,000, of whom 4,000 were killed or wounded, a casualty rate of 27 per cent.

A few months after Fontenoy had been lost, Prince Charles, the Young Pretender, raised his standard in Scotland and marched south upon England with an army of Highlanders. Initially he achieved a good deal of success, for the best of the British troops were in Flanders and the units opposed to him were full of recruits. At Prestonpans the Highlanders, charging out of the mist with broadswords, shattered the small British force opposing them and for a time it looked as though the road to London might be open. Charles however also had his problems, for his Highlanders, in spite of their initial triumphs, showed no great enthusiasm for an invasion of England and many streamed off northwards, ladened with plunder, to look to their farms. The Scots had one more victory at Falkirk where 12 weak battalions, so full of recruits as to be little more than militia, broke and ran at the mere sight of the Highlanders; only the 4th and 48th stood firm, beating off the charging swordsmen with volleys of the kind which had broken the French at Dettingen.

In the meanwhile the Duke of Cumberland had been hastily recalled from Flanders and was back with his army and some Dutch allies, and with his arrival on the scene the end was certain. It finally came at Culloden where 12 battalions, drawn up in two lines with pairs of guns in the intervals of the front line, and with their flanks covered by dragoons, broke and almost destroyed Charles' force. The battle was essentially one of massive fire power opposed to brawn and muscle, and as we shall see later bore a marked resemblance to certain others fought by the British Infantry in Africa in the second half of the nineteenth century.

As soon as the Scottish rising had been quelled the army returned to the Continent where it continued to fight well until the war petered out in the Treaty of Aix-la-Chapelle. Once the war was officially over retrenchment naturally became the order of the day, and 10 battalions were quickly disbanded, while the survivors were cut down drastically by reductions to their establishments. So many men were discharged from the two services that a scheme was devised to settle them in Nova Scotia. The offers of grants of free land were tempting, and sufficient men came forward to make the settlement a success. One odd result of this was that it caused some apprehensions amongst the French settlers in Canada, which was to be the next scene of operations.

In spite of the fact that the British Infantry had a great deal of practical experience both at home and abroad between 1715 and 1746, very little new tactical doctrine emerged. The basic teachings of Marlborough had proved sound, and what was good enough for the great Duke was good enough for his followers, a cry which we shall hear again a century later.

The infantry still fought in three ranks and relied for its main success on its well tried system of musketry, usually firing by platoons but occasionally, as at Fontenoy, by whole battalions. The supreme importance of controlled fire power had been made clear, not only abroad but also against the Highlanders. All three ranks continued to fire together, standing, although occasionally the front rank knelt and sloped bayonets.

Tactics remained unimaginative, so that the height of the art was to bring a line of infantry to within effective musket range of its opponents and then let gunpowder (and discipline) take over. The result of this was that manoeuvre remained slow and clumsy. The only infantry formations were a line of three ranks or column of route, which was that same line doubled and turned to a flank. Frederick of Prussia, it is true, was then experimenting with a new and more flexible system of battlefield manoeuvre, but that had not yet come to fruition – or, at least, not to the notice of the other armies of Europe. The result of this was that cavalry, although less and less able to tackle steady, well-formed infantry, continued to be the arm *par excellence* for movement and pursuit.

Weapons had changed very little. The infantry musket had become relatively standardized in the form of the Long Land pattern flintlock with a 46-inch (117-centimetre) barrel which may fairly claim to be the first of the series referred to unofficially but extensively as Brown Bess. The early models had wooden ramrods but these were exchanged for steel ones from about 1740 onwards, which helped to speed up the rate of fire. The quality of powder had also improved, and although the priming horn of fine powder was carried, officially at least, until 1756, it is probable that practical soldiers had found some time before that a pinch of the ordinary propellant powder could safely be used for priming; this further reduced the time taken to reload.

Improvements in the rate of fire inevitably led to increased ammunition consumption and the number of rounds carried by the individual soldier had to be increased. In 1715 the usual scale per man was 24 rounds, although an extra half dozen might be issued when an engagement was expected, but by the middle of the century the scale had risen to 36. The cartridge pouches were by then fitted with wooden blocks pierced with vertical holes each just large enough to hold a round, this being a great improvement. The old system of packing cartridges horizontally in layers had made them difficult to get out in a hurry, so that soldiers expecting action had tended to place a few ready to hand in the top of their waist bands, a practice which though sensible, inevitably led to lost or damaged ammunition.

The only other personal weapon carried by the infantry soldier was the short sword or hanger. These seem to have fallen into disuse in the War of the Spanish Succession, but in 1721 George I had made it clear that he expected them to be carried, not indeed for any real practical reason but because they were the traditional mark of a soldier. In addition to individual weapons the battalion also retained its two light fieldpieces.

One major administrative improvement was the introduction of numbers, based and allotted strictly on regimental seniority, to replace the older and more haphazard method of designating regiments by their colonels' names. This system, which had caused confusion, had gone by 1753. One example was in the case (not uncommon) where colonels of different regiments had the same name. At one period the 3rd and the 19th were both Howard's Regiment and in order to differentiate them they were prefixed with the colour of their facings, hence the Buff Howards and the Green Howards. The former soon settled for its traditional title of Buffs, but the latter still exist under the old title. The allocation of numbers was not initially quite strict, so that if a numbered regiment ceased for some reason to exist, while others junior to it continued in being, they were all renumbered accordingly, which must have caused worse confusion than ever. It may be as well to note here that the numbers used in this book are in every case the final ones.

In 1751 George II, assisted by the Duke of Cumberland, produced a Royal Clothing Warrant in a tidy-minded attempt to regularize the dress of appointments of the various regiments. Although the subject is outside the stated scope of this book the warrant is interesting in a more general way because of its specific reference to the 'Six Old Corps' and to the 'Royal Regiments', all of which had certain privileges regarding dress. The Old Corps are listed as the 3rd, 5th, 6th, 8th, 27th and 41st, while the Royal ones are the 1st, 2nd, 4th, 7th, 18th, 21st, 23rd and the Highland Regiment (42nd). The existence of these favoured regiments is not in doubt, but the reason for the inclusion of some of them is still a matter for speculation amongst military historians.

An attempt was made in 1742 to establish permanent depot companies for infantry regiments, the object of these being to raise and train recruits, particularly when the regiment concerned was overseas. This was a laudable attempt to abolish the worst abuses of drafting but it was unfortunately short-lived and in a very short time the depot companies had been deployed elsewhere.

Although Great Britain and France were at peace in Europe in the early 1750s, they were involved in such extensive 'unofficial' warfare in North America and India that a formal declaration of hostilities could not be delayed for much longer. In 1755 therefore the British Government thought it prudent to prepare for large scale operations, and as a preliminary measure ordered 15 regiments to raise second battalions; this deliberate measure (as opposed to the simple splitting of oversized regiments), was a new departure and did not last long, for in 1758, 10 of the new battalions were constituted as separate regiments in their own right. The original regiments were as follows, the numbers in brackets being those allotted to their newly-independent off-spring: 3rd (61st), 4th (62nd), 8th (63rd), 11th (64th), 12th (65th), 19th (66th), 20th (67th), 23rd (68th), 24th (69th) and 31st (70th). The remaining second battalions, those of the 32nd, 33rd, 34th, 36th and 37th Regiments were reduced at the end of the war, which had as anticipated, broken out in 1756. A number of new regiments were also raised in 1756 and were numbered 50th to 59th. As the highest numbered previously mentioned in this chapter was the 48th (the last of the regiments raised for the War of the Austrian Succession) it may be as well to note here that the missing one, the 49th, had been formed in the West Indies in 1743 by the regimentation of various previously independant garrison companies in Jamaica.

There were three main theatres of war; India, Europe, and North America. The Indian operations, although important, can be dealt with briefly since they were fought mainly by troops, both European and Indian, of the East India Company. One important exception to this was the presence of His Majesty's 39th Regiment, which arrived in India in 1754 and which thereafter bore the proud motto *Primus in Indis*.

The British intervention in Europe was intended primarily as a diversion, to keep the French employed while the Royal Navy and various military detachments began the systematic seizure of what was to form the basis of an empire; the allied army in Europe was under the overall command of Prince Ferdinand of Brunswick and consisted of the British and the Prussians, the latter under the command of the celebrated Frederick the Great.

The most important event in the European theatre of the Seven Years War as far as the British Army was concerned was undoubtedly the remarkable performance of six British regiments at Minden in 1759. On this occasion the French were in a strong defensive position, but drawn up in a somewhat unusual fashion in that their centre was formed of cavalry with infantry on both wings, an odd reversal of the more usual custom. The French mounted troops consisted of 51 squadrons in two lines, with a reserve of a further 18 squadrons behind them.

A British force consisting of six British and three Hanoverian battalions was in process of forming up in order of battle opposite the French centre when the brigadier commanding the first line, consisting (from right to left) of the 12th, the 37th and the 23rd, suddenly decided to advance. The reasons for this odd action are not clear even now, though it is possible, as it was with the flank attack at Fontenoy, that a verbal order carried by an allied staff officer may have been misunderstood.

The second line, consisting (from right to left) of the 20th, 51st, and 25th with the three Hanoverian battalions on their left, were still in process of forming but as soon as the process was complete they too advanced in support of their first line, which by then had got some distance ahead. The advance at once came under heavy artillery crossfire; the French guns firing on the British left were at extreme range and thus did relatively little harm but those on the other flank were very close and inflicted heavy casualties. Nevertheless the advance continued, leaving the ground behind it scattered with fallen redcoats, until it was close to the enemy, when it halted.

The leading rank of the French cavalry at once charged but were broken by steady platoon fire at point-blank range. The second line then came forward, supported by a body of infantry which moved towards the British left flank, but both these attacks were shattered in their turn by the relentless, rolling musketry of the leading brigade. The French reserve then tried its luck and actually succeeded in riding through the depleted ranks of the first line. Then it met the six battalions of the second line, waiting expectantly in the smoke, and suffered the same fate as its comrades.

Although Lord George Sackville's failure to bring the British cavalry forward made the victory less decisive than it might have been, the blow to the morale of the French cavalry was as serious as the casualties inflicted. As was to be expected the allied casualties were not light, particularly in the right-hand battalions of the first and second line which had borne the brunt of the French artillery fire during the advance. The six British battalions went into action 4,434 strong and lost 1,330 killed and wounded, or almost exactly 30 per cent of their effectives. The Hanoverians suffered relatively lightly, not through any lack of courage but because they happened to be in the most sheltered position; even so their casualties amounted to 12 per cent, which can hardly be considered negligible.

One feature of the action was the absence of the grenadier companies of the regiments concerned, these having been withdrawn and formed into an ad hoc grenadier battalion under Major Smith of the 20th. This custom, which had started a few years before, and which was later extended to light companies, was a common one since it gave commanders battalions of high grade troops for special tasks. It was fundamentally a vicious system in that the worst casualties tended to fall disproportionately heavily on the best troops; nevertheless it lingered into the nineteenth century.

During their approach to the battlefield the British battalions involved at Minden had picked roses from the gardens along the way and many of them went into action with them stuck into their hats. The regiments concerned still keep up the custom of wearing roses on the anniversary of the battle.

Probably the most important innovation to emerge from the fighting in Europe was the new tactical system of Frederick the Great. Instead of moving his battalions in the long jointless lines then customary, he divided them into 10 equal divisions and by wheeling these to the right through 90 degrees he then formed a compact battalion column which, allowing 60 men per division in three ranks, gave it a frontage of only 20 men. This system, which like so many other things was fundamentally so simple that one is astonished that it took so long to evolve, enabled him to manoeuvre safely and freely in the close presence of an enemy in order of battle and allowed him to form line across the flank of his opponents, who being less mobile were hard put to change front to meet the new threat. Great attention was also paid to speed of musketry so that his infantry was able on occasion to deliver an astonishing volume of fire. Being produced by soldiers packed like sardines, its actual physical effect was surprisingly small, but its moral effect was great.

The Prussian system depended on extreme accuracy of drill, for unless distance and interval were exactly maintained chaos could result. When we consider that these various movements had to be put into operation by thousands of men moving across country we can only wonder at the success it achieved. It demanded above all things a high standard of activity and intelligence on the part of the regimental officers and non-commissioned officers, for although inexperienced soldiers in the ranks could be pushed and shoved into position by their more experienced comrades it was essential that commanders, guides and markers should know their business thoroughly. Even at best the drill had to be done slowly, so that Frederick sensibly left wide flanking movements and pursuits to his excellent cavalry while his infantry manoeuvred majestically on the main field.

Although perhaps not considered very sporting by the more reactionary soldiers of Europe, Frederick the Great's system caught on rapidly and by the end of the Seven Years War formed the basis of the tactical systems of every civilized army. Once introduced moreover it remained in use, although of course with some modifications, until modern times. Indeed many of the movements used in present day ceremonial parades – Trooping the Colour and the like – have their origins in the system devised by the Prussian king.

As long as campaigns were restricted to north-west Europe, or even to the open plains of India, there was no real and obvious need for light infantry. It is true that in the sixteenth century, when hand firearms were in their infancy, small bodies of mobile musketeers had been employed to cover the main battleline, but once firearms became universal the chief need was for extension so that every infantryman had a clear line of fire. These linear formations were, however, clumsy to manoeuvre in the presence of an enemy, so that tactics became heavier and less flexible until the general introduction of the Prussian type of battlefield drill.

Marshal Saxe had employed the wild Pandours of the Palatinate as light irregulars in Europe, and had demonstrated conclusively that even the textbook formations of Frederick could be seriously disrupted by the fire of mere handfuls of bold, active partisans. Nevertheless the real requirement for specially trained light troops only became apparent in the early campaigns against savage irregulars and it is thus clear that North America was the true cradle of this sort of soldier; it is to the Red Indian that we owe light troops in the eighteenth and nineteenth century meaning of the term.

The early European settlers in North America had learnt the techniques of irregular warfare by hard experience, and this was perhaps particularly true of the French. The British colonists had always tended to expect protection in the form of regular troops from their mother country but the French, having been left largely to their own devices, had learnt their business as a matter of hard necessity. They had, moreover, intermarried with the Indians and had thus produced a considerable number of half-breeds who combined the best (militarily speaking at any rate) of both their parent races.

The first and very clear example of the shortcomings of orthodox military tactics when applied to unorthodox situations was the defeat of General Braddock on the Monongahela River in 1755. It occurred in the strange twilight period when the British and French were officially at peace in Europe while conducting quite considerable campaigns against each other elsewhere.

Braddock's disaster, for it was nothing less, is well covered in the standard books on military history and can be dealt with briefly here. He advanced on Fort Duquesne with a detachment of good regular troops, almost all infantry and comprising 86 officers and something over 1,300 other ranks, plus a few locally recruited provincials, and he moved this force with great care. He was neither surprised nor ambushed in the strict sense of the word. He simply met a force of French, half-breeds, and Indians in the dense forest and was soundly beaten by a more flexible system of tactics. The British fired steady volleys in neat ranks; the enemy took cover and fought in the only fashion they knew, and the results were hideously decisive. Sixty-three officers and over 900 soldiers were shot down where they stood, after which the rest withdrew, if indeed such a military term may properly be applied to what was in effect a rout. Braddock fought gallantly and received terrible wounds from which he died a few days later, a surprised and disillusioned man. Those of his force too badly wounded to flee died too, and died unpleasantly under the knives and over the fires of the Indians, who did not share the European concept of the usages of war. Nor could the few French officers present do much about it except keep out of the way until the horrid slaughter was finally over.

The British, though steeped in the traditions of formal warfare, were by no means stupid, and they very quickly saw that drastic steps had to be taken to avoid any repetition of Braddock's unfortunate affair. Almost the first result was the raising of a four-battalion regiment at first known as the Royal Americans but later to achieve fame as the 60th Rifles. The leading figure in this was Colonel Bouquet, a Swiss officer with a long and distinguished record, and as soon as he had assembled a nucleus of some 40 officers, mostly Germans, he departed for Pennsylvania. That part of America was popular with settlers of British, Swiss, and German origin and it was there that he recruited the great bulk of his rank and file and not a few of his officers.

Bouquet's system was simple but revolutionary. He first taught his recruits the elements of cleanliness and discipline, after which they learnt to walk, to run and to manoeuvre across all types of terrain in open order, a process which automatically assured their physical fitness and activity. They had to handle their arms easily, load quickly, and shoot fast and accurately. They had to be able to swim, to handle canoes, to use snowshoes, to dig, to cook, to make their own clothes, and generally to fend for themselves, mostly things which as frontiersmen they took for granted. Nor were their moral standards neglected. General Fuller, in his book *British Light Infantry in the Eighteenth Century*, compares them favourably with what he described disparagingly as the 'modern board-school products joining the British Army in the 1920s:'

> They lived and fought like men, they were recruited not from the unemployed but from the skilled of the forests and the backwoods, where they had been brought up in an atmosphere of danger, not of blue-coated policemen but of scalp-hunting Indians. They worked like men and they learnt what a man should learn; to fight at times and at times to build himself a peaceful home ... there is only one true training for the soldier, namely, to act like a man under the certain circumstances of peace and the uncertain circumstances of war. The men of the 60th were not only admirable soldiers but good carpenters, masons, tailors, butchers and shoemakers; in an English company of the present day it would be difficult to find five men who could, or can, boil a potato or wash a handkerchief properly, let alone build a house or plough a field.

These strictures, though true, are very severe, for it is hard to blame a man for the shortcomings of his environment. Bouquet's men learnt most of their skills as part of their day-to-day life, but in the 1920s and indeed even more so in the 1980s, soldiers have to be taught them. Perhaps even General Fuller (who survived World War 2) would have agreed that the infantrymen of 1939–45, when well-trained, had proved remarkably adaptable in spite of their generally narrow city upbringing.

Lord Howe, who arrived in America in 1757 in command of the 44th Regiment, had no false pride but took as his mentor the famous leader of rangers, Robert Rogers, and had soon taught not only himself but also his regiment the rudiments of forest fighting. Much of it was common sense: powder and pipeclay disappeared; uniform was simplified; equipment was lightened; fights, for they could hardly be called battles, became a matter of loose order, speed, flexibility, and self-reliance, and the soldiers learnt fast. Best of all perhaps were the Highlanders whose background made them much closer to General Fuller's ideal soldier than the general run of British infantry, and two regiments of these, Montgomery's and Fraser's, did sterling service, though neither survived the Seven Years War. Yet all did well in the hard school of practical experience. One regiment, Gage's, was specially raised and equipped and also did well; it briefly held the number 80 in the line but was disbanded when the war was over.

General Wolfe, an officer with advanced but eminently sensible views on warfare, was an acknowledged leader in this field. Before the siege of Louisberg in 1758 he had raised a corps of light infantry 500 strong, carefully selected from the troops available for their intelligence, activity, and marksmanship. They wore inconspicuous clothing and carried the light artillery carbines in preference to the more clumsy musket generally issued to the infantry. Fire power – mobile, flexible, intelligently directed fire power – was everything and to maintain it each man carried 70 rounds. In order to achieve lightness they even discarded the bayonet, initially in favour of the tomahawk, but a year or two later it was brought back, partly because of its value for night work, but also to encourage the soldier to stay in action even after his last cartridge had gone.

Parkman, writing in his book *Montcalm and Wolfe*, says of the troops at Fort Edward in 1759 that they were: 'Drilling every day, firing by platoons, firing at marks, practicing manoeuvres in the woods, going out on scouting parties, bathing parties, fishing parties.' Even the sergeants abandoned their halberds, long cherished as a mark of rank, and reverted cheerfully to fusil and cartridge box.

By an odd quirk of fate, General Wolfe, the light infantryman *par excellence*, was to go down in history chiefly for his victory at Quebec which won Canada for Britain; strangely enough this battle was won not by any new light infantry tactics, but by steady, devastating volleys of the kind which had shattered the French horsemen at Minden.

Apart from the introduction of light infantry tactics, which was essentially a local phenomenon peculiar to Canada, there were few changes in the method of handling infantry on the battlefields of the Seven Years War, with the one important exception that by the end of hostilities most battalions had developed systems of drill based on the Prussian model. There was however no real uniformity of method as yet, so that when two or three units were ordered to manoeuvre together it was first necessary for the brigadier to reduce the different systems to some acceptable common denominator.

Establishments and the general details of arms and equipment remained very much unchanged. When a battalion of the 1st Royals was despatched on the expedition to Belle-isle in 1760 it took with it a fairly full scale, which as it appears by comparison with other units to have been a reasonably typical one, is worth setting out in detail.

Most of the items listed are straight forward but a few may require amplification. It is noticeable for example that the gun

CAMP EQUIPAGE

20 officers tents	160 hatchets
1 quarterguard marquee	160 mallets
160 soldiers' tents	160 tin kettles
320 standard poles	160 tin kettle covers
160 ridge poles	750 canteens
12 bell tents (for arms)	12 camp colours
12 standards (for arms)	20 drum covers
24 cross-sticks	10 powder bags
2,560 tent pins	

BATTALION GUNS

2 guns	7 horse halters
2 carriages	7 collars
1 bomb cart	3 saddles
	4 traces, iron
	4 cruppers
	4 dragropes

AMMUNITION AND ACCESSORIES

60 grape	2 lambskins
40 roundshot	2 powder horns
112 tubes (priming)	2 wires
24 portfires	2 hammers
1 strain of metall (sic)	2 spikes
2 tube boxes	1 lintstock
2 portfire stocks	1 pinchers
2 leather haversacks	500 springe tacks

ARMS AND EQUIPMENT

30 halberds	2 colours
20 drums	30 sergeants sashes
700 firelocks	700 pouches with shoulder belts
700 bayonets	700 waistbelts
700 swords	700 slings
700 cartridge boxes	70 grenadier matchcases
700 iron ramrods	

PIONEERS

10 axes
10 saws
11 aprons

equipment was apparently entirely horsedrawn, no reference being made to man-harness. Presumably each gun was drawn by three horses in single file and the bomb cart by one. The scale of ammunition and accessories for the guns is also self-explanatory with the exception of 'strain of metall'. Various experts in artillery matters have been unable to explain this, which suggests that it may be a misprint; the best suggestion was that it was some sort of sieve for removing lumps from gunpowder but this is pure speculation. The wires were for piercing the paper cartridges through the touchhole to ensure that the fire from the priming tube actually ignited the charge. The lambskins were for wrapping around the end of the sponge rod used for cleaning the bore of the guns, and the springe tacks were intended to keep them in place. It was of course necessary to remove and wash them regularly. No loading or cleaning tools are listed unless, as is possible, the word 'hammers' is a misprint for 'rammers'.

The 700 cartridge boxes may have been designed to carry extra rounds on the waistbelt, a practice sometimes adopted, but it is more likely that it was the term used to describe the pierced wooden containers which fitted into the pouches. It is noticeable that the iron ramrods are shown separately from the firelocks.

One odd omission is the lack of any reference to knapsacks or haversacks. These were usually classed as camp equipage at this period and one would have expected them to have been listed with 700 canteens which are obviously individual water containers, although whether of miniature barrel type or white metal bottles it is impossible to say.

4   1763–1805 RIFLEMEN AND LIGHT INFANTRY

The end of the Seven Years War brought the usual reductions in strength, but this time they were even more serious than before, because the war had resulted in the acquisition of vast new colonial territories which had somehow to be garrisoned. Recruiting was particularly difficult because the country was prospering and the pay of the soldier had not kept pace with that of the classes from which he was usually drawn. The result of this was that home battalions were reduced to little more than cadres, full of worn-out soldiers who could not be dispensed with because they could not be replaced. Decrepit they might have been, but they filled a place in the ranks and could at least take their turn on guard, so that commanding officers were loath to lose them.

Battalions overseas were usually made up to a reasonable strength by drafting before they went, but thereafter they were often left to rot from drink and disease because they simply could not be replaced.

The first mild crisis came in 1770 when the threat of a war with Spain made it necessary to augment the size of the Army. Infantry recruits were hardly to be found in England, so resort was had to the Catholic Irish, the beginning of a long and fruitful tradition of British regiments full of Irishmen. They made fine soldiers too, for if they had but little allegiance to the Crown they dearly loved a fight and the chance to loot which often followed it; nor, having regard to their habitual poverty, is it easy to blame them. They gave the British Army excellent value for its money and it is hard to see how it could have managed without them for the following 150 years.

The lessons of the Seven Years War, particularly those of Canada, were set aside, and training soon reverted to the showy drills of European warfare in the style of Frederick the Great. Everything was done at the customary dignified speed of 75 paces a minute, which in view of the age of many of the men in the ranks was probably just as well, for broken-down veterans are not the best material out of which to form light infantry.

The historian of the Queen's Regiment describes the manoeuvres performed by his regiment in Gibraltar in 1771 when being inspected by Lord Cornwallis as:

A General Salute, the manual Exercise, marched past by Grand Divisions, Fired by Companies and Grand Divisions from Flanks to Centre twice each, Fired by Companies and Grand Divisions from the Centre to the Flanks twice each to the Rear, Formed the Battalion to the Right and to the Left obliquely and to the Front, Advanced from the centre of Wings, Retreated from the Flanks of Wings, Advanced from the Centre of the Battalion, faced outwards and fired by Companies twice, Retreated from the Flanks of the battalion, Formed column from the Centre by Companies, Formed and fired by Companies twice, Changed the front to the Right and fired by Companies twice, the same to the left, by Companies formed rank intire, Formed two lines, Retreated and Fired by Companies twice, Formed two-deep, Lined the works and each man fired four rounds, retreated from the Works, Fired a Volley and Charged bayonets, General Salute.

It makes the modern reader breathless simply to read it, and it is to be hoped that the men in the ranks were not too exhausted after it. The most remarkable thing perhaps is the omission of any form of light infantry movements. Light companies had been reintroduced into the infantry in 1770–71, although they tended to be so in name only. Orthodox colonels did not much like them because they tended to spoil the symmetry of a battalion on parade. The old system of having half the grenadier company on either flank was hallowed by long tradition, as were its differences in uniform, but the new light companies in short jackets and strange leathern caps were much disliked and thus tended to become repositories for all the bad characters and all the clumsy, awkward, undersized or mishapen men of the battalion. It was a very remarkable thing to have happened less than 10 years after a war in which the value of light infantry had been well proved.

In 1775 the American War of Independence broke out, and it is hardly necessary to say that the British Infantry was ill-prepared to deal with it. The causes of the war are outside the scope of this history, but ironically enough the event which finally made the rebellion possible was the British capture of Canada a few years earlier. Before then the colonists, fearing the French, had relied largely on British protection, but with the French beaten there was no other power able to threaten them and it was this fact which finally enabled them to rise.

As was usual, the prospect of a war stimulated recruiting and the offer of engagements for three years or until the end of the war probably attracted a good many men who would have been reluctant to bind themselves for life. The British Infantry regiments which went to America were therefore reasonably strong and in good shape, although sadly enough there were far too few of them. Parliament had in fact approved the raising of an extra 20,000 men but as this would take time, recourse was had to German mercenaries. This caused an immediate outcry, presumably on the illogical grounds that as this was a domestic squabble between people of the same race, foreigners should keep out of it. Irrespective of logic there was an understandable emotional basis for this kind of feeling, but the rebellion had to be tackled and the government would have been failing in its duty had it not taken positive action. The real problem was, as ever, the chronic opposition of a large and influential sector of British opinion to anything which looked like a standing army.

It is clear, if perhaps understandable, that the capacity of the colonists was seriously underrated, an error which we shall see repeated in South Africa a century and a quarter later. In the absence of scarcely a vestige of the hard-won experience of a dozen years before, the British Infantry was despatched to the scene of operations in the confident hopes that pipeclay and powder, steady drill, and mechanical musketry, would soon settle the business.

The first serious clash came when General Gage, commanding the British troops in Boston, sent off eight flank companies of a total strength of about 400 men, to seize or destroy a quantity of warlike stores which the rebels had collected at Lexington some 20 miles (32 kilometres) away. The colonial militia turned out in force and the British were soon compelled to retire; the affair became a running fight with the Americans firing from behind trees and walls and from the windows of houses along the route. The British infantry were tired and heavily laden; but above all the were completely untrained in the sort of irregular hedge-fighting to which they were committed. It is inconceivable that a body of proper light infantry of the type trained and led by men of the stamp of Wolfe or Howe would not have cleared away their gadfly opponents in short order, but no such body existed. Gage sent out a relieving force of some 1,400 men and the affair finally ended at sunset when the survivors crawled exhausted into Boston. The total losses on the British side were 260, or about 15 per cent of the force engaged, which considering all things was light. Fortunately for the British the bulk of their opponents were raw and inexperienced, which is all that saved them from annihilation.

The next major action was at Bunker's Hill where a party of rebels had prepared a strong position with earthworks and logs. It was however sited in an amateur fashion and could have been outflanked or cut off fairly simply, but General Gage, who from his previous experience should certainly have known better, ordered a frontal attack. His reasons for this are not known, but it is reasonable to assume that he thought that one severe reverse might nip the thing in the bud, as indeed it might well have done had things gone differently.

Twenty-five hundred British infantry set off up the broken, grassy hill in heavy marching order on a blazing summer's day, and delivered a classic attack without any vestige of fire support. This attack was promptly shattered by heavy fire from the rebels. Contrary to generally held opinion it seems likely that the bulk of the defenders was armed with smooth bores; Israel Putnam, who commanded them is said to have used, and may indeed have invented, the expression 'Don't fire until you see the whites of their eyes', which is clearly not the language of long-range marksmanship. There were however a number of skilled riflemen present and these had been ordered to concentrate on the British officers, a task which they accomplished with great efficiency.

A second attack suffered the same fate as the first and General Howe, the commander on the spot, then ordered the survivors to throw off their knapsacks and take the position at the point of the bayonet. By this time the rebels were getting short of ammunition and a number of them made off. Many more however died where they stood when the British, coming forward over the bodies of their comrades, swept over their defences. Their success, which was due entirely to the almost incredible gallantry of the troops engaged, had however cost them dear, for some 1,150 had been killed or wounded, or about 46 per cent of the total engaged.

General Fuller, writing of this battle in his *British Light Infantry in the Eighteenth Century*, commented that:

> . . . the very winning of it was a moral disaster; for though the British troops behaved with magnificent courage they were at first severely repulsed by the raw American Militia . . . General Gage had much experience in the handling of light infantry; he had witnessed Braddock's disaster on the Monongahela, he had raised a battalion of light infantry, commanded it, and had been present with Abercrombie and Howe at Ticonderoga; he was a contemporary of Bouquet, Rogers and Washington, and yet at Bunker Hill, in place of

attacking the Americans as he had seen Beaujeu attack the red coats of Braddock, he attempted, against expert riflemen, to carry a position by a direct frontal assault unprepared by a skirmish fire-fight.

These were hard words indeed but almost certainly justified, for a good corps of light infantry, or even a sensible tactical plan, must have won the action at small cost, and might even have ended the rebellion.

Unfortunately the British then had one or two orthodox successes against the new American army, which perhaps made them persist in their error. In the meanwhile the rebels, who were at first small in numbers and inclined to despair, gained hugely in strength as the flames of the revolt spread, and having the good sense to stick chiefly to guerrilla tactics they soon notched up a number of successes. The British commanders eventually realized what the regimental officers had seen clearly for some time, namely the fact that fighting irregulars with lines and columns in the Prussian style was like trying to swat gnats with a club, singularly exhausting to the assailant but not often doing the would-be victim much harm; but by then the situation was out of hand and America, practically speaking, had become unconquerable with the means then at the disposal of the British. The country was vast and primitive and was inhabited by people of the same stock as those who fought to subdue them. Communications were poor and the long lines of communication were standing targets for guerrilla attacks. Even more important perhaps was the existence of a great and influential body of opinion in Britain itself which regarded the war as being cruelly oppressive and did all it could to hamper operations. Finally there came the decisive, large-scale intervention of the French, an ironical enough development in view of the fact that it had previously been their presence in Canada which kept the colonists quiet, but sufficient to tilt the scales.

Although the war was eventually lost, the British Infantry had no cause to be ashamed of its conduct. As had happened in the Seven Years War, battalions had adapted themselves to the peculiar tactical needs of the situation as a matter of hard necessity, and in many cases had achieved a considerable measure of success. A number of British commanders also proved to be adept guerrilla leaders and their bands of mounted riflemen often beat the rebels at their own game. The best known are probably Tarleton and Simcoe, but there were many almost equally competent if less well known. Many of the Hessian officers also became notable leaders of light troops, perhaps the most famous being von

Ewald whose practical ability in the field was only equalled by his facility with the pen, as witness his many books dealing with the handling of light troops.

Captain, later Lieutenant-Colonel, Patrick Ferguson of the 71st Regiment invented a breechloading rifle with which to oppose the backwoodsmen: he persuaded the authorities to raise at least one, and possibly two, rifle companies and led them with great success until a bad wound put him out of action. When he returned, crippled in one arm but still very ready to fight, he found that his rifles had been withdrawn during his enforced absence, presumably by some senior officer who did not approve of British soldiers skulking behind trees to fight. Ferguson was then given command of a battalion of American loyalists, armed with orthodox smoothbore muskets, and died with them at Kings Mountain in 1780, the rebels who defeated him being riflemen to a man.

Although this is a book on the British Infantry we shall do well not to forget the gallant services rendered by the very large number of colonists who remained loyal to the crown. They paid dearly for their devotion and at the end of the war many went to Canada where they played a considerable part in opening up that great country.

The basic tactical requirement in North America was for a looser, more flexible system, based on small bodies of men fighting in rough lines, often of one rank and never more than two; the third rank had never been of great value as far as its fire power was concerned, and in thick country it became a positive menace. Extension was everything, so that if you could lap round the flanks of your enemy you were well on the way to beating him. The rifle was by no means universally advocated due to its slowness, though it provided an admirable weapon for a proportion of skirmishers. Many officers believed that a well-made, carefully loaded musket was a perfectly adequate weapon, given that the soldier had some proper individual instruction in its use. Troops on service needed light, practical equipment based on essential needs – arms, ammunition, a hatchet, some sort of covering and the means of carrying basic food, and that was all.

All this was very obvious to the experienced regimental officers on the spot, so that they were somewhat surprised to find on their return to England that their views were by no means universally accepted. A number of senior and influential officers, many of whom had not served in America, felt that the whole thing had got out of hand, and that although special tactics might be necessary in the conditions usually found on the North American continent they could see no real need for them in Europe, and although it is easy to deride them for hiding their heads in the sand, there was perhaps a certain sense in what they said. Amongst them was a colonel on the staff by the name of David Dundas, a dry and somewhat humourless Scot who had attended the Prussian manoeuvres in 1785 and had been deeply impressed with the speed, flexibility, and above all uniformity, with which thousands of troops had been handled.

Most British regiments manoeuvred in the style of the Prussian drill but their systems were all their own, so that before a brigade, for example, could be handled in the field a great deal of preliminary coordination had to be done. Dundas rightly saw that this was ludicrous, and by 1788 he had compiled a drill book which after preliminary trials was introduced officially into the British Army in 1792. This at least laid the basis of a universal system, and one upon which all subsequent works were more or less closely based.

Although the value of the book was almost universally acclaimed as far as its basic drill, manual exercise, and other barrack-square teachings were concerned, it came in for some sharp criticism on its tactical doctrine. Drill was to be in three ranks, although understrength units might be practiced in two (a good get-out, of which the British Infantry took full advantage), but the whole system of movement on the actual battlefield was reduced to 18 manoeuvres which Dundas considered would meet any conceivable contingency. Light infantry work was hardly mentioned. All movement remained slow: ordinary time was 75 paces per minute, quick time 108, and wheeling time 120, so that evolutions in the field were ponderous in the extreme. Before being too critical however we must bear in mind that the accurate manoeuvring of large numbers of men is difficult on a level parade ground, and very difficult indeed across country.

As the Eighteen Manoeuvres tend to be mentioned frequently in many military works of the time it may be as well to list them. They were:

1 Forming close column in rear of the right company
2 Forming close column in front of the left company
3 Forming close column on a centre company facing to the rear
4 Changing position in open column
5 Throwing back the wings
6 Changing position by a countermarch
7 Countermarching by files on the centre of the battalion
8 Marching in open column
9 Echelon change of position
10 Taking up a new line by echelon movement
11 Changing position to right or left

12   Retreating in chequered lines
13   Marching to a flank in echelon
14   Forming the hollow square
15   Retiring by filing
16   Advancing in line, fire and charge
17   Retreating in line by wings
18   Advancing in line

Although sound in principle they were complicated in practice and tended to lead some of the more stupid commanding officers into strange errors. Years afterwards in 1804, Bunbury tells us that Moore, by then a major-general, commented to Dundas, 'That book of yours, General, has done a great deal of good, and would be of great value if it were not for those damned eighteen manoeuvres.' To which the author replied, slowly, 'Wy-ay; ay; people don't understand what was meant. Blockheads don't understand!'

Although, as often happens, the exponents of both the old and the new systems insisted that they and they alone were right, what was really required was a sensible blend of the two; this however was some distance in the future. In the meanwhile a number of thinking officers, among them John Moore to whom reference has already been made above, continued to plan and experiment quietly in the certain knowledge that sooner or later their ideas would be needed.

As usual a number of regiments were raised for the American War of Independence, and of these the 71st, 72nd and 73rd survived. Soon after the end of hostilities four more new regiments were also given permanent places on the British establishment. They had originally been raised for the East India Company, but when the latter refused financial responsibility for them they were allotted the numbers 74 to 77 of the line.

The outbreak of the French Revolution made relatively little initial impact in England, where it was regarded as a purely domestic upheaval in a country for which Britons had no great love. If anything there was a certain amount of sympathy of the kind shown to the American colonists a few years earlier, and had the new regime shown reasonable restraint they might well have cultivated these sentiments. Unfortunately both for themselves and for Europe the French overplayed their hand. Their extensive interference in the affairs of other countries in their desire to spread liberty caused considerable apprehension amongst all established governments, while their execution of King Louis XVI turned public opinion firmly against them; relations with Britain deteriorated steadily and war inevitably broke out in 1793.

The British Army started the war in its usual state of peacetime weakness. The establishment of a battalion was 495, which gave it

10 companies of 40 privates with a proper proportion of officers, non-commissioned officers, and drummers, but even this weak strength was rarely achieved. Battalions were mere cadres, many of the men they had being either boys, or cripples, or worn out by long service; the units in the Guards brigade which went to Flanders in 1793 were a little better off but even they were far from efficient. A line brigade which followed them, and which consisted of the 14th, 37th, and 55th Regiments, was reported as being quite unfit for service, a sad reflection of the state to which three fine regiments had been reduced. When we consider that this was probably the best brigade available, we can only wonder what the really bad regiments must have looked like.

The situation regarding reliefs overseas was chaotic, and as had happened after the Seven Years War was largely shelved as being too difficult. The battalions already overseas were simply left there to wither and die, and as a large proportion of them were in disease-ridden tropical stations the process of complete deterioration did not take long. The West Indies in particular were the great graveyard of the British Infantry, and the existence of the garrisons there was probably the greatest single cause of bad recruiting, for although men were ready to take their chances in battle against the French the prospect of yellow fever understandably appalled them. Soldiers under sentence, even of death, could commute their punishment if they agreed to serve in the West Indies, but although death was perhaps somewhat slower in coming it was almost as certain as the gallows and a good deal more painful. It was of course a chance worth taking for a man already under sentence of death; he might be lucky and survive, while at worst he would have a few months extension in which to soak himself in cheap rum. Other recruits, faced with less drastic alternatives, were not quite so willing. The raising of negro regiments recruited from slaves in the period 1794–8, went far towards solving the problem, although it was done against the orders of the home authorities and in the teeth of the opposition of the planters. They feared, above all things, the prospect of slave risings and considered that the policy of arming the blacks could only precipitate such horrors. In the event, the black regiments were loyal and efficient; military service was several steps above slavery and as the climate suited them they were well content with their lot.

On the outbreak of war with France, Parliament authorized the raising of 25,000 extra men; the bulk of these were required to bring the ranks of the existing regiments up to something approaching fighting strength, but 100 independent companies, each of 100 men, were also raised, to be used as drafts where required. It was however one thing to authorize the raising of men, but quite another to implement it, with the not unnatural result that the whole thing developed into a huge and cynical commercial enterprise with ample opportunities for speculation of all kinds and on the largest scale. The basic iniquity was the device of raising men for rank, under which virtually any individual who could bring a certain number of recruits was given a commission quite irrespective of his suitability. This system did but little to help the Army, although it was of great benefit to a large number of other people, crimps, commission-brokers, agents, go-betweens and a host of hangers on.

Let us consider a purely hypothetical case in which a young man bought 100 recruits for £10 apiece. For this outlay he probably obtained a captain's commission but of course did no duty; instead, he at once went on half pay which at about 4s. 6d. per day gave him a trifle over eight per cent for his investment, as safe as the Funds and a good deal more profitable. The men obtained for such a low sum (bearing in mind that much of it went in commission) were mostly useless and were at once discharged, when they were quickly seized for resale.

Very fortunately the real nature of the war soon made itself clear to the people of Britain. This was no eighteenth century dynastic struggle for limited aims but a fight for very survival, and Captain Collingwood of the Royal Navy perhaps expressed the nation's feelings when he wrote that the outcome would decide, '... Whether Britain is to be enrolled in the list of nations or disappear'. Once this had become clear the country responded reasonably well considering the small population and the diverse calls made on it by industry, agriculture, and the fleet. The main forms of non-regular land forces then in existence were the militia and the volunteers and these proved very popular initially because people equated survival with home defence. Once things had settled down however, discreet pressure on the volunteers tended to drive men into the militia, which being drawn by ballot was a form of conscription. There was generally no requirement for principals to serve provided they could find a substitute, and the price of these rose sharply and attracted the very sort of man who might otherwise have enlisted as a regular soldier. Once into the militia however, men could be persuaded into the line by the offer of bounties, and although this was expensive it did ensure that men transferring could be selected with some care; it was also an advantage in that they had at least some basic training.

It must not be assumed from this that recruiting was ever easy, and for most of the war regimental recruiting parties were scouring the country. As always the militia was a prime target, so that a few well set-up soldiers, full of tales of wild doings abroad and inevitably assisted by alcohol, could often attract large numbers to their regiments. The Irish, as ever, enlisted in large numbers, partly out of poverty, partly out of the love of a fight, and every regiment was full of them. Rifleman Harris, newly transferred from the 66th Regiment, helped to escort a party of recruits to England and after great efforts got them onto a ship, only to find that his troubles were just starting for:

> No sooner were we out to sea, however, than our troubles began afresh with these hot-headed Paddies; for having now nothing else to do, they got up a dreadful quarrel amongst themselves, and a religious row immediately took place, the Catholics reviling the Protestants to such a degree that a general fight ensued . . .

Nor were things better in England. The recruits all carried immense shillelaghs which they would not relinquish for a moment, and used them at the slightest provocation. There was a running fight across Salisbury Plain, in the course of which an officer of the party who attempted to pacify the participants was promptly knocked down, and only fatigue finally got them into Andover. A short rest however soon restored them for:

> Scarcely had we been a couple of hours there, and obtained some refreshment, ere these incorrigible blackguards again commenced quarrelling, and collecting together in the streets, created so serious a disturbance that the officer, getting together a body of constables, seized some of the most violent and succeeded in thrusting them into the town jail; upon this their companions again collected, and endeavoured to break open the prison gates.
> Baffled in this attempt, they rushed through the streets knocking down everybody they met. The drums now commenced beating up for a Volunteer Corps of the town, which, quickly mustering, drew up in the street before the jail and immediately were ordered to load with ball. This somewhat pacified the rioters, and our officers persuading them to listen to a promise of pardon for the past, peace was at length restored amongst them.

If this was typical behaviour, and it probably was, it is remarkable that such material could be reduced in a few months to disciplined, well-trained soldiers. The discipline however tended to be fragile, as witness some of the later irregularities in the Peninsula:

the wildness was always there, which accounts to a great extent for
the severity of the military disciplinary code. It was easy enough for
humanitarians to fulminate against it, yet in the last resort there
were always at least a few wild and savage characters who could
only be controlled by the threat of the lash or the gallows.

The great task of knocking such varied material into shape fell
almost entirely on the shoulders of a relatively small corps of
capable and devoted officers, who strove successfully to form an
army capable of dealing with the French. These were the subalterns, captains and majors, many of whom were to be generals (or
dead) before the war ended and they were ably and loyally
supported by the best of the young non-commissioned officers,
many of whom were to rise to sergeant-major or quartermaster;
nor was it impossible for a really good soldier to rise even higher.
One example was Colonel South of the 20th Regiment who, having
enlisted in about 1780, rose steadily thereafter through every
grade in the regiment until he finally commanded its 1st Battalion, and there were others who did as well. It was by no means
easy but a man of character, courage and determination could
sometimes achieve it.

Such men were sometimes handicapped by their wives who were
often inclined to refuse resolutely to become officers' ladies. One
such was the wife of the sergeant-major of the 28th. Her husband
was given a commission at the end of the eighteenth century but
she preferred to stick to her three-legged stool by the kitchen fire
with an old red jacket round her shoulders, a battered straw hat on
her head, and a short clay pipe in her mouth. When asked why, she
replied forthrightly that the king might make her Jack a gentle-
man if he liked, but that neither he nor the Sultan of the 'Ingees'
would make her a lady.

One fruitful, although necessarily long-term, measure to improve recruiting was the enlistment of boys for long service. There
were always plenty of orphans and other homeless boys and the
parish authorities, whose responsibility they were, were always
happy enough to be rid of them. From 1795 onwards several
regiments were ordered to recruit boys between the ages of 12 and
16. The 9th Regiment did so, but as they were soon overflowing
with volunteers from their county militia regiments they soon
handed them over to other less fortunately placed units. The 16th
did the same, but they too soon transferred their boys to the 34th
and 65th Regiments, who together with the 22nd Regiment then
retained them to maturity. The three latter regiments were sent to
the Cape in 1800 where they served well.

One notable recruit to the 22nd Regiment was John Shipp
(already referred to earlier) who wrote an interesting and amusing

account of his career entitled *Memoirs of the Military Career of John Shipp*. A born soldier, he enlisted in 1797 as a parish boy at the age of 13, was a sergeant in the light company at 20, and commissioned the following year for gallantry at the siege of Bhurtpore. Financial difficulties compelled him to sell out in 1807, but he at once enlisted as a trooper of dragoons and achieved a second commission in 1815, a remarkable, indeed a unique, record.

The first 10 years of the French Revolutionary and Napoleonic Wars saw the British Infantry involved in a series of operations. They were by no means uniformly successful but they taught the new British Army at least the rudiments of its business, and if the lessons were sometimes costly they were on the whole assimilated. The campaign in Flanders in 1793/4 ended in disaster, although the troops as a whole fought surprisingly well. A certain young lieutenant-colonel named Arthur Wesley, who we shall meet again though under a slightly different name, commanded the 33rd Regiment in this campaign with some distinction; many years later he remarked that it had at least taught him how not to do things, which probably sums up the value of these operations very adequately.

The next major campaign in North Holland in 1799 saw a much improved, though still very raw, army. Many regiments were full of superficially trained young militiamen who were enthusiastic to start with but were soon discouraged at the apparent technical superiority of their opponents. Quartermaster Surtees of the Rifle Brigade, who served in this campaign as a very young private soldier in the 44th, having volunteered from the militia only a few weeks previously, commented shrewdly on the difference between old soldiers and young. His regiment though still full of fight, was retiring in some confusion before a superior French force when the 23rd Regiment, which had been ordered forward to support them appeared on the scene and drove the enemy off with a couple of highly effective volleys. He tells us in his *Twenty-five Years in the Rifle Brigade* that:

> Nothing could surpass the steadiness and fine appearance of the 23rd on entering into action; but they were all old soldiers while our two battalions were composed altogether, I may say, of volunteers from the militia, who had as little idea of service in the field as if newly taken from the plough. I would just remark here, that for what I have witnessed upon different occasions I should never be inclined to put much confidence in raw troops of whatever nation, or of what stuff soever they may be composed, for it is certain that without being at all deficient in point of courage, they have not that confidence in

their own powers which soldiers who are inured to service possess . . . So it was on this occasion. Nothing could exceed the material of which these two battalions were composed had they had the advantage of a little more experience; and no troops could fight better than they did after gaining the support and countenance of the old regiments which were sent to reinforce them.

The expedition to Egypt under Abercromby in 1801 may fairly be classed as a considerable success. Although ill-equipped, the young British regiments soon demonstrated their capacity to deal with the famous French infantry. On 8 March the army made an opposed landing from the boats of the fleet, sitting packed like sardines under a heavy fire of roundshot and shell from the French batteries which caused a good many casualties. Fortunately the operation had been so frequently rehearsed on the shores of the Sea of Marmora that there was very little confusion. As the blue jackets ran the boats onto the beach the markers doubled out and in a very few minutes a solid line of battle had been formed. General Moore, who landed first with the reserve, consisting of the 23rd, 28th, 42nd and 58th Regiments, the flank companies of the 1st and 2nd Battalions of the 40th, and a locally enlisted unit known as the Corsican Rangers, at once stormed a prominent sandhill which formed the centre of the French defences, and within 20 minutes of the first boats grounding the main objective was firmly in British hands. The 42nd had hardly got ashore before they were charged with great élan by a regiment of French cavalry, which they fairly demolished with two terrible volleys before advancing majestically upon the French infantry in the rear.

The Guards, who had suffered heavily in their boats, landed in unavoidable confusion and they in their turn were also charged by the French horse. Although in no sort of order they quickly formed rallying squares, mere irregular hedgehogs of bayonets, and held them off until the 58th, wheeling up on the French flank, drove them off with the sort of volley which was rapidly beginning to typify the British Infantry. A few days later the 90th, although caught from a flank while deploying into line from column, also drove off their mounted opponents, from which it finally became clear that steady infantry, even if caught in confusion, had little to fear from cavalry provided they kept their heads.

Several more days of fighting culminated in a great night attack by the French on 20/21 March; this too was shattered and virtually decided the campaign. It was in this battle that the commanding officer of the 28th, attacked from the rear while engaged in front, calmly turned his rear rank about and dealt with both sets of opponents simultaneously. Not the least interesting aspect of this gallant action is that it indicates clearly that the British Infantry were now habitually fighting in two ranks, regardless of what the drill book said. In the same year as the Egyptian campaign a General Order was finally issued stating that battalions might parade in two ranks 'even at reviews', which meant in practice that the Duke of York had sensibly surrendered to informed opinion. Abercromby was killed during the battle of Alexandria but his successor Major-General Hutchinson, though an odd character, was competent enough and soon brought the campaign to a successful conclusion.

The outbreak of the French Revolutionary Wars led almost immediately to radical changes in the French tactical system. The vast expansion in strength, plus the large loss of royalist officers who had either been removed or fled the country, made it impossible to train the huge new levies in the old, precise system, so that battles from the French point of view at first degenerated into mass attacks by swarming, untrained volunteers in little or no order. These had some failures but they also had some remarkable successes, in which their fluid probing so disorganized the formal, static line of battle opposed to them that it broke. The swarms were essentially skirmishers, and although initially quite untaught they instinctively made use of ground and cover so that the Frederician volleys hurled at them rarely did much harm, particularly since the firers were themselves under a constant fire from hundreds of concealed muskets.

By the time Napoleon came to power the system had begun to be regimented, so that the leading swarms had become thick skirmish lines and the mobs following had been drilled into columns; once the troops had been taught to manoeuvre as formed bodies the system proved highly successful. The battalion columns were usually formed on a frontage of two companies in three-rank line with succeeding pairs of companies immediately behind them. Assuming there were eight companies of 90 men, two of which were employed to skirmish, this gave a compact formation with a frontage of 60 and a depth of nine which could quickly deploy into line if a fire fight was imminent. On occasion, when objectives and frontages were narrow, the columns were deeper, three battalions being formed one behind the other which gave great impulse but reduced the available fire power considerably.

The real tactical problem from the British point of view was to neutralize the skirmishers as far as possible so that the main line might be preserved intact to deal with the following columns, and by the end of the eighteenth century it had occurred to a number of the more professionally-minded officers of the Army that one possible means might be to have at least a portion of the British Infantry armed with rifles. Although the rifle was almost as old as hand firearms themselves, it had never attracted great attention as a military weapon, partly because it was expensive to make, but principally because it was extremely slow to load. If the spherical lead ball, then the only form of projectile known for military small arms, was to be spun by the rifling it had to be a tight fit and with a muzzle-loaded weapon this caused serious difficulties in ramming down the ball, particularly after a few shots had made the barrel foul. Various means of overcoming this problem had been tried, and apart from Ferguson's breechloader (which although it solved the problem of ramming gave rise to others, notably the clogging of the mechanism by fouling), the best compromise seemed to be to wrap the ball in a circular patch of lubricated linen or thin leather. This had been the method customarily used by the American riflemen in the loose irregular forest fighting of 20 years previously and it seemed to be sufficiently effective to permit the military use of the rifle, although only as a strictly specialist weapon.

The first British troops to recommence experiments with rifled weapons were the 60th, whose long experience in North America had made them familiar with arms of this type, even though they had never carried them officially. As early as 1794 two battalions had been rearmed with German rifles of the jäger type and two others had formed rifle companies; by 1795 the 5th Battalion had not only become a rifle regiment but was clothed in green.

In 1800 it was decided to form an experimental rifle corps, the original intention apparently being to give each infantry battalion a proportion, probably a company, of men armed with a rifle and trained in its use. It is not clear who first got the idea officially approved by the Duke of York, although it is at least possible that Sir John Moore had a hand in it; but very early in the year the following circular letter was sent to the commanding officers of the 1st, 21st, 23rd, 25th, 27th, 29th, 49th, 55th, 67th, 69th, 71st, 72nd, 79th, 85th and 92nd Regiments:

Horse Guards
January 17, 1800

Sir

I have the honor to inform you that it is His Royal Highness, the Commander in Chief's intention to form a Corps of detachments from the different Regiments of the Line, for the purpose of its being instructed in the use of the Rifle, and in the system of exercise adopted by Soldiers so armed. It is His

75

Royal Highness' Pleasure that you shall select from the Regiment under your Command 2 Serjeants, 2 Corporals, and 30 private men for this duty, all of them being such men as appear most capable of receiving the above instructions, and most competent to the performance of the duty of Riflemen. These N.C. Officers and Privates are not to be considered as being drafted from their regiments but merely as detached for the purpose above recited; they will continue to be borne on the Strength of their Regiment, and will be clothed by their respective Colonels. His Royal Highness desires you will recommend 1 Captain, 1 Lieutenant, and 1 Ensign of the Regiment under your Command who Volunteer to serve in this Corps of Riflemen, in order that His Royal Highness may select from the Officers recommended from the regiments which furnish their quota on this occasion, a sufficient number of Officers for the Rifle Corps. These Officers are to be considered as detached on duty from their respective Regiments, and will share in all promotion that occurs in them during their Absence.

Eight drummers will be required to act as Bugle Horns, and I request you will acquaint me, for the information of His Royal Highness, whether you have any in the . . . Regiment qualified as such, or of a Capacity to be instructed.

I have, &c., &c.,
HARRY CALVERT,
A.G.

The regiments duly complied, not always, regrettably, with their best men, and by March 1800 the various detachments had assembled at Swinley Camp, near Horsham, and begun training.

The two officers principally concerned were Colonel Coote-Manningham and Lieutenant-Colonel the Honourable William Stewart, both enthusiastic riflemen who had served in an experimental light infantry corps raised by Sir Charles Grey in the West Indies in 1794. The Corps broke up in July when the bulk of the Army was due to embark for operations in the Mediterranean and the bulk of the soldiers were returned to their units; Stewart however managed to retain a slightly unofficial detachment of three companies which formed part of the expedition to Ferrol, and although the operation proved to be largely abortive the practical value of riflemen in the field was convincingly demonstrated.

When the expedition returned to Malta these riflemen were also dispersed, and it appears that for a few weeks at least the corps virtually ceased to exist except for Stewart and a handful of officers. By the end of August it had been reformed with volunteers from the Irish Militia, but under the same officers, and in October of that year its establishment was finally fixed at a headquarters and eight companies of a total strength of 893 all ranks.

Colonel Stewart was then detailed to command the troops ordered to be embarked on Admiral Sir Hyde Parker's expedition to the Baltic. These consisted of the 49th Regiment under Isaac Brock and a company of rifles under Captain Beckwith, both officers who were later to achieve a measure of military fame, and they were present at the battle of Copenhagen in 1801. There and thereafter the riflemen did well both at the unfortunate affair at Buenos Aires and the not very arduous campaign in Denmark in 1807.

In 1803, at about the same time that the new Rifle Corps was being redesignated the 95th Regiment, Major-General Sir John Moore was ordered to set up a camp of instruction at Shorncliffe, the principal object of which was to give ordinary line battalions additional instruction in the loose and more flexible tactics of light infantry. Moore was an officer of ability and experience and perhaps one of the greatest trainers of troops which the British Army has ever produced. Although a strict disciplinarian when necessary, he regarded it as essential to treat soldiers as intelligent human beings and to encourage them to think of themselves as military craftsmen rather than robots. The first regiment to come under his hand was the 52nd of which he was colonel, and he decided that his first task was to make it a model of what a light infantry regiment should be. He was extremely fortunate in having the whole-hearted support of the Duke of York, which enabled him to weed out unsuitable officers and men and replace them with carefully selected volunteers. The first commanding officer was Lieutenant-Colonel Kenneth Mackenzie, a capable and experienced officer who had already commanded the 90th Regiment in Egypt, and between them they very soon had their regiment in a high state of training and morale.

A few months later the 43rd joined the camp. Although a regiment with a distinguished record, its reputation at that particular period was low, but under Moore's firm hand it had soon reached the same high standard as the 52nd. The 95th Regiment was then also placed under Moore's command, thus completing the famous trio of regiments which were to form the Light Brigade, and later the Light Division, of Peninsular fame.

There is perhaps some misapprehension as to what constituted a light infantry regiment in the early nineteenth century. Moore was clear, from the first, that the basis of all the training should be that of normal infantry since that was inevitably how they would have to fight for a great deal of the time. Only when they had

77

reached a high standard in that respect did he go on to teach them to fight extended. He never claimed to have invented everything he taught, but had the flair for picking the best from the considerable amount of written material available. As good light companies were to battalions, so good light battalions were to be to armies, troops well trained in orthodox movements but with the extra capacity to skirmish, hold outpost lines, and generally act as a cover and screen for the main force, whether on the move or at rest.

The 95th Rifles were trained on similar lines though it was of course expected that from the nature of their armament they would fight principally in extended order. Nevertheless they too were highly trained in the basic manoeuvres of line infantry and not infrequently fought as such. A company was broken down into two half companies or platoons, each of which was further divided into two sections or squads. Half-companies were commanded by subalterns, while sections were commanded by sergeants, each with a corporal to assist him. There also existed a system of appointing one rifleman in each section to be a chosen man, a sort of unpaid non-commissioned officer whose duty it was to assist the sergeant. There is no evidence to indicate any further subdivisions below sections, which consisted of a paper strength of some 20 riflemen, often reduced by sickness and wounds to perhaps a dozen or so. Extension was not great by modern standards, not usually more than three paces between men, which made it possible for the sergeant to control his section by voice, signal, or whistle.

It may now be as well to consider the basic weapons with which Moore's troops were equipped. The standard infantry arm of the period was the flintlock musket, known affectionately but unofficially as Brown Bess, which as far as its basic principle and capacity were concerned hardly differed from the one used in the Seven Years War, nor indeed was it to change very much during the remaining 40-odd years of its existence. The barrel length varied from 39 inches to 42 (99 to 107 centimetres) according to pattern, the tendency after about 1797 being to rely more and more on the shorter one, principally the so-called India Pattern. Some reference is occasionally made to light infantry muskets in the early nineteenth century, but these were not significantly different from the standard infantry arm. The musket was of about 0.76 inches (19.3 millimetres) calibre and fired a spherical lead bullet, which in order to facilitate loading was made a very loose fit, thus having serious effects on both its accuracy, and velocity. Militarily speaking the effective range at which one man might hit another was about 40 yards (36 metres), although the musket might kill in random fashion at up to 10 times that range. Normal fire effect was achieved by volleys, usually by half-companies, but light infantry extended often employed file firing in which the right-hand man of the front rank fired, followed by his rear rank man, followed by number two of the front rank then number two of the rear rank, and so on down the line. Each man reloaded independently, thus ensuring that a good proportion of muskets were always ready in an emergency. This system allowed a continuous fire to be kept up, with the additional advantage that as men had more time both to reload and to aim carefully their shooting tended to be a good deal more accurate than that of the mechanical volley, where speed was everything.

The rifle used by the 95th was named after its inventor Ezekiel Baker, a noted London gunsmith, and was a weapon much superior to the musket as far as individual accuracy was concerned; it was shorter and lighter than the musket and the seven grooves of rifling in its 30-inch (76-centimetre) barrel gave sufficient spin and stability to its bullet (which was a leaden sphere of 0.62 inches (15.7 millimetres) calibre) to make it possible for one man to hit another with some certainty at 250 yards (230 metres). Although customarily loaded with a separate greased patch it was still relatively slow in operation, one well-aimed shot per minute being probably a fair average rate.

Unlike the smoothbore musketeer, who used paper cartridges containing powder and ball, the rifleman habitually charged from a powder horn, which gave him a more consistent quantity of powder and thus more reliable shooting. All riflemen carried a proportion of cartridges for use in emergencies at close quarters, when speed was more essential than absolute accuracy, and by the time of the Peninsular War this seems to have become a fairly universal practice. It is possible that the balls in the cartridges were prepatched, but as evidence is scanty on this point this is no more than speculation.

Neither musket nor rifle was completely reliable, particularly in wet weather when the priming was very liable to be spoiled. Both weapons were equipped with bayonets. That of the musket was usually fixed in battle, and in view of the close range of fighting in those days its use, or at least the threat of its use, was common. The riflemen carried heavy brass-hilted sword bayonets which so affected the accuracy of the rifles that they were usually only fixed in emergencies.

The structure of an infantry battalion changed very little after the introduction of the light company in 1770, and although as we have seen the strength varied considerably due to fluctuations in recruiting, the basic framework of grenadier, light, and eight battalion companies remained in existence. One beneficial change was the abolition of field officers' companies in 1803. Since 1744 the colonel, lieutenant-colonel and major had each drawn the pay of a company in addition to that of their rank. The actual command of these companies devolved on the senior subalterns, of whom the one commanding the colonel's company bore the title of captain-lieutenant. Until 1770 this strange appointment carried no privileges with it, but after that date its holder ranked as a captain in the Army while continuing to draw a subaltern's pay. Once the system had gone, three extra captains were placed on the establishment so as to give each company its own proper commander.

In 1793 it was officially ordered that field officers and the adjutant should appear on parade mounted. Apart from any questions of prestige or comfort this was in fact essential when a battalion was manoeuvring because the officers concerned had then to dress markers, ensure that proper direction was kept, and supervise the movements generally, all of which made it necessary for them to be mobile. When the order came out, the commanding officer of the 29th Regiment, presumably anxious to combine appearance with economy, laid down that mounts should be fit for the duties assigned to them but not showy, stout hardy animals of between 14 and 15 hands being considered suitable.

Establishments varied surprisingly between one battalion and another so that it is impossible to be precise, but by 1797 most were at a normal strength of 44 officers, 52 sergeants, 50 corporals, 20 drummers, and 950 privates, a total of 1,116, this being the highest reached for the remainder of the war. As early as 1792 extra recruiting companies were also authorized for battalions, but these came and went in a somewhat confusing manner so that it is impossible to be precise about them.

In 1802 an Army of Reserve to the strength of 50 battalions was raised by ballot for home defence, the battalions being affiliated to existing regular battalions; discreet pressure was then applied to persuade these units to volunteer for general service, and as we shall see in the next chapter this was rewarded with almost complete success.

There were of course a number of individual changes in the establishment, perhaps the most surprising of which was the late appointment of a sergeant-major. Staff-sergeants in the capacity of quartermaster-sergeant and pay-sergeant had been authorized in 1787 but it was not until 1798 that the sergeant-major first appeared officially, although he had existed for some years, presumably by the regimental elevation of a senior sergeant. The letter of authority for raising the 79th Regiment in 1793 makes specific reference to a sergeant-major and we know that William Cobbett held the appointment even earlier than that. In addition a drum-major, again a post of long (if unofficial) standing, together with an armourer, were added in 1805. At this stage there was no non-commissioned officer in a company above the rank of sergeant, although the 95th Regiment habitually employed the senior sergeant of each company as a company sergeant-major, his section being commanded by the senior corporal.

The tactical changes have already been referred to. The massing of flank companies into ad hoc battalions, a favourite expedient of eighteenth century commanders, had begun to fall into disuse, and battalion guns had very properly reverted to the Royal Artillery.

Inevitably the scale of operations led to the raising of a number of new infantry regiments. Many were broken up for drafts or disbanded, but a considerable number remained in being; the most senior of these surviving units was the 78th and the most junior was the 95th. In 1782 all infantry regiments were allotted county titles in addition to their numbers. Although colonels of regiments were consulted, the allocation appears to have been more or less arbitrary and did not apparently lead to many closer county/regimental links.

5 1806–1815 THE NAPOLEONIC WARS

The opening years of the nineteenth century saw considerable improvements in the general state of the British Army, for the Duke of York, although by no means an unqualified success in the field, had proved to be an excellent commander-in-chief, and under his firm guidance military affairs had made considerable progress. The country as a whole had begun to appreciate that there could be no just peace in the world until the French were finally and decisively beaten, and this realization led to increased support for the prosecution of the war.

Great Britain continued to flourish, for the Royal Navy had swept the seas almost clear of French ships so that commerce was booming and the country was prosperous, although the prosperity was by no means evenly distributed. The Industrial Revolution had led to a considerable increase in manufacturing capacity and agriculture was efficient, although it was becoming difficult to feed an increasing population from domestic resources.

The real need was men, for home defence, for the fleet, and for offensive operations. After Trafalgar the risk of invasion was much reduced and defence could be left largely in the hands of the militia and volunteers. The combined needs of the Navy and commercial shipping had however led to a shortage of professional seamen so that the Navy was to some extent in competition with the Army for the limited manpower available. Fortunately the various schemes for recruiting the ranks of the Army had begun to have some effect and battalions were filling up with good volunteers, mostly from the militia. The new second battalions were strong and so many of the men in their ranks had volunteered for unlimited service that they had become in every respect regular units.

Training and tactics for the infantry as a whole were still largely based on a somewhat simplified version of Dundas' system, although two ranks had become almost universal. Experience in the field had shown the need for certain basic movements which could be carried out with reasonable certainty under fire and the tactical system had been streamlined. There were three fundamental formations: line for fire, column for movement, and square against cavalry. The fast movements of the French had made it necessary to speed everything up and the old dignified battlefield pace of 75 paces a minute (which still lingers on in modern ceremonial as 'slow time') had given place to one of 108. Above all was the steady attention paid to improvement in musketry; although still largely mechanical, in as much as the volley remained the standard type of fire, file firing, in which front and rear men of each file fired in succession down the line, had become more common. The infantry was at least given practice with ball ammunition – which was by no means the case with most other European armies – and the fire of a British battalion had reached a deadliness never before achieved.

One of the earliest battles to demonstrate this was Maida in Southern Italy. In 1806 Major-General Sir John Stuart, commanding the considerable British garrison in Sicily, decided to strike a blow at a small French army in Calabria which reports suggested was unsupported, and at once embarked a force of seven battalions, a few light guns and a handful of cavalry with which to carry out this task. This force, numbering something over 5,000, was organized into four weak brigades, and when it came close to the French it advanced in echelon from the right. The French, numbering about 7,000, advanced in similar formation but with their left leading, so that the two leading brigades came into collision first. They exchanged volleys at rather long range and in the course of this fire the British brigadier, noticing that the musketry of his men was hampered by the rolled blankets which they were wearing bandolier fashion, ordered them to be removed. The rear rank helped the front rank to remove theirs, and the front rank then turned about to perform a similar service. In the smoke the French mistook this for the beginning of a retreat and at once dashed forward, but were met by a shattering volley which dispersed them. They at once retreated, followed in a somewhat uncontrolled fashion by the excited redcoats.

The next two brigades then clashed in their turn, the French again being broken by one terrible volley at point-blank range. The further advance of the British was then halted by the threat of some hovering French cavalry until presently the 20th Regiment, which had just landed, hastened up from the rear and dispersed them, after which its commander wheeled it in line onto the flank of the remaining enemy infantry. One of the young officers of the

20th at that time was a certain John Colborne, who nine years later was to conduct a similar operation against the French Guard at Waterloo.

After the battle was over the British, being unable to pursue for lack of cavalry, were allowed to bathe. While this was going on a nervous staff officer, seeing a herd of cattle stampeding across the plain, cried out that the French cavalry were approaching upon which the 27th Regiment and a composite battalion of grenadier companies dashed out of the sea, hastily flung on their crossbelts, unpiled their muskets and formed up stark naked on the beach, perfectly ready to deal with any contingency.

The existence of this composite battalion may require explanation. The massing of flank companies into ad hoc units had been quite common in the eighteenth century but had gradually fallen into disuse, principally because it deprived battalions of their best men. Battalions in Sicily had also tended to train the best men of their battalion companies to act as skirmishers; these men were known locally as flankers and General Stuart, not content with combining the flank companies of battalions left behind, had also taken the flankers from these units, forming the whole into two composite battalions.

Not all operations were as successful as Maida. In South America a small force, badly led and short of food, blundered into disaster when it attempted to capture Buenos Aires, for the inhabitants, although relatively useless as soldiers in the open, defended the place stubbornly and finally compelled General Whitelock's scattered columns to surrender. A similar thing happened in Egypt at much the same time, when a British force was repulsed from Rosetta by a scratch body of Turks and Albanians. These two events demonstrated the ability of determined defenders, even completely untrained ones, to hold a town against good troops; it was a lesson which the French were also to learn a little later at the Spanish town of Saragossa.

It is now necessary to consider the opening moves of what was to culminate in the Peninsular War, the greatest campaign fought by the British Army until the early twentieth century. In 1806 Napoleon, dismayed by the effects of the British naval blockade, instituted a countermeasure known as the Continental System, the effect of which, had it been fully implemented, would have been to ban British vessels from every port in Europe. One country reluctant to join was Portugal, so the French Emperor issued one of his famous ultimatums to her in 1807; when this had no immediate effect he despatched a small army to march across Spain with the connivance of Godoy, then virtual ruler of the country. Lisbon fell without resistance but fortunately the Regent of Portugal had been persuaded by the British Ambassador to flee to the then Portuguese colony of Brazil, taking with him the Portuguese fleet.

Napoleon, having obtained a footing in Spain, then decided to seize that country also. He was greatly helped by a serious quarrel between the Bourbon king of the country and his son, both of whom he removed from the country by trickery and forced to abdicate. This led to a serious revolt in Madrid which was bloodily suppressed, after which Napoleon, abandoning all pretence of diplomacy, placed his unwilling brother Joseph upon the Spanish throne; upon this the whole country rose spontaneously and called upon Great Britain for assistance.

The Portuguese also rose in June 1808 and the British Government at once decided to help its old ally. In August 1808 Sir Arthur Wellesley landed in the country with some 15,000 troops and inflicted two sharp defeats on the French army under Junot before being superseded by the successive arrival of two elderly generals of considerable seniority but no great talent. The French duly capitulated but the terms were so lenient that the senior British officers concerned (including Wellesley) were recalled, leaving command of the army to Sir John Moore.

Affairs in the Peninsula were by that time in a state of deep confusion. Napoleon had intervened personally, and a few weeks before Christmas 1808 had entered Madrid virtually unopposed. Bad communications led Moore to understand that the Spaniards were resisting and he determined to go to their help. Fortunately he discovered just in time that the capital was quiet and that Napoleon was advancing on him with a force much superior in numbers to his own, whereupon he turned northwest and made for Corunna. There he fought a successful defensive action and although he himself was killed, his army was then able to embark undisturbed and return to England. In many ways the campaign was a disastrous one, but not wholly so. It led to the loss of a great many men and horses and much material and it showed that British discipline in adversity still left a great deal to be desired. On the credit side it undoubtedly disrupted French plans for the systematic subjection of Spain and almost certainly saved Lisbon, which was to prove such a valuable British base for much of the remainder of the war. The troops left behind in garrison in Portugal by Moore, 20 British battalions and four of the King's German Legion, thus remained undisturbed, and in April 1809 they were joined by Sir Arthur Wellesley who had been appointed to the Chief Command. He brought with him seven extra battalions thus bringing his strength up to some 25,000 men.

The total disposable force of infantry available to the British Government in 1809 consisted of three regiments of Guards and

103 of the line, plus 10 battalions of the King's German Legion (these being the remains of the old Hanoverian army), and 10 more which can only be described as 'assorted', being for the most part composed of a variety of foreigners, largely under French émigré officers. There were also eight veteran battalions for home garrisons and eight of the West India Regiment which could not be deployed outside their own local sphere. The actual availability of battalions was as follows:

60th Regt.	7
1st Regt. (Royal Scots)	4
1st Guards, 14th, 27th and 95th Regts. with 3 each	12
2nd and 3rd Guards and 61 other regts. with 2 each	126
37 single-battalion regts.	37
Total	186

The single-battalion regiments were mostly in remote garrisons overseas where they had little or no chance of raising second battalions. A few which returned to Europe later, and even one or two abroad, did succeed in raising them eventually, but in general they remained as single-battalion regiments.

As had happened for many years the establishments of infantry battalions fluctuated somewhat in the early nineteenth century according to their location and role, although by 1809 it had become reasonably uniform. This was helped by the abolition of the separate Irish establishment in 1800, which at least put all home-based units on the same footing. There were however still some variations so that the figures discussed below, although generally correct, may not be universally so. It must also of course be borne in mind that for various reasons actual strengths were often appreciably lower than the official entitlement.

A standard first battalion serving in Europe in 1809 consisted of 1,114 of all ranks, the breakdown being as detailed opposite. These figures were sometimes increased by a paymaster and pay sergeant for the colonel; the establishment of second and subsequent battalions was one less, the difference being the colonel. A battalion in overseas garrison was usually about 210 less than this in nominal strength, the difference consisting of 10 sergeants, 10 corporals, and 190 privates.

Drum-majors had no official existence until 1810, having previously held the vacancy of a duty sergeant. Colour-sergeants on a basis of one per company were authorized in July 1813,

OFFICERS	OTHER RANKS
1 colonel (not with battalion)	1 sergeant-major
1 lieutenant-colonel (in command)	1 quartermaster-sergeant
2 majors	1 armourer-sergeant
10 captains	50 sergeants
12 lieutenants	50 corporals
8 ensigns	22 drummers
1 adjutant	950 privates
1 quartermaster	
1 surgeon	
2 assistant surgeons	

although the 95th Rifles had always employed one of its section sergeants in the role of company sergeant-major in each company since its first formation.

The usual system with a two battalion regiment was for the first battalion to be either abroad (especially when active operations were involved) or first for overseas duties if both were in the country. When a first battalion was ordered abroad it transferred all its sick, convalescents, absentees and other ineffectives to its second battalion, taking in exchange effective soldiers. This naturally had a serious effect on the second battalion, whose business it then became to recruit itself back up to strength, and as long as it remained virtually as a home-based depot this was not too difficult. The sick either recovered or were discharged, immature soldiers grew up, and in due course the unit was again effective. The problem of course was that there were never enough fully effective battalions available for service. After Corunna for example the first battalions which had been with Moore were in no state for active operations for some time, with the result that when Wellesley resumed command many of the new battalions sent to him were second battalions. Except in rare cases of three- or four-battalion regiments, these had no reliable source from which to draw reinforcements, but simply shed their ineffectives and departed understrength, sometimes alarmingly so. The seven battalions which actually accompanied Sir Arthur back to Portugal in 1809 averaged almost exactly 700 rank and file. This was a deficiency of some 30 men per company, a very serious matter for any unit embarking on what was likely to prove an arduous campaign. The British line battalions in Portugal at that time consisted of six first battalions, two single-battalion regiments, eight second battalions, one third battalion, and the 5th/60th.

The situation as far as the Guards were concerned was noticeably better because their establishments were much more generous than those of the line. Professor Oman, discussing the matter in *Wellington's Army* lists the 1st Guards (three battalions) at 4,619 all ranks, and the 2nd and 3rd Guards (both with two battalions) at 2,887, which meant that they could provide full-strength battalions up to their regimental limit and still leave themselves the equivalent of a depot battalion. At one time the brigade was even able to provide a bonus in the form of a composite battalion of 11 companies which served in the Barossa campaign of 1811 under Graham.

In practice the system as regards line regiments in Spain and Portugal was as follows; when a first battalion in England, as for example one recuperating after a campaign, was fit for service, it drew reinforcements from its second battalion, if in England, and went overseas at full establishment. If its second battalion was already in the Peninsula it absorbed its rank and file on arrival there, leaving a cadre of officers and non-commissioned officers to go home and recruit. When a second battalion in the Peninsula had its first battalion abroad in another theatre, say in Canada or the East Indies, the custom at first was to run it down until it was virtually ineffective and then send it home to recruit, but this did not last long. The reason was that when many of Moore's first battalions were recovered and fit for operations they were sent on the Walcheren expedition in 1809. There they all became riddled with malaria, and although some were sent back to the Peninsula as effective battalions, their sick rate was so high that Wellington refused to have any more sent to him. This put a premium on seasoned battalions, however weak they might have become through the normal ravages of campaigning, and Wellington held on to them as long as he could. After Albuera in 1811 for example, the casualties had been so great that for a short time the remnants of no less than seven units, 1st/3rd, 1st/29th, 2nd/31st, 1st/48th, 2nd/48th, 1st/57th, 2nd/66th, were worked as a provisional battalion.

The 1st/3rd and 1st/57th were soon reformed, both having second battalions at home; the 1st/48th absorbed the rank and file of its second battalion and survived; the 29th, a single battalion regiment, was sent home to recruit; the 2nd/31st and 2nd/66th, both of whose first battalions were abroad in other theatres, remained as a provisional battalion until the end of the war. The strengths of the 2nd/66th in the period are probably typical. It embarked in April 1809 with a strength of 720 rank and file, and returned to England in July 1814 with 409, having in the interval received drafts of 336. Thus its losses overall were 647 or about 90 per cent of its embarkation strength.

There was also a system of depot companies; when things went according to plan, i.e. the first battalion went abroad and the second battalion stayed at home, the second acted as a depot, but as we have seen the system rarely worked as tidily as that. The rule appears to have been that single battalion regiments were allowed an extra depot company when ordered abroad, as were each battalion of a two battalion regiment when both its units were overseas. These depot companies, being too small to be administratively self-sufficient, were usually grouped more or less arbitrarily into depot battalions under a field officer and housed in some convenient barracks, if possible close to one of the major ports of embarkation.

Sir Arthur Wellesley (he was born Wesley but changed it later) was the third and youngest son of an Irish peer, and entered the Army by purchase in 1787 at the age of 18. He commanded a battalion with some distinction in the campaign of 1794–5, after which he departed for India. There he served for 10 years, latterly in command of considerable armies in considerable campaigns, and if it can be said that family influence pushed him on, it is but fair to add that it was skill and competence that made him uniformly successful. His earlier battles in Portugal have already been alluded to; he returned there in chief command in 1809, principally because he had convinced the British Government that Portugal, or at least the vital Lisbon peninsula, was defensible against any force that the French could employ against it in the foreseeable future. Although his recent experience against the French had been limited, if highly successful, it is clear that he had made a careful study of their methods and had evolved various countermeasures to them; these methods it is now necessary to consider.

The broad principles of French tactics had changed relatively little; the early revolutionary armies had consisted of swarms of skirmishers supported by masses of men in rear, and Napoleon had done little more than regiment and regularize this system, which had indeed been uniformly successful. The skirmishers first harassed the opposing line and as they made the maximum use of cover they were not seriously inconvenienced by the machine-like volleys fired at them. When this probing had found a weak place the columns came up with a rush and being by then reduced to eminently manoeuvrable bodies, two or three could if necessary be directed on any one point.

The standard formation of a column was a six-company battalion on a frontage of a double company. Assuming a company to be about 75 strong and formed in three ranks, this gave a solid block with a frontage of about 50 men and a depth of nine. If space was limited, two or three, or for that matter a dozen, battalions could be formed one behind the other in the same formation making one huge column; this was clumsy in theory but in practice it was an easy way to manoeuvre a mass of relatively ill-trained conscripts, since all that was required was experienced officers and non-commissioned officers in front and on the flanks.

Such columns were practically projectiles in themselves and did not reckon to produce much effective fire. They simply rolled on under their own impetus and with luck smashed their way through the enemy line. As the range of the standard musket was then short, the column was only exposed to effective small arms fire for a very short time; often only one volley was possible, and with the poor standards of musketry which then prevailed in Continental armies, this was rarely sufficient to stop it. As time went by the French skirmishing lines grew a good deal thinner; trained light infantry were hard to find and Napoleon soon found that it was easier and more economical to pound the enemy with massed artillery as a prelude to the advance of his infantry. These guns could also neutralize those of the enemy, and this was essential because the solid mass of a column provided an ideal target for artillery fire.

On occasions when some small arms fire seemed to be essential the French employed a formation known as *ordre mixte*, in which battalions in column alternated with battalions in line. When a flank was particularly exposed to a sudden dash by cavalry, Napoleon sometimes found it expedient to march a battalion in file on that flank so that a simple turn left or right brought it into line. There seems in fact to have been no case when this system was employed in the Peninsula.

Wellesley appreciated that initially at least he would be considerably outnumbered, since the French had something like a quarter of a million men to oppose his 30,000. This of course was not as bad as it looked because the French, being an army of occupation in a bitterly hostile country, were compelled to disperse widely to maintain control. Worse still, they had no proper supply system save foraging, which in a country where agriculture was barely above subsistence level, made concentration very difficult. Nevertheless, in spite of these difficulties, the small British Army might often be faced by three times its own numbers, and in circumstances like these a false move could mean disaster.

In particular the British general appreciated that he would be short of both cavalry and guns. Long years of littoral warfare had left the British Government with the somewhat defeatist attitude that any campaign would probably end with a hasty evacuation over open beaches, with horses being shot and guns abandoned, and as these were both expensive items they naturally preferred to depend on infantry, which at best could be easily embarked in ships' boats and at worst could be replaced and equipped relatively cheaply. In these circumstances it was clear that Wellesley would first have to prove his ability to hold his ground before a proper proportion of the more expensive arms would be allotted to him.

It was clear that much time would have to be spent on the defensive, and very fortunately much of Portugal was eminently well-suited to that type of warfare, being in the main poor cavalry country, rocky, broken and seamed with ravines and gullies. It was upon these conditions that Wellesley formulated his system.

One of the disadvantages of the defensive is that the initiative is largely surrendered. The enemy is not normally compelled to attack; he can retire, or outflank as may seem best to him; in practice in the Peninsula the French were reluctant to retire because of loss of face, and often unable to spend much time on manoeuvring because of their chronic shortage of supplies. What they needed were quick successes which could be magnified in despatches into major victories.

Another disadvantage of the defensive is the need for time to find, reconnoitre, and occupy a suitable position. This in the main depends on good information and here the British were at an advantage because in spite of a shortage of cavalry they were operating in a friendly country with the full cooperation of its inhabitants. The shortage of mounted troops was also to some extent off-set by Wellesley's employment on reconnaissance of single well-mounted staff officers rather than cavalry patrols. All this gave the British general the opportunity to employ an offensive/defensive, that is he could approach a more or less isolated French force and offer battle in the reasonably certain knowledge that the enemy would be forced to take quick action, which usually meant attack, before the failure of its supplies compelled it to disperse.

Wellesley's basic defensive technique was to establish his front line on a reverse slope, preferably one with a long even forward slope. This made enemy reconnaissance difficult since his troops were concealed behind the crest which also protected them from aimed artillery fire. His second line, usually somewhat weaker than the first but deployed on the same frontage, was some 200 yards further back, with a reserve behind that again. In view of the French superiority in cavalry it was necessary for Wellesley to protect the extremities of his line by resting them on streams, ravines, steep hills, or defended villages. If all else failed he presumably might have made do with a battalion in square, although in practice this never seems to have become necessary; he usually placed his cavalry in support of any flank which appeared to be the most exposed. It is of interest to note that as early as 3 August 1808, at a time when his force had not fired a single shot in the Peninsula, Wellesley issued a General Order in which appeared the bald statement, 'The order of the battle is to be two-deep', thus finally banishing the third rank.

These dispositions set the scene for the main battle, but first there was a preliminary resistance by a strong skirmishing line which lined the crest and even the forward slope if a covered line of withdrawal was available. A number of guns were also placed well forward so that the harassment of the enemy could begin as early as possible. The scale on which these light troops were employed was very considerable, so great indeed that the French were at times under the impression that they were the first line. In April 1809, Wellesley had broken up the 5th Battalion of the 60th Regiment so as to be able to attach a rifle company to each British brigade (those of the King's German Legion had their own riflemen) which gave it a skirmish line of one rifle company and three battalion light companies. Early in 1810 the Portuguese army, which had been retrained and reorganized by Marshal Beresford and a strong cadre of British officers, was also incorporated into the British Army, usually on a basis of one brigade to each division; the Portuguese brigades consisted of two infantry regiments, each of two battalions and one battalion of *cacadores*, light troops armed with rifles.

This addition strengthened the skirmishing element considerably; if we assume the average division consisted of six British and four Portuguese infantry battalions, the light troops employed in advance consisted of six British and four Portuguese light companies, plus two companies of the 60th and the *cacadore* battalion of six companies. Assuming battalions averaged 800 men with companies of 75, divisional strength was about 9,000, of whom nearly 1,400 (or about 15 per cent of the available infantry strength), were skirmishers. This compared very favourably with the French proportion, particularly since the latter had no riflemen while the British division had about 600. The brigades in the light division usually comprised two strong battalions of light infantry and half a battalion of rifles, so that they too were well equipped to deal with their French counterparts. The advance of a French column against a concealed British line was therefore through a series of belts of fire of ever increasing intensity. Assuming visibility to be good, the guns opened first with roundshot at half a mile (800 metres) or more. Then the riflemen, stationed as far forward as was possible, joined in, retiring steadily by sections as the column approached; then the light companies opened fire, the whole being well supported by the artillery which changed from roundshot to grape and from grape to case as the range lessened.

The critical moment came when the head of the column neared the crestline. At that stage the guns might either limber up and retire or simply be left by their detachments in the reasonable expectation that the column would have more to occupy it than the removal or immobilization of temporarily deserted guns. At this stage the skirmishers really had to move fast and clear the front because it was absolutely vital for them not to mask the fire of the first line. The usual drill was for companies to turn inwards on the centre and then double back in file. At Talavera they cut things rather fine and it was this which impelled the usually placid General Hill to exclaim, 'Damn their filing. Let them come in anyhow!' This of course was how they often did come in, racing for the intervals of the battalions or hurling themselves breathlessly under the poised muskets of their comrades in the battalion companies. Skirmishers in action were usually placed under the command of a field officer from one of the battalions on a brigade basis; this it must be realized was a very different thing from the semi-permanent flank battalions which had been popular a few years previously.

The custom was for the British first line to hold its fire as long as possible. The smoothbore musket was at its best at ranges of 100 yards (90 metres) or less; it was not a particularly accurate weapon even then, but with the huge size of the target presented to it even the worst piece in the hands of a bad shot could hardly miss, provided only that it was held horizontally. A French column of two battalions would have a frontage of about 50 men and a depth of 18 which after allowing for the inevitable straggling probably meant a block 60 yards (55 metres) wide and 25 yards (23 metres) deep – a solid third of an acre (0.8 hectares) of close-packed infantry.

A British battalion of about 600 men would be in a two-deep line on a frontage of some 200 yards (180 metres). As the French approached the flank companies might wheel slightly inwards so as to be able to fire at the flanks of the column, and at the critical moment 600 pieces went off together. The French, already tormented by the skirmishers, were often fairly blasted to a halt with heavy casualties and while they were reeling from the shock the British line reloaded so as to be ready for either a second volley or a bayonet charge as circumstances might dictate. If the latter, it was a limited one, designed only to drive the remnants of the column back in confusion, and was not pushed more than 100 yards (90 metres) or so.

93

The real problem for the French in the Peninsula was their reluctance, or possibly their inability, to deploy their masses at the right time. Their original well-drilled battalion columns had been very flexible, but the deeper they became the more difficult was their deployment. The matter was made even worse by the low standard of training of most of the reinforcements sent to the French army in Spain, and it may even be that in latter years the French used their columns virtually as projectiles as a matter of hard necessity rather than risk a slow and confused deployment under fire, which could at best lead to a serious loss of impetus, and at worst to a complete and disastrous shambles.

Nor were they helped by Wellesley's habitual use of the reverse slope positions, which often made it difficult to decide exactly where his first line was until it was too late. Timing was everything, as Napier made clear in his great history of the Peninsular War, when he wrote:

> The column is good for all movements short of the actual charge; but as the Macedonian phalanx was unable to resist the open formation of the Roman Legion, so will the close column be unequal to sustain the fire and charge of a firm line aided by artillery. The repugnance of men to trample on their own dead and wounded, the cries and groans of the latter, and the whistling of cannon-shots as they tear open the ranks, produce disorder, especially in the centre of attacking columns, which, blinded by smoke, unsteadfast of footing, bewildered by words of command coming from a multitude of officers crowded together, can neither see what is taking place, nor advance, nor retreat, without increasing confusion. No example of courage can be useful, no moral effect produced by the spirit of individuals, except upon the head which is often firm and even victorious while the rear is flying in terror. Nevertheless columns are the soul of military operations; in them is the victory, and in them also is safety to be found after a defeat. The secret consists in knowing when and where to extend the front.

Although it is possible to describe Wellesley's concept of a defensive battle it is not so easy to find one which fitted it in every respect. It may therefore be as well now to consider briefly some of his better known defensive actions and see how far it was possible to achieve the ideal.

Talavera (July 1809) was a defensive battle forced on Wellesley by circumstances beyond his control, and he had to take up the best position he could find in some haste. The Spaniards on his right were firmly ensconced in the town with a tangle of walls and enclosures in their front, and his own left wing was reasonably well posted on a piece of high ground with a brigade of cavalry in support. His centre however was on flat, level ground, and thus suffered more than usual from artillery fire. At one stage in the battle the Guards and the Germans of the 1st Division having repulsed a column in good style, pursued it too far, got into confusion and suffered heavily at the hands of the French reserve. The third brigade of the Division was swept away by the first wave of fugitives and for a time there was a dangerous gap in the line. An intelligent brigadier filled part of it and Wellesley, present as always near the vital point, hastily sent forward the 1st/48th to close the rest. They quickly formed a line, but it was clear that the mob of retreating Guards and Germans would inevitably break it, so its commanding officer wheeled back by companies into open column, allowed the fugitives to go through, then swung forward into line again in perfect time to stop the pursuing French with one devastating volley; it is but fair to say that the Guards and Germans halted a few yards in the rear, threw out markers, reformed quickly, and were soon back in line as steadily as ever.

Busaco, fought in September 1810 during the retreat to the lines of Torres Vedras, was perhaps the nearest possible to the British commander's ideal. Wellington (as we must henceforward call him, he having received his peerage for Talavera) chose the position carefully, apparently in the hopes of finally stopping the French advance, and he chose it well. It was a very strong position indeed, its chief weakness being that it could be turned on its northern flank. It was also somewhat too extensive for the troops available although there were certain compensating factors. In the first place the sierra was so high and visibility then so good that the direction of any French attack could be noted in good time to move reserves to the threatened point. Secondly the hill was so steep as to be virtually inaccessible for horses so that the excellent French cavalry could not be used; thus it was possible for Wellington to accept gaps between his divisions in the absolute certainty that they were not liable to sudden dashes by light horsemen. Lastly, the position was so high that it was almost out of reach of the French artillery; in the ensuing battle one or two enemy howitzers, presumably heavily overcharged, succeeded in lobbing a few shells onto the crest but their effect was negligible. The configuration of the ground made it possible for the British line to be concealed, so that the French commander completely miscalculated its length and attacked its centre under the impression that he was in fact turning its right flank.

Busaco demonstrated very clearly on several occasions the

weakness of a column when faced by a steady line, and the effect was particularly marked here because of the long preliminary climb up a steep rocky slope which brought the French infantry to the summit in no sort of order. The attack by General Regnier's column on Picton's 3rd Division was met by the 74th Regiment in line with a Portuguese battalion on either flank. As there was no threat from cavalry the two Portuguese battalions, reinforced by a composite light battalion, wheeled inwards so that the unfortunate French were struggling upwards into a horseshoe of muskets which presently blasted them back down the slope.

The column which tackled Craufurd's Light Division on the left suffered even worse, for Craufurd had a battalion of British rifles and one, later two, battalions of *cacadores* well forward in ideal skirmishing country and ably supported by a battery of horse artillery; the French had first to run this formidable gauntlet before being shattered by a charge of the 43rd and 52nd Regiments which their divisional commander had held back under cover until the critical moment arrived.

Albuera (May 1811) was fought by Beresford. He was a good trainer of troops and a brave man but did not shine in his only essay in independant command. In spite of criticisms, the position he took up was by no means a bad one; its principal defect was that its right was weak and Beresford compounded the error by placing his Spaniards there. The French did not oblige with the anticipated frontal attack but made a circuit and came in on the weak flank; the Spaniards, brave enough but poorly trained, made some shift to change front and the battle degenerated into a static and very prolonged fire fight.

A brigade of Stewart's 2nd Division was sent forward under the temporary command of Colonel Colborne of the 66th to extend on the right of the Spaniards but wheeled slightly inwards so as to take the French in the flank. Colborne, a thoroughly competent soldier, whom we last met in command of the grenadiers of the 20th at Maida, wished to form line well back and move up the slope in that formation but with his right-hand battalion in quarter-distance column; Stewart, however, brave but impetuous, ordered him to move forward in column and deploy on arrival. Colborne, faced with a direct order did as he was bid, deploying his battalions as they reached the crest, each one edging off to the right front as it did so in order to leave room for its successor. The brigade was actually engaged in a fire fight with the French when a heavy storm intervened and under cover of it the French cavalry charged the right rear and broke the whole to fragments; only the left-hand battalion, possibly still in column when the blow fell, got into square and beat off the horsemen, who were Poles in French service.

More British troops then came up and the strange and bloody static battle continued in a manner reminiscent of the early eighteenth century. The seven British battalions principally engaged were in line; the leading French corps was in *ordre mixte* with its supporting corps jammed up close behind it so that the whole formed a solid block of men on a frontage of about 400 yards (366 metres) and a depth of over 50 yards (45 metres). Some deployment had taken place on the French left to meet the threat of Colborne's attack, but similar attempts on the right were driven back by fire. Therefore, although almost every British musket was probably in action (some at very long range) only the leading three ranks of the French were able to reply. General Cole then brought up his 4th Division at the insistence of one of Beresford's staff, and placed it on the French left flank. This finally turned the scale and the French withdrew, leaving the British as victors on one of the bloodiest fields ever seen.

Apart from Colborne's disaster, the cavalry on either side largely neutralized each other. Cole, when he advanced, did so in line with a square, or at least a close column ready to form square, on either flank, thus offering no opportunity for the sort of sudden swoop of cavalry which had earlier proved so destructive. Had the French been in simple column they would probably have either broken the Spaniards immediately or been repulsed. As it was, the *ordre mixte* lacked the impulsion of the column but on the other hand placed sufficient muskets in line to allow a static fire fight to take place. Once this started they had no power to stop it; they could not deploy and dared not attempt an orderly retreat since once they turned their backs the British would have charged them. So they simply stood with enormous, hopeless, courage, for although the rear ranks were largely protected from musketry by those in front they were still torn through and through by roundshot from the British artillery. The French infantry were famous for their élan in the attack, but this battle showed them to be equally steadfast in a heavy pounding match.

At Fuentes d'Onor the British right flank was in the village and thus defensible, but the flank itself was open and the French were in a position to get behind it and cut Wellington off from his only line of retreat, the single bridge over the deep chasm of the Coa at Castello Bom. The British 7th Division which had been sent off earlier to stop, or at least delay, a French turning movement, were compelled to withdraw and Wellington therefore sent out the Light Division and his cavalry to take the pressure off them. This they did, the Light Division retiring steadily in battalion squares across a vast level space well suited to cavalry action with remarkably few casualties. In this they were of course greatly assisted by the British cavalry which, though much inferior numerically, delivered numerous gallant and successful charges against the swarming French horsemen. A strong defensive flank was then established between the village and the Coa and the situation was saved. Wellington himself admitted to his brother later that, 'If Boney had been there we should have been beat.'

Apart from the retreat of the Light Division there was of course heavy fighting elsewhere, particularly in the village itself, which was tactically the key to the position. At one stage the place was held by the 79th Highlanders, of whom Costello of the Rifles noted:

> Poor fellows! they had not been used to skirmishing, and instead of occupying the houses in the neighbourhood and firing from the windows they had, as I heard, exposed themselves by firing in sections. The French, who still occupied part of the town, had not escaped a rough handling as their dead also evinced.

As was perhaps to be expected, the fighting in the village saw the bayonet used extensively. At one stage 150 grenadiers of the Guard were driven into a blind alley by the 88th Regiment and were killed to a man by the bayonets of the excited Irishmen.

The battle of El Bodon saw Picton's 3rd Division withdrawing over an open plain in much the same way as had happened south of Fuentes and with a similar successful outcome. Probably the most remarkable feature of this battle however was the famous attack of the 5th Regiment under Major Ridge. The French cavalry had just captured a Portuguese battery and were milling round it triumphantly but in no sort of order when the British commanding officer advanced his battalion in line to within 20 yards (18 metres) of the astonished French, shattered them with two or three volleys, and retook the guns.

Although it is still fashionable in some quarters to consider Wellington as being primarily a defensive general, this is demonstrably not so since any check through a list of his principal battles in the Peninsula will make it clear that the bulk of them were offensive. Even in the early days he was ready enough to seize the initiative, as witness Rolica and the Douro, and from the end of 1811 onwards almost every battle he fought was offensive in character.

His broad tactical movements are well enough shown in the various histories of the campaign. As far as his infantry was concerned he manoeuvred it in battalion or sometimes brigade columns at deploying distance, and always formed line in good time for the final assault. Occasionally he seems to have moved for quite long distances in line, although it is a slow and difficult formation to maintain properly, even on level ground. At Salamanca the 3rd Division, swooping down past the British right, remained in open column until the last moment and then deployed into line on the march by doubling the rear companies diagonally forward. This avoided the necessity of halting the division to change formation under the close fire of the French. There seem to be few, if any, instances of the British finally closing in column, except of course in sieges when the narrowness of the breach made this course inevitable. Night attacks (except, again, at sieges) were also avoided when possible. The principal exception was at Talavera, and here the French took the initiative by seizing part of the left of the British position under cover of darkness, a feat which made a prompt British counterattack essential.

Long practice had taught the British infantry to manoeuvre well and the system of drill, though still closely based on Dundas, had been simplified and speeded up for the sake of flexibility. A number of commanding officers had begun to teach the battalion companies to skirmish, a fact which was to prove useful in the later scrambling sort of fighting in the Pyrenees. Various line regiments were actually converted to light infantry in the course of the war, these being the 68th and 85th in 1808, and the 51st and 71st in 1809.

When the Peninsular War ended in 1814, the Army dispersed quite quickly, many of the infantry battalions being despatched direct to other theatres. The operations in Portugal, Spain, and the South of France have tended to conceal the fact that considerable bodies of British soldiers were engaged in active operations elsewhere. Great Britain had been at war with America since 1812, a somewhat unnecessary affair brought on by the Americans who objected to British warships searching American vessels for deserters, who were in fact numerous. It constituted a stab in the back at a time when the British were engaged in a life and death struggle with one of the greatest tyrannies the world had ever seen, and was provoked largely by a relatively small number of rabidly anti-British American politicians. It was by no means popular with the northern states who considered, very prophetically as it turned out, that their commerce would suffer badly because of it. Success on land was achieved by a handful of neglected regular battalions, under the leadership of some generally second-rate officers; from this category we must of course exclude Brock, but as he was killed at Queenstown at the head of his own 49th Regiment soon after the war began he was not able to influence operations except in the earliest days.

Once the Napoleonic wars were over, or apparently over, in

1814, the British were able to divert considerable forces, both military and naval, to North America. Sergeant Cooper of the 7th Fusiliers, author of *Seven Campaigns*, had enlisted in 1807 under Windham's scheme so that at the end of the Peninsular War he was in fact time-expired and looking forward to discharge. The papers were actually made out and only awaiting his colonel's signature, but this was not forthcoming, so Cooper found himself en route for America and another campaign.

There was also considerable fighting at times in the East Indies. Battalions were posted there with a higher establishment of about 1,134, and thereafter allowed to dwindle under the normal wastage of casualties on service, death or incapacitation from disease, or old age; this was often a matter of hard necessity since the other battalion was often in the Peninsula and therefore inevitably got priority for reinforcements. The 1st Battalion of the 66th Regiment may perhaps be quoted as a fairly typical case. It sailed for the East Indies in March 1804 having been made up to full establishment from the unlimited servicemen of the second battalion. It then served in Ceylon, in India, and in the Nepalese War of 1815 and returned home the next year, a trifle over 400 strong.

Battalions not required for reinforcement of other overseas theatres were brought back to England and run down to a strength of 570 private soldiers. Large numbers of men who had joined under Windham's scheme were discharged and many more were invalided out through wounds, disease, or simply old age.

Napoleon's return took the nations of Europe very much by surprise. Great Britain, having as usual done her best to disperse her available forces, was then faced with the task of improvising an army as quickly as possible in pursuance of her treaty obligations; this army Wellington subsequently described as an infamous one and if we consider some of the allied forces the description is no bad one, but it hardly does justice to the British infantry present. These consisted of four battalions of Guards, 23 of the line and two of rifles, a total of 29, of which 17 had been in the Peninsula and 10 in the Low Countries with Graham. The main problem was their strengths which were in general low to start a campaign. Two battalions of Guards and the 1st/52nd were over 1,000 strong and the 1st/71st was over 900, but the remainder averaged not much over 500. The eight battalions of the King's German Legion, who were usually regarded as equivalent in fighting capacity to British battalions, were even weaker since their total strength, including officers, was 3,738. These figures it should be noted do not include the British brigade of the division left at Hal.

The first fighting at Quatre Bras fell on Picton's 5th Division, which was nominated as the reserve. Its eight British battalions had all served in the Peninsula and still had a relatively large proportion of old and experienced soldiers in their ranks, and its Hanoverian militia units, though raw *landwehr*, were ready enough to fight. It was a straightforward encounter battle between French cavalry and British infantry and as usual the latter came off best, their main losses being inflicted by the French infantry skirmishers who crept forward between the cavalry attacks and fired away at the huge targets offered by the squares.

The French cavalry suffered heavily. At one stage the 42nd and 44th Regiments were caught unsupported in line by cavalry charging from the rear; the 42nd tried to form square but the horsemen were upon them before the rear face had formed, whereupon the Highlanders promptly faced inwards and shot them all down. The 44th simply turned their rear rank about and fired a volley which brought down so many that the remainder sheered off. It was at this stage that Picton, despairing of allied cavalry support, formed the rest of his division into close columns and marching them boldly into the French cavalry, formed square, and opened fire in order to relieve the pressure on the two isolated battalions.

Halkett's brigade, coming up in support were less fortunate, due partly to inexperience and partly to the Prince of Orange's odd habit of ordering battalions to form line in the close presence of French cavalry, with whom it was unwise to take liberties. The 33rd got into square, as did the 30th, but the unfortunate 69th were broken while the 73rd only saved themselves by seeking refuge in a wood.

The position taken up by the allied army at Waterloo was in many ways a typical Wellingtonian one, with the line on a reverse slope and both flanks well supported by defended buildings, with a similar central bastion. The defence of these again demonstrated the resisting power of troops in stout buildings against many times their own numbers. On the right the Guards held Hougoumont to the end while in the centre the French only succeeded in capturing La Haye Sainte when the gallant German rifle battalion holding it ran out of ammunition.

The French infantry attacks were pressed in deep column with battalion after battalion behind each other, and these suffered heavily from the fire of the extended British lines. The French cavalry charges, though gallantly pressed, were invariably repulsed in square, and after the first couple of attacks these were so hedged round with dead horses that the succeeding waves could make no impression on them. As at Quatre Bras the French skirmishers pressed close in to the squares trying to tempt them into firing a volley which might give the French a chance to charge while the British were reloading. Fortescue quotes the case of a staff officer who, seeing that the Guards were disregarding this fire, rode up to Lord Saltoun, their commander and cried, 'God damn you, don't you see those are French! Why don't you fire at them?', only to receive the reply, 'Why, damn you, don't you think we know better when to fire than you do?', upon which the staff officer disappeared as suddenly as he had come.

The inexperience of the bulk of Wellington's army made it almost impossible for him to manoeuvre. He said later that had he had his old Peninsular army with him he would have swept the French away, but as it was the battle degenerated into what he described as hard pounding.

Harry Smith of the Rifles said later of Waterloo that:

> As a battle of science it was demonstrative of no manoeuvre. It was no Salamanca or Vittoria, where science was so beautifully exemplified: it was as a stand-up fight between two pugilists, 'mill away' till one is beaten. The Battle of Waterloo, with all its political glory, has destroyed the field movements of the British Army, so scientifically laid down by Dundas, so improved on by that hero of war and drill, Sir John Moore. All that light-troop duty which he taught, by which the world through the media of the Spanish war was saved, is now replaced by the most heavy of manoeuvres, by Squares, centre formations, and moving in masses, which require time to collect and equal time to extend:

These were hard words yet they contained a good deal of truth. There was to be no major war for almost 40 years after Waterloo, and in that time the Army stagnated. It was accepted as axiomatic that what had been good enough for the Duke must be good enough for his successors, but even this somewhat complacent acceptance of the status quo was largely fictitious. Over the years the skills and techniques of the old Peninsular army were lost, and when the next major test came it was to find the British Army wanting in many important aspects. Its formal training continued to be based on *Field Exercise and Evolutions of the Army*, a manual essentially similar to Dundas' original work, but somewhat modified by the experience gained in the Peninsular War and issued in 1824. This was an extremely complex and comprehensive work designed to cover every contingency, but in practice much of it was rarely if ever used on service, where simplicity was essential. The three basic formations in battle were line for a fire fight or a fairly short attack, column of various types for more extended movement and manoeuvre, and square as a defence against cavalry, and a battalion which had been really well-drilled in these fundamentals could take its place on a battlefield with some confidence. Line consisted of the companies of the battalion side by side in two ranks, and once paraded this line was then divided (or to use the technical term 'told off') into divisions, usually eight in number and thus equating to the original companies. These were then further told off into half-battalions or wings, grand divisions (each of two normal divisions) subdivisions (or half-divisions) and sections (quarter divisions).

A column could be based on a frontage of any of these subunits, each in line but formed one behind the other. In open column the distance between subunits was equal to their frontage, so that a simple wheel through 90 degrees brought them back into line, but column at half or quarter distance was also extensively used. All of these were more or less compact formations and relatively easy to manoeuvre, and also had the advantage that square could be formed from them very rapidly. The quickest and easiest square was one formed from a column of companies at quarter distance, to which a brief reference has already been made in Chapter 2. If we assume a battalion of eight companies or divisions, each told off into four sections the basic drill was as follows:

The second division from the front, number 2, halted and number 1 dressed back to it, thus forming a four-deep front face. The sections of the divisions numbered 3 to 6 then wheeled outwards through 90 degrees and the rear sections closed up to those in front, thus forming the left and right faces; number 8 division closed up on number 7 and both then turned about to form the rear face, and the square was formed. If there were more or less than eight divisions the drill remained substantially the same but the side faces were slightly shorter or longer than the others, so that geometrically speaking the square was in fact a rectangle. There was also a system of forming square from line by the wheel-back of flanking divisions, but this was less commonly used. These drills it may be said, remained in use substantially unchanged until the twentieth century.

6   1816–1859 AN ERA OF NEGLECT

The decisive defeat of Napoleon at Waterloo made it clear that the Napoleonic Wars were finally over, and once this was obvious to the British Government the usual dismemberment of the Army began. Until 1818 the need for occupation forces in France remained, but in that year they were finally withdrawn, and the proper run-down started. Within 12 months virtually all second or more junior battalions of infantry had gone, the only exception being the Guards, the 1st Royals, the 60th, and the Rifle Brigade (formerly the 95th Regiment). Of these the 1st Guards, who had been honoured for their services at Waterloo by the additional title of Grenadier, retained three, the remainder two each. The various foreign regiments and two battalions of the West India Regiment were also reduced at the same time.

Battalions were cut down to a total all ranks strength of 697, of whom 570 were private soldiers, unless they were in the East Indies when they were marginally higher. Battalions guarding Napoleon at St. Helena were often the strongest of all, being apparently on a special establishment.

The various colonies, old and new, appear to have sustained unnecessarily large garrisons, due probably to the Duke of Wellington's desire to keep as strong an army in being as possible by keeping it out of the public eye, and in the nature of things the great bulk of these garrisons consisted of infantry. This serious imbalance between the number of units abroad and at home however, although understandable, inevitably led to serious and chronic problems of reliefs. The theory was that infantry battalions should spend five years in the United Kingdom and 10 abroad, but in practice this could rarely be achieved. It was based on a sort of notional Empire-wide state of peace which rarely existed, so that few battalions ever achieved five years at home while a great many served much longer periods abroad than the statutory 10 years.

Soldiers conditions were bad everywhere. No one worried very much about their food, their accommodation, or their health; even in England the soldier was only given 40 per cent of the cubic space allotted to a convict, while conditions abroad were often unspeakable. The average mortality figures per thousand per annum speak for themselves. The healthiest station in the world apparently was the Cape, with a figure of 13. Next came the British Isles with 15, then Bermuda with 28 and the Windward Islands with 71. The figures for the East Indies are not available but fell somewhere between the Windward Islands and Jamaica with the horrifying figure of 120, one which in theory at any rate (and in practice almost) ensured that a battalion died in six years. The figures for West Africa were something over 75 per cent per annum, but West Africa was of course a penal station to which normal battalions were rarely if ever sent.

In order to establish even a semblance of regularity of relief, battalions due for overseas service had to be made up to the higher establishment by ruthless drafting from other units, so that the infantry in the United Kingdom was almost always under strength and full of recruits. The situation was made worse by the fact that in the absence of any properly organized system of civil police, most of the responsibility for maintaining law and order fell on the Army. Much time was spent preventing smuggling, searching out illegal stills, and dealing with the various manifestations of rural discontent – rick-burning, machinery breaking, animal maiming and the like – brought about by the serious post-war decline in agriculture. Much of the work fell on the cavalry, for whom there was relatively little need abroad except in India, and on occasions the yeomanry helped, but a great burden still fell on the infantry. The principal problem was that troops were necessarily dispersed in a multitude of small detachments which made proper command and supervision impossible and which had a serious adverse effect on training and discipline. The situation, bad as it was in England, was nevertheless a great deal worse in Ireland where a considerable proportion of the population was in a more or less chronic state of insurrection.

Fortunately things were improved relatively soon after Waterloo by the formation of civilian police forces. The Irish Constabulary was founded in 1819 and was followed by the Metropolitan Police in 1829 and various county constabularies thereafter. These properly trained keepers of the peace removed a great burden from the shoulders of the Army in the United Kingdom (except in Ireland where its active participation in the maintenance of law and order continued to be essential) and greatly improved its popularity in the eyes of the general public. The new police forces, being initially at any rate paramilitary organizations, also offered a suitable career for steady ex-soldiers and many hastened to join them.

By 1822 the situation as regards the infantry had achieved a very precarious (and very temporary) balance, and establishments had been fixed. Battalions in India and the East Indies were on an establishment of 1,071 and were organized on a basis of 10 companies, nine service and one recruiting company in the United Kingdom. Battalions elsewhere had a basic establishment of 654 all ranks and were organized on an eight company basis.

In 1824 the combination of a large-scale war in Burma and considerable disturbances amongst the West Indian negros made it impossible for the British Infantry to carry out its role, and with some reluctance the Government approved the raising of six new regiments numbered 94 to 99. This measure, though it gave some temporary relief, did nothing to solve the problem of how to keep battalions abroad effective without a proper depot organization at home, and in 1825 all line battalions (less those in the East Indies which already had small home-based depots) were raised to a strength of 10 companies of which six were to be service and four depot. The total strength of a battalion then became as described below.

The service element consisted of one lieutenant-colonel, one major, six captains, eight lieutenants, four second lieutenants, a surgeon with an assistant, four staff sergeants, 36 colour-sergeants and sergeants, 24 corporals, 12 drummers and 516 private soldiers, giving six companies of 86 privates with a proper proportion of officers and non-commissioned officers. The depot element, usually referred to as the depot battalion, consisted of a major, four captains, four lieutenants, four second lieutenants, a surgeon, 26 staff sergeants and sergeants, 26 corporals, eight drummers, and 224 privates, giving four weak companies each of 56 privates.

This system was for practical purposes a reversion to the concept of 'feeder' second battalions originally introduced by the Duke of York in 1803, and offered certain advantages. Service battalions were not particularly strong but under this system they could return ineffectives to the depot and be posted serviceable replacements, which kept their actual fighting strength reasonably close to their posted strength. The existence of a strong and efficient depot also facilitated recruiting, particularly since there was now every prospect that recruits obtained would go on to their own service battalion and not be faced with the prospect of being drafted.

The overall problem of reliefs was not affected by this change, and the number of battalions in the United Kingdom at any one time remained low. When it became necessary to send an expedition to Portugal in 1826 it was only with the greatest difficulty that nine effective battalions (two of which were Guards) could be found; and when the Duke of York died the next year he was perforce given a civilian burial because there simply were not enough troops available in the country to provide a military funeral for a field marshal. The Reform Parliament of 1832 continued to whittle away at the Army, so the situation could not improve. Anything done had to be done with inadequate resources and there seemed no prospect of any improvement. It is true that in 1837 a new system of rotating battalions (other than those in the East Indies) was introduced under which units leaving England on overseas tours went first to the Mediterranean, then the West Indies, and then Canada which at least gave them a reasonably gradual acclimatization; this however was no more than a laudable attempt to make the best of the available resources. In the autumn of 1837 there occurred a rebellion in Canada, and although it was a very small affair indeed the British Government found the greatest difficulty in raising sufficient troops to put it down. The situation was made worse by a dispute with the Americans over the Maine boundary which occurred at the same time. Palmerston at first took the high hand and ordered the British commander in New Brunswick to repel aggression, but as the unfortunate officer had no more than a single weak battalion of some 350 of all ranks, his position was precarious. No battalions could be found to reinforce him, nor was there a British naval squadron in American waters, so that the British Government eventually had to back down and agree to every demand made on it.

After this things were bound to improve, though the initial improvements were small; in 1839/40 battalions received an increase of five private soldiers per company which was at least a step in the right direction, but as no new battalions were raised the vexed question of reliefs was still not tackled. In 1841 there were 78 line battalions abroad, six on passage, and 19 in the United Kingdom, of which only 11 could be classed as even reasonably effective.

One significant improvement in infantry armament which occurred at this time was the gradual introduction of the percussion musket to replace the old flintlock. The complex and relatively unreliable system of ignition by flint and steel was abolished and in its place came the use of fulminates, that is, chemical compounds which would explode when struck. Caps filled with this were placed on a hollow nipple which communicated with the main charge and were set off by a simple hammer. Although this gave no greater range or accuracy it made the musket easier to load and more reliable in action, thus increasing the column of effective fire. As will be seen, it also opened the way to the eventual adoption of a reliable breechloader, and so may be classed as an important advance. At the same time a new rifle, worked on the same system, the Brunswick, was issued to rifle regiments. A few years previously, in 1830, infantry sergeants had also lost their half-pikes, being issued with muskets in lieu there of, although they still retained their swords.

In 1840 it was decided to raise a special regiment in Canada, its principal object being to prevent desertion, which had always been a serious problem along the border. The United States offered an attractive refuge to deserters, and the authorities there had rather encouraged it, so that the wastage rate of battalions in Canada was high.

The men for the new regiment were drawn from the 19 battalions then serving in Canada, and had to have a minimum of 15 years service and be of good character. The idea was that men might be given grants of land on final retirement and become settlers. The corps was at first called the Royal Canadian Veteran Regiment, but the word veteran was soon dropped. In August 1840 it finally became the Royal Canadian Rifle Regiment and was dressed in green and armed with the Brunswick rifle; as befitted a rifle regiment, no colours were carried.

The regiment was established at 1,078 other ranks in 10 companies, and considerable difficulty was soon experienced in keeping it up to strength, one of the problems being that as it was classed as a rifle corps it was expected to manoeuvre at high speed which soon wore the men down. The standards were then lowered somewhat and things improved. The establishment dropped at one time to six companies, but by 1860 had risen to 14. The regiment was finally disbanded in 1870, when the bulk of British regiments were withdrawn from Canada.

In 1842 Lord Hardinge was appointed Secretary at War. He was a distinguished soldier and administrator who had perhaps moved more with the times than most of his contemporaries. He first distinguished himself in the Peninsular War as a young staff officer by ordering up Cole's 4th Division at Albuera on his own responsibility and thus winning the battle at a time when Beresford, the British commander, was contemplating retreat. He subsequently served in the Waterloo campaign as Wellington's liaison officer with the Prussians and lost an arm in action. He had always been a stout advocate of the British Army in Parliament so that his appointment was a fortunate one.

Soon after his appointment the relief situation got so bad that he was driven to improvise units by raising a number of depot battalions (initially six) to six-company strength and using them as service battalions. This raised the number of infantry battalions in the United Kingdom from 25 to 31, thus greatly easing the problem.

The establishment of the six regiments concerned was increased to 1,338 made up as follows: one colonel, one lieutenant-colonel, two majors, 12 captains, 14 lieutenants, 10 ensigns, six staff sergeants, 67 colour-sergeants and sergeants, 25 drummers, and 1,200 rank and file. The latter were broken down into two battalions of 540 and a depot of 120, the officers and non-commissioned officers being distributed accordingly. The lieutenant-colonel retained overall control if possible, although in practice it was usually necessary for the second battalion to be commanded by the senior major. When such battalions were employed in a completely separate role a lieutenant-colonel and an adjutant were appointed to them. These improvised units, which were known as reserve battalions, had no colours, no band, and no flank companies; they were intended for service in temperate climates and several saw action against the Kaffirs in South Africa. In the period 1842 to 1846 no less than 12 such units were formed, their parent battalions being of the 5th, 6th, 12th, 20th, 36th, 42nd, 44th, 45th, 67th, 71st, 91st and 97th Regiments. The bulk of them had been reabsorbed before 1854 but at least one, that of the 12th Regiment, was still in existence in 1858.

In 1843 there were considerable disorders in the rural areas of England. The new civilian constabularies were not strong enough to deal with disturbances on that scale, and as few infantry battalions were available it became necessary to recall out-pensioners and form them into units. This was only possible by the fact that the ex-soldiers concerned had enlisted for life and were thus technically available until the day they died; it is difficult to believe that men recalled in that way showed much enthusiasm, but presumably they forfeited their pensions if they did not appear.

This recall did however demonstrate the need for a reserve of reasonably active men and in 1847 a bill was introduced to establish one. Limited service had been abolished in 1829 and since then men had enlisted for life. This was done away with in its turn, when the standard initial term of enlistment became 10 years, with the option of serving a further 11 for a pension. The idea was that a proportion of men would opt out at the end of their first engagement but remain as an unpaid reserve for the next 11 before qualifying for a deferred pension, but in the event this proved unpopular and was not proceeded with.

The mid 1840s were a period of considerable unrest in the world, for apart from the Sikh wars and a dispute with America over the Oregon boundary, there were several revolutions in Europe which made the Government consider very seriously its arrangements for internal security requirements on a large scale. No new battalions were raised, but the establishment of the four depot companies in England was raised considerably so that at a pinch they might be constituted as weak battalions for home service. The threat of revolution in Britain came and went in 1848 with the organization of a huge Chartist rally and a march on London. No troops were actively involved but they were present in considerable numbers, although discreetly concealed on the orders of the 80-year-old Duke of Wellington who had inevitably been called in to advise a number of very frightened politicians.

The Army, and perhaps particularly the Infantry, continued in a poor state. Recruiting was bad, so that when in 1850 some tension with France was thought to necessitate a small augmentation of 2,000 men it proved very difficult to raise them. This was to some extent due to the fact that the population of Ireland had dropped considerably after the great famines of the 1840s and thousands of young men who might otherwise have enlisted into the British Army had emigrated to America. Another cause was the general lowering of physical standards amongst the civil population of England, which was increasingly being crammed into the slums of the new manufacturing towns.

One of the fallacies of all governmental planning in the post-1815 period had been the bold assumption that because Great Britain was not at war with any major foreign power she was therefore at peace. Elements of the British Army had in fact been more or less continuously employed in warlike operations, often of an extremely arduous nature, either within, or at least on the remote fringes of, the large and rapidly growing British Empire. There had been a campaign against the Gurkhas, extensive operations against the Mahrattas and their licenced freebooter auxiliaries the Pindaris, an unpleasant war in Ceylon, and even more unpleasant and deadly ones in Burma and West Africa. Britain had fought the Kaffirs, suffered a disaster in Afghanistan, brought the so called Opium War in China to a successful conclusion, conquered Sind, beaten the Sikhs in a series of extremely hard-fought campaigns, attempted to subdue the Maoris, had a brief brush with the Boers and a second more extensive campaign against the Kaffirs, and in 1852/3 were engaged in yet another war in Burma. This list, which does not include minor 'police' operations, makes it essential that the word 'peace' should be written in inverted commas. In spite of the almost

worldwide nature of the list of operations, the main emphasis in
terms of size and extent of active operations was on India, and it is
true to say that the quality of our adversaries there improved
considerably in the period under review.

In the eighteenth and early nineteenth centuries the enemies
encountered, although numerous, had rarely been either organized or trained. They had often been no more than vast mobs
moving slowly across open plains, and the only really formidable
aspect of them had been their brave and numerous cavalry.
Cavalry however had long been disregarded by good infantry,
which the British-trained sepoys soon became, and much of the
earlier history saw comparatively small but well-trained forces,
usually predominantly Indian, manoeuvring freely and shattering
cavalry charges by the traditional method of steady volleys which
had proved so effective against the French. Therefore, although
there had been setbacks, the general rule of 'never retreat from
Orientals' had proved sound, and the redcoat infantry, European
and Indian, had for long had a reputation for invincibility. The
first really grave setbacks came with the Afghan disaster in 1842,
when the word went round India that the armies of Great Britain
could, after all, be beaten; this must have had some considerable
effect on the decision of the Sikhs to fight soon afterwards.

The Sikhs were fighting men of high calibre, organized on
European lines and trained by European officers and drill
sergeants, and the possessors of a large and well-handled artillery.
Gough, the British commander, was a head-down fighter of the old
school who put his trust in British bayonets and came very near to
disaster. The first day of the battle of Ferozeshah in December
1845 ended in near defeat, but fortunately the second day resulted
in a victory, although a costly one. The bulk of the casualties fell on
the British regiments, at least two of which, the 9th and the 31st,
lost 300 men each in fighting of an intensity not experienced since
Waterloo, and there was to be a good deal more almost equally
fierce fighting before the campaign was won. One fortunate result
of the war was that it left the Sikhs in no doubt as to the fighting
qualities of the British soldier and almost certainly led them to
support Great Britain a few years later when the mutiny broke out
in the Bengal Army.

The most useful campaigns from the point of view of tactical
innovations were almost certainly those in New Zealand and
against the Kaffirs. They were both brave, active and elusive
enemies against whom line and column were quite ineffective and
this led to a welcome loosening of tactics. Battalions in South
Africa in 1852/3 were allotted a small proportion of the new Minié
rifles and these, supplemented in many cases by privately owned

sporting rifles belonging to regimental officers, led to the fairly widespread use of tactics which had hitherto been confined to light infantry and rifle regiments.

In 1853 the decision was taken to set up a camp of instruction at Chobham in Surrey, at which up to three infantry brigades with a proper proportion of other arms might be exercised, units being changed over from time to time. This was practically the first time since the end of the Napoleonic Wars that such an attempt had been made; troops in England were usually too widely scattered to make formation training possible, while those on foreign service were simply grouped into ad hoc brigades where they learnt the art of cooperation as best they could, and often on the field of battle itself.

Command of the camp was given to General Lord Seaton who may perhaps be better remembered as John Colborne, of Maida, the Peninsula, and Waterloo fame. Although 75 years of age he was still an alert and active officer and his extensive experience in handling light infantry made him particularly well fitted to the task. A few years earlier he had written to his soldier son that:

> The details of the field-exercise must be constantly studied. An officer with common capacity may become a good drill with practice and knowing the principles of our field exercise; and yet, how rarely do we meet officers up to their business in this respect! Every officer of the 52nd could work a regiment in the field perfectly because he was compelled to begin early and frequently tried.

It is clear that he did useful work in the short period available. The major war by then looming on the horizon was to make it regrettably clear that such camps should have been instituted years before.

When the Crimean War broke out in 1854 the British Infantry in the United Kingdom consisted of a collection of virtually independent battalions, well enough trained in a limited way, but knowing very little about the manoeuvre of higher formations, a deficiency which the hastily improvised staffs were quite unable to make good. Most of them were also considerably under strength and had to be made up in the usual way by hastily drafting from other regiments not nominated for the original expeditionary force. The inevitable result of this was that when the scale of the war made it clear that many more troops would be required, these battalions, denuded of their best soldiers and given ineffectives in return, had to be filled up with recruits and sent off with little more than a cadre of experienced soldiers in their ranks. In spite of the various small wars which had been fought in the previous few years, not many of the battalions in the first wave had ever seen action. Of the 30 line battalions which fought at the battle of the Alma a bare half dozen had seen any form of active service in the preceding 12 years.

The infantry of the expeditionary force, which included three battalions of Guards, was organized into four infantry divisions and a light division, each of two brigades of three battalions. Battalions going to the Crimea were made up to a strength of 16 companies, eight service and eight depot, thus giving them what amounted practically to second battalions. The service element consisted of a lieutenant-colonel, two majors, eight captains, 16 lieutenants, eight second-lieutenants, a surgeon and three assistants, four staff sergeants, 50 colour-sergeants and sergeants, 50 corporals, 20 drummers, and 950 men, organized on the basis of a grenadier company, a light company, and six battalion companies. The depot element was weaker in officers, being commanded by a major with eight captains, eight lieutenants, and eight second-lieutenants; no surgeon was provided. The figures of other ranks were theoretically identical with those of the service element but must in practice had been very much lower until recruiting got under way. This establishment was soon found to be far too ambitious and after being authorized for only one month it was altered in June 1854 by the reduction of the depot element to four companies. The officer and non-commissioned officer element of these remained unchanged but the drummers came down to eight and the private soldiers to 380.

One most important accession to the fire power of an infantry battalion was the almost general issue at this time of the Minié rifle in place of the smoothbore percussion musket. Until then the rifle had been considered as a specialist weapon due to the difficulties of reloading it; obviously if a bullet is to be spun by the rifling it must be a tight fit and a tight bullet had to be coaxed down inch by inch with a heavy ramrod so that the edges of the lands of the rifling actually bit into the soft lead. This was a slow process and various attempts had been made to overcome the problem for some years. Minié's rifle fired an elongated bullet with a hollow base containing an iron plug. The bullet was made so as to be an easy sliding fit going down, but when the charge was fired the plug drove into the soft lead causing it to expand into the grooves and thus be effectively spun on its way out.

The Minié was authorized in 1851 by the Duke of Wellington, albeit somewhat reluctantly, although its introduction appears to have been largely due to the Marquis of Anglesey who was Master General of the Ordnance until 1850, and to Lord Hardinge who succeeded him briefly in the post before becoming Commander-in-Chief on the death of the Duke in 1852. A few were in use in South Africa in the Kaffir War of 1852, but production was slow until 1854. The battalions of Guards despatched to the Crimea had 250 Miniés and 650 smoothbore muskets, while few line battalions had anything except smoothbores. A good many more rifles were however soon despatched, with the result that before the fighting started three out of the four British Infantry divisions were fully equipped with them. No one, except the rifle regiments, knew very much about rifle shooting and there was very little time to learn. Units hastily improvised ranges wherever they could so that their men might have fired at least a few rounds before they were called upon to use their weapons in action. Colonel Bell, a Peninsular veteran then commanding the 1st Royals, tells us in *Rough Notes by an Old Soldier*, how he inadvertently blundered into the vicinity of one of those impromptu ranges and had to ride for his life even though the firers were half a mile (0.8 kilometres) away.

The Minié was by no means a perfect weapon. In the first place it was very heavy because some one (reputedly Wellington) had insisted that the bore should be sufficiently large to take the standard spherical ball. The latter weighed a trifle over an ounce but an elongated projectile of the same calibre naturally weighed a good deal more, which made an appreciable increase in the soldier's load. There was also the occasional risk that when the barrel was fouled the bullet was liable to stick, so that the plug was blown clean through it and out at the muzzle leaving an irregular lump of lead in the breech which effectively put the piece out of action until it could be attended to by an armourer. Even before the Crimean War had started a new and superior weapon was in train. This was the Enfield of 0.577-inch (14.7-millimetre) calibre (as opposed to the 0.702-inch (17.8-millimetre) of the Minié), numbers of which had appeared in the theatre of operations by 1855.

In spite of this the Minié gave good service. Russell, correspondent of *The Times* wrote 'It is the king of weapons . . . the volleys of the Minié cleft them [i.e. the Russians] like the hand of the destroying angel and they fell like autumn leaves before it.' This is purple prose, yet there is much truth in it, for it was indeed only the fact that the British Infantry had rifles which gave any interest or novelty to the tactics, being otherwise surprisingly like those of the Peninsula, although not as well applied. The Russians, armed with smoothbores, habitually moved in ponderous columns while the British fought in line, and it was not unusual for mere handfuls of British to take on thousands of Russians, secure in the knowledge that their superior training, allied to their rifles, would enable them to do so with reasonable impunity.

As only two battles were fought it is difficult to discuss tactics profitably. The British attack on the Alma was a scrambly affair, largely because of inexperience on the part of brigade and divisional staffs who did not allow the army sufficient frontage in which to deploy. The result was that the attack looked forward to the thick skirmishing lines of 1870 rather than to the neat and orderly advances of the Peninsula. Inkerman was a surprise, a savage, shapeless battle fought in a thick fog, and even now it is difficult to paint an accurate picture of what occurred. The British fought by battalions, wings, and companies, without much order, and their victory was due largely to the courage and activity of regimental officers and men. This was of course nothing new; it had happened before and would happen again. One thing clearly demonstrated was that whatever the drill book might say, the soldiers in action were making their own rules in the light of practical experience. There was relatively little volleying at Inkerman or even file firing; small bodies of British infantry shook themselves out into thin single-rank skirmishing lines and plied their new and deadly rifles independently, with enormous effect.

The rest of the war developed into a huge siege, a type of operation never popular with the British Infantry, who traditionally disliked scrambling about in trenches as much as they disliked digging them. Enough has already been written of life in the works in front of Sebastopol and the author has no intention of adding more to it than an anecdote or two which demonstrate very conclusively the remarkable capacity of British infantrymen to infuse a sporting element even into war. The first is a rather macabre little episode related by Major Henry Clifford V.C. of the Rifle Brigade:

> I could not help laughing the other day I was in the advance trench. I saw groups of six or seven men with their rifles full cock and sights up watching anxiously over the parapet. 'What are you on the look-out for' I said. 'Oh, sure Sir' said the old soldier 'We're waiting for the Russians to go to the rear.' About six hundred yards off was the quarry in which the Russians had lodged a strong party of men, but not having provided them with a patent water-closet the enemy are obliged to go a distance of about fifteen yards for the purpose. Our men watch out for them, and when one makes his appearance they all fire at him. One ran out as I was looking on. The bullets went all round him but he got off safe. My friend the Irishman remarked that at any rate it would be as good as a dose of opening medicine to him. On the return of the poor devil a second volley was fired and he came over like a

rabbit, as dead as a stone, and was hailed with a merry shout by our men.

One can only wonder how long the Russians tolerated that sort of loss before they improvised some kind of covered way to their latrines. Perhaps they just did not believe that it was anything more than luck, for their own few Brunswick-type rifles were hopeless beyond 300 yards (275 metres).

Eighteen-year-old Lieutenant Vaughan of the 21st Fusiliers was another keen shot whose letters home are equally full of regrets at missing the pheasant season, and of his exploits with the rifle at sterner game. On 27 November 1854 he wrote to his father:

> I was on a working party the other day down at the trenches, and I took one of the Minié rifles and went to the front and I picked off three men at about eight hundred yards in about 30 or 40 shots.

This was remarkably good shooting and probably only made possible by the fact that distances in the trenches were known to the yard by long experience.

The casualties in the Crimea, both from battle and disease, were huge and proved virtually impossible to replace. Certainly as far as quality was concerned the standard had dropped alarmingly. The original expeditionary force had only been brought up to war strength by ruthless drafting from other battalions and as the initial losses fell on those picked men the effect was grave. Regular battalions, coming out in the second wave, were of noticeably poorer quality as a result, while later drafts often consisted of mobs of half-trained frightened boys, a sad change from the steady battalions of mature men who had fought the Russians to a standstill in the earlier battles. By March 1855 infantry regiments in the Crimea had again been raised to 16 companies in a desperate but much belated effort to restore the situation. Service battalions in the theatre still consisted of eight companies with a four-company depot (which practically amounted to a weak holding battalion) in Malta, and a further four-company depot in the United Kingdom.

Once the war was over the establishment of the Army was of course reduced, but rather surprisingly there was not the great rush to cast off every last surplus soldier which had characterized the end of previous wars. Units were gradually run down by the normal processes of discharge of 10-year men who did not wish to re-engage, and by the disposal of ineffectives. Surprisingly enough the war had practically been fought on the peace establishment; no new regiments had been raised and only two regiments had raised extra battalions. These were the 60th and the Rifle Brigade, which had raised 3rd battalions in 1855, both these battalions being retained at the peace. Some assistance had been given by the Militia in providing overseas garrisons.

In view of the considerable surplus of soldiers, recruiting almost ceased and the large depot organizations were quickly run down, so that single-battalion regiments were soon down to a strength of 952 private soldiers in eight service and four depot companies. In spite of the casualties incurred in the Crimea, most battalions still had a fair cadre of experienced soldiers, while the frightened boys of the Sebastopol trenches had filled out, and with good food, strict discipline and proper training, were well on the way to becoming thoroughly effective soldiers. The overall situation was therefore as satisfactory as might reasonably have been expected at the end of a major war, and in view of the new crisis looming ahead this was just as well.

The causes of the Indian Mutiny of 1857 were complex ones and it is difficult to sum them up briefly without running the risk of appearing unfair to one side or the other. The trouble in Bengal had been brewing for some years; British rule in India had become more bureaucratic and consequently less personal, and there was a certain lack of sympathy for the problems of the sepoys as regards pay and allowances. Many of them, particularly those of Oudh, were either land owners or at least from land-owning families, and the various extensive annexations of the 1850s had unsettled them. There also had been grave fears regarding what they considered, perhaps with justification, to be threats to their religion and caste, and there is no doubt that a good many of the British in India at the time would have liked to have seen the whole thing swept away and replaced by Christianity. Caste had always been a particular problem in the Bengal Army; in the other armies, those of Madras and Bombay, caste of course existed but was kept within reasonable bounds. Once their men were away from their own particular villages they were prepared to relax a little, particularly on active service, so that no serious problems arose, but with the high-caste Hindu element of the Bengal Army it had become a predominant factor.

The real defect seems to have been the lack of good man management. Promotion was slow and the best of the British officers sought more attractive and more profitable outlets outside the Army, which thus remained to a considerable extent in the hands of ancient colonels and majors, and too many second-rate junior officers. The sepoys were many of them simple souls in an increasingly strange world and needed not only discipline but firm guidance and sympathy, whereas all they got was neglect. In all, an explosion was inevitable and perhaps, after a certain stage had been reached, even desirable.

In particular, from the military point of view, there was the question of the greased cartridge which finally sparked things off. Mention has already been made of the new Enfield rifle, and in 1857 issues were just beginning to a few selected Bengal regiments. The cartridge for this rifle was made up in a tube of what is still known as cartridge paper, about 0.6 inches (15.2 millimetres) in diameter and three inches (76 millimetres) long. The bullet was placed at one end, base outwards, and the paper below it tied with packthread. The space above the bullet held the powder charge, the top of the paper being sealed by twisting it; the whole was then dipped into lubricant, mainly to render it waterproof.

To load the rifle the cartridge was held in the palm of the right hand, bullet downwards, the rifle being held vertically in the left hand with the butt on the ground. The twisted end was then torn off in the teeth and the powder poured down the barrel, after which the bullet was pushed base first into the muzzle, the surplus paper torn off and the whole rammed down. The problem arose from the fact that although the lubricant was a mixture of beeswax and tallow or some similar compound, in Bengal the rumour soon spread that it was a mixture of pig and cow fat; as the one was unclean to the Muslim and the other sacred to the Hindu, the simple act of biting the paper would involve pollution and loss of caste and it was this rumour which finally united the two religions in the Bengal Army.

It is highly improbable that there was any deliberate intention of defiling the sepoys, but it is possible that unacceptable ingredients were used experimentally. The real truth will never be known, but the real truth is unimportant. It was what the sepoys believed which was important; they believed that it was deliberate, and rose accordingly.

There were 29 European battalions nominally in India in 1857, 20 of the Queen's troops and nine of the East India Company's. In fact three of these were in Persia, three in Burma, with a wing of another in Aden, while of those in the country no less than 12 were in the Punjab, leaving somewhat less than 10 available in Bengal, a ludicrous number when it is considered that the Bengal native infantry alone consisted of 72 strong battalions.

The course the mutiny ran was perhaps inevitable. There were the first risings, the first massacres, the first indecisions, after which things began to happen, albeit in a hesitant and disorganized manner. The bulk of the rebels concentrated at Delhi, where they reinstated the last of the Mogul emperors, and there the

British followed them. A mixed force of British, Gurkhas, and loyal Indians (of whom there were many) some 4,000 strong seized the ridge outside Delhi and fought 30-odd actions in three months before they assaulted, and almost incredibly, took the place. Thereafter the end was certain; there was still much fighting to be done but the British soon established their superiority, after which the campaign degenerated into an arduous punitive expedition.

The British soldiers tended to hold the sepoys in contempt, and it is a fact that the Bengal troops had not shone in their various operations in the field in the previous 20 years. It is easy to compare the fine, mature battalions of the native army with the immature boys (if such they were) of the British battalions; nevertheless it was the latter who had always done the hard work and they knew it. In addition of course they felt a very real hatred for the perpetrators of the various massacres which had occurred, and if some of these were rumoured, many were real and hideous enough. We have but to read the furious eye-witness accounts of Cawnpore and elsewhere to understand why the British soldier, rightly or wrongly, looked upon the whole thing as a kind of crusade.

Many of the sepoys fought well; indeed when cornered they fought with the very real desperation of men who knew that they faced defilement followed by the gallows, but their leadership was poor. A few natural commanders appeared, but it was too much to expect that ancient native officers, sunk in lethargic routine, should have blossomed into Napoleons overnight.

It is perhaps ironic that one of the causes of the Mutiny, the new Enfield rifle, should have also been one of the principal instruments in its suppression. The rifle proved an excellent weapon and the troops, many of whom were Crimean veterans, handled it well. At one stage in the very hottest weather it was found that the barrel expanded to such an extent as to make loading difficult, but a small reduction in the diameter of the bullet solved the problem without in the least affecting range or accuracy.

In no real sense was the rising a country-wide affair for with minor exceptions the other armies remained loyal, as did many soldiers from Bengal. There were civilians involved of course, but many of them were the usual riff-raff to be found in any large city, and certainly the bulk of the population remained at least neutral. The Sikhs, remembering the fighting qualities of the British, were only too glad to join them, as were the Gurkhas who still provide a number of fine battalions for the British Army. It is one of the odd facts of the Mutiny that it was a campaign waged against people that had always been trusted, and only won with the help of native allies who until relatively recently had been bitter enemies.

119

Soon after the outbreak of the Mutiny it had become obvious that more infantry would be required, and in August 1857 the British Government authorized the raising of 10 second battalions. The first eight were allotted to the 2nd to the 9th Regiments (the 1st Royals already having a second battalion) while 4th battalions were also raised by the 60th and the Rifle Brigade.

As time went by, and India continued to soak up more and more infantry, the home authorities became seriously perturbed at the lack of troops in England and in March 1858 a further 16 regiments, the 10th to the 25th, were also ordered to raise second battalions. Very fortunately recruiting had by then improved enormously; the campaign in India had attracted attention, and the gallant and well publicized deeds of the regiments there (plus possibly the attractive rumours regarding rich loot) had brought many young men to the recruiting sergeants. Most of these second battalions had to be raised from scratch, although at least one, the 2nd/12th, was based on the last of the old reserve battalions. In June 1858 another regiment was also added to the British line in the shape of the Royal Canadians, a unit composed almost entirely of Canadians who had volunteered to help with the suppression of the Mutiny. The outbreak was in fact over before the new regiment could be sent to India, but it was brought onto the establishment as the 100th.

All these new battalions were raised on the basis of 10 service and two depot companies and had a total rank and file strength of 1,000. One obvious lesson from the Crimea had been that all infantry should be able to skirmish, so that in 1858 flank companies were abolished and companies numbered serially from right to left. The new battalions were naturally also all raised on this basis.

As was to be expected, the repercussions of the Mutiny were considerable. It was of course obvious that the East India Company could not continue to rule, and on 1 January 1859 the Crown assumed control of India by a Royal Proclamation, after which it became necessary to consider how best India might be garrisoned in the future. A Royal Commision was appointed to consider the case and in spite of opposition from Indian officials, who considered a local European army desirable, it was eventually, and inevitably, decided that the Crown could only have one army, and that India should be an imperial responsibility like any other.

This decision naturally led to certain problems as far as the existing European regiments of the old Company's army were concerned. The British Government, with a certain lack of tact, proposed simply to convert them to Queen's troops by a stroke of the pen, but the soldiers in the ranks thought differently. They considered that they should be re-enlisted with bounties, and for a time discipline, perhaps never very strong in the Company's European regiments, almost ceased. Eventually one regiment was disbanded and large numbers of individuals in the others took their discharge, when the trouble ceased. Soldiers coming over to the Queen's service were allowed to count an extra two years towards pension, and in due course nine new regiments were added to the British line and numbered 101 to 109. At first they were somewhat weak in numbers but as recruiting was good they soon filled up and became effective units. Thus in a matter of two years 10 new single-battalion regiments and 26 new battalions had been added to the establishment.

At the end of the campaign in India there were no less than 77 battalions of British troops in the country, of which 68 were the Queen's and the remainder Company's troops. This was the greatest concentration ever achieved in a single theatre, and although it was clearly unnecessary to keep such huge numbers there once peace had been restored, the Royal Commission soon came to the conclusion that the acceptable minimum in the foreseeable future would be 50. Thirty-seven were also required for other overseas garrisons which, allowing for the fact that battalions would serve, on the average, two thirds of their time abroad, made a further 44 necessary for the defence of the United Kingdom and for reliefs. This made a minimum total requirement of 131 battalions and this total was in fact slightly exceeded. There were 109 regiments of the line plus the Rifle Brigade. Of these the 60th and the Rifle Brigade had four battalions, 26 had two and the remaining 83 were single battalion corps, giving a grand total of 141. Until well into 1862 the recently transferred Company's regiments were however only shown in the Army list in skeleton form. These figures do not include the Guards, the Royal Canadian Rifle Regiment, or the various colonial corps.

The year 1859 saw a period of sabre rattling on the part of the French, which caused some apprehension at the time. The bulk of the British Infantry was abroad and most of the new battalions were only in skeleton form, so that even the vague threat of invasion was alarming. The affair, which led directly to the resurgence of the volunteer movement, eventually blew over, although it was the first of a chain of circumstances which led to a major reorganization of the British system of home defence.

The general introduction of the rifle quickly made it clear that some uniform system of instruction was essential if the soldiers were to get the maximum value from their new and more deadly weapons. In the days of the smoothbore musket individual accuracy had hardly been possible except at point-blank range.

Reliance had therefore been placed on the volley, but volley firing was a purely mechanical business and thus strictly within the province of the drill sergeant, whereas the new rifle, sighted to 900 yards (825 metres) and certainly capable of good individual accuracy at 400 to 500 yards (365 to 455 metres), required a new and specialist approach to the problem. Lord Hardinge had another requirement too, in that he needed an establishment under his own control in which new infantry firearms could be tested and reported on. In those days the various ordnance committees tended to consist largely of artillery officers, but although their excellent technical knowledge qualified them for such posts he could never be quite sure of their impartiality. The new infantry rifles were already beginning to outrange the standard smoothbore field guns of the period, and he may have thought that artillery officers were not always keen to recommend the adoption of infantry arms which might eventually render their own pieces obsolete. He was possibly reinforced in his opinions by the knowledge that in the recent past at least two self-expanding bullets, the one invented by Captain Norton of the 34th Regiment and the other by the well-known gunmaker Greener, had been turned down without any clearly stated reason being given. In 1853 therefore he obtained authority to set up an establishment at which to study the scientific use of the rifle, to evolve a doctrine on it, and to develop a uniform system of instruction which could then be passed on to the soldiers in the ranks.

The site chosen for this new establishment, which was to be called the School of Musketry, was at Hythe in Kent. An excellent barracks, built originally to house the by then defunct Staff Corps, already existed there, while the miles of shingle beaches on the eastern side of the great Dungeness headland were admirably suited for the construction of rifle ranges. No time was wasted for, although no final authority as yet existed, the first commandant arrived in June 1853. He was Lieutenant-Colonel C.C. Hay, a thoroughly practical officer late of the 19th Regiment, who brought with him Colour-Sergeant John M'Kay of the same regiment; he was followed a few weeks later by two sergeants of the Grenadier Guards and one of the 97th Regiment, which gave a small but highly effective nucleus of staff.

The first function of the School was to carry out exhaustive tests on the new Enfield rifle, and in particular to compare it with Lancaster's oval-bored weapon of the same type. Colonel Hay came down in favour of the former, and it was duly adopted. The School finally came into official, if somewhat belated, being on 22 September 1854 and thereafter expanded steadily. In addition to the resident staff, all battalion and depot musketry instructors were at first also held against the Hythe establishment; the total of these was considerable, being 100 captain-instructors, 50 lieutenant-instructors (for depots), 100 second-class instructors (sergeants) and 100 third-class instructors, many of whom were corporals with a few private soldiers amongst them. By 1856 the School was well established and had adopted for its badge the familiar and famous crossed rifles surmounted by a Royal crown.

The first batches of instructors were all trained on the Enfield, and instruction at the School was on reasonably modern lines. A good deal of time was spent on theory but this was probably essential for soldiers who had hitherto handled only the old smoothbore. Much of the instruction was mechanical and repetitive and laid great stress on word perfection in the various handbooks then in use, although as this was to a great extent equally true until World War 2, it can hardly be considered a criticism.

The soldier was first taught to aim on a rest of a type very similar to the modern one, great emphasis being placed on keeping the sights upright; correct holding and trigger release were also rightly considered vital and a great deal of dry training and strengthening exercises were carried out so that the student was thoroughly familiar with his weapon before he ever discharged it. The standing position was still considered as being the important one, although the kneeling position was also encouraged as being a steady one which could be adopted quickly. As the Enfield had a muzzle velocity of only about 1,000 feet per second (300 metres per second) its bullet travelled along a relatively high trajectory at all but the closest ranges, and this led to the need for accurate judging of distance, which thus became an important item on the syllabus.

The targets then in use were cast iron plates, six feet (1.8 metres) high by two feet (0.6 metres) wide and marked off by serrations into six-inch (15-centimetre) squares. They were propped up by rear supports and were so designed that several could be locked together for practice at longer ranges. They were usually whitewashed, with a circular bull and various other rings marked out in lampblack; some were equipped with a separate iron bull suspended on wires which made a gratifying clang when struck. At ranges between 400 and 600 yards (365 to 550 metres) double targets were generally used, the bull being a solid black one two feet (0.6 metres) in diameter; from 600 to 900 yards (550 to 825 metres) a three-foot (0.9-metre) bull was usual.

Markers watched the targets from behind protective earth and iron barriers and signalled scores by means of different coloured flags, red and white for a bull, blue for an inner, and white for an outer. The soft bullets made a considerable and easily visible splash of lead on the target so that shots could be spotted. When there were so many on the target that the quick identification of new ones became difficult, the marker waved his red flag horizontally to indicate to the firing point that he intended to 'wash-out' his target and rewhiten it, hence the modern term. All shots were carefully recorded in a squad register so that the progress of individual students could be gauged. The usual method of collective fire was by file firing, although volleys might exceptionally be ordered, either at very long ranges or when a cavalry charge had approached sufficiently close to make that type of fire desirable.

Other shorter special courses were run for senior officers, for students from other arms employing weapons of the carbine-type, and later for officers of the volunteers. A special course was run for Guards' adjutants in 1858, and one student, Brevet-Major Robert Lindsay V.C. of the Scots Fusilier Guards explained to his mother that:

> We plunged on my arrival into musketry and have been immersed in it ever since. Theoretical principles and the whole history of Small Arms from the first invention of gunpowder down to the latest invention of modern days, occupy our whole time . . .

Although a gallant and very competent officer he clearly found technical details somewhat confusing, and later described the Enfield rifle as having 'a hundred parts, and each part having two ends, and each end a different name.'

By 1860 it had become clear that the School of Musketry was a valuable institution which had come to stay. It was in fact so busy, chiefly with students from the new second battalions, that in 1861 a second school was opened in Fleetwood, Lancashire to help deal with the backlog. As soon as this was cleared in 1867 the Fleetwood establishment closed, but the main school of course continued. Training was on sound, if stereotyped, lines and the reputation of the place was high. As far as the British Army was concerned Hythe meant the School of Musketry, and 'Hythe-trained' was synonymous with competence in that particular field. It was a tradition which remained in being until Hythe finally closed in 1969, and is still carried on at the School's new location at Warminster.

7 1860–1898 THE BEGINNING OF REFORM

The first 12 years of the period under review in this chapter were important ones in the history of the world, for they saw a virtual transformation in the nature of war, which led in turn to great changes in the balance of power in Europe. In 1860 the French were dominant on land, but a new star was rising. In 1864 the Prussians inflicted a short, sharp defeat on the Danes, following it two years later by an even more decisive victory against Austria which had hitherto been regarded as a major military power. Finally, in 1870–71 she virtually destroyed the French army in a brilliantly fought campaign which left her as undoubtedly the most powerful military state in Europe.

Outside Europe there was the American Civil War. This was a major conflict, which although overshadowed at the time by events in Europe, nevertheless offered many valuable lessons in the new art of war. The major changes came about as a result of the employment of huge armies, consisting for the great part of short-service soldiers reinforced by reservists, and armed with rifled, and in some cases breechloading, weapons. The maintainance and movement of these huge forces was only made possible by modern improvements in communications, noticeably the railway, the steamship, and the electric telegraph, and although Great Britain was not directly involved in any of these campaigns they were inevitably to have a profound effect on her military developments.

By 1860 the British Army had recovered from its major operations of the previous six years, and was largely occupied with recruiting and training the numerous new battalions made necessary by her new responsibilities in India, responsibilities which were to dominate her military thinking for many years to come.

Various Royal Commissions were appointed to consider the

question of manpower. The one of 1861 made the sensible suggestion that recruits should be taken when available without too much regard for establishment, as a form of insurance against possible lean years later, but then apparently ran out of ideas. The one of 1866 was more constructive; it proposed the localization of infantry regiments to stimulate recruiting and advised the appointment of an inspector-general of recruiting with a suitable staff. It suggested that the initial period with the colours should be raised to 12 years (this was adopted in 1867) and felt that re-enlistment ought to be encouraged, but although all this did help to build up the regular army it did nothing to establish a reserve, the need for which had been one of the major lessons of the Crimea and the Mutiny.

One step towards modernization occurred at this period with the proposal to adopt a breechloading rifle. The resounding success of the Prussian needlegun against the Danes in 1864 had shown the superiority of this type of weapon, and by the time of the next major European conflict, the Austro-Prussian war of 1866, the conversion of the existing muzzle-loaded Enfield rifle by means of the Snider breechblock had been approved and issues begun soon afterwards. This was a temporary expedient, and by 1871 the Martini-Henry, a purpose-built breechloader, had been approved; it was to remain as the standard arm of the British Infantry for almost 20 years.

In December 1868 a major event occurred, particularly as regards the infantry, in the appointment of Mr Cardwell as Secretary of State for War. He was a practical, forward-looking administrator and a number of sensible changes were soon in train. The situation in Europe showed the need for adequate regular forces at home, and this he gradually achieved by careful reductions in colonial commitments. It was made clear to the old 'white' colonies that in future they could have to take a much greater part in their own defence than hitherto, while the various non-European colonies were largely left in the hands of locally enlisted troops or constabularies under British officers. All this was made possible by the great improvements in communications of all kinds, for the telegraph, the steamship, and the Suez Canal had suddenly made it possible to move reinforcements in weeks rather than months. By March 1870 Cardwell was able to announce that the number of infantry battalions in the United Kingdom had risen from 46 to 68, a very significant increase. A less important but nevertheless useful alteration made at the same time was the reduction of battalions on the Indian establishment to 10 companies, which brought them into line organizationally with battalions elsewhere and thus facilitated reliefs.

The next significant step was the Enlistment Act of 1870 which confirmed Cardwell's belief in the need for a reserve. Men were to enlist for an initial term of 12 years of which the period spent with the colours might be varied at the discretion of the Secretary of State. He considered that the minimum should be three years and the maximum six or seven, and that only a limited number of soldiers, mostly non-commissioned officers, should be allowed to re-engage to complete 12 years or longer. He announced at the same time his belief that non-regular infantry units, i.e. those of the militia and the volunteers, should all be brought under common command and onto a common system.

In 1871 a committee, usually known as the Localization Committee, was set up to consider the future structure of the British Infantry on the lines envisaged by Cardwell; it was presided over by Major-General P.L. Macdougall, an officer of great practical experience, and one of its members was a certain Colonel Garnett Wolseley, a capable and dashing officer with a growing reputation. The committee duly reported to the Commander-in-Chief, who early in 1872 produced a memorandum on the subject for the benefit of the House of Commons; as this was to outline the future organization of the Infantry it was an important document, its full recommendations being set out below.

1 Double battalion Regiments to be worked as one Corps, to be formed into three distinct bodies, – one Battalion abroad at whatever fixed establishment may be required with 1 Lieutenant-Colonel, 2 Majors, 8 Captains, 16 Lieutenants and sub-lieutenants, 1 Adjutant, 1 Quartermaster, and one Paymaster; one Battalion for home service at a reduced home establishment, with 1 Lieutenant-Colonel, 2 Majors, 8 Captains, 14 Lieutenants and sub-lieutenants, 1 Adjutant, 1 Quartermaster, 1 Paymaster. The Depot centre to be formed by two Companies from each of the two Battalions, with 1 Captain and 1 Subaltern to each Company.

2 The Local or Depot centre to be in the charge of a Lieutenant-Colonel assisted by a substantive Major, 1 Quartermaster, and 1 Paymaster. Two Militia Regiments to be included in each such District, with the Volunteer Corps of the District and the Army Reserve men and pensioners making up the entire force of the Local centre. The two Militia Adjutants and the permanent Militia Sergeants to do duty with the Depot Centres, when their Regiments are not embodied or out for Training.

127

Each Militia Regiment to have its Sergeant-Major, Quartermaster sergeant, and Orderly room Clerk as part of its fixed establishment of non-commissioned officers.

The Depot Companies to have one Colour and one Company sergeant at all times distinct from the Militia Sergeants.

3   All other Regiments to be linked by Brigades of two and two, and to be in every respect organised as the double-battalion regiments as regards one Regiment at home, one abroad, with a combined Depot Centre as specified above.

4(a)   The present number of Battalions of the Army, 141, to be maintained as at present and the Regiments linked to continue as separate Corps for the officers, and made to act as much as possible in mutual support. The Majors for the Depot Centres to be taken from the Home Regiment or Battalion, and to take this duty in alternation by periods of two years.

4(b)   All recruits to be raised and drilled both for the Line and the Militia at the Depot Centres and to be passed from these as rapidly as possible into the two Service Battalions or Militia Regiments, as the exigencies of the Service may require; but in cases of war and Militia embodiment these Depot Centres to be the nuclei for the formation of a Local Reserve Battalion. The Reserve men of each District to be trained equally for a certain number of days in each year at these Depot Centres.

The present accommodation to be thoroughly examined into and made available for the above purposes, and supplemented wherever necessary by additional accommodation.

5   The first Battalions for Foreign Service to be on an increased Establishment, and these to form the first Corps d'Armée for service abroad.

The system was soon approved and put into operation, the new 'brigades', or subdistricts as they were usually called, being numbered 1 to 70. Very few suitable barracks existed where required, so that a considerable building plan had to be put in train. Many of the new depots were built in a distinctive and typically Victorian style, with a great deal of red brickwork ornamented with deep purple, although a few were built of local stone. All, or almost all, of these new barracks included a three- or four-storey battlemented 'keep' of pseudo-Norman design, which was generally used for the storage of arms and ammunition for the militia and reservists. They must also have been built with a vague idea of defence, since some at least were equipped with loop-holed steel window shutters.

As far as regiments with two or more battalions were concerned things worked well from the start, because everyone was a member of the same family, wore the same badge, and was accustomed to pull together. Not surprisingly however the system of linking single-battalion regiments led to endless friction, so much so in fact that in the late 1870s there was considerable agitation to end the system. This however the Government resolutely refused to do, and in this they were right, for the new arrangements had great advantages, particularly as far as the training of recruits was concerned. Previously the depot companies had been grouped into more or less ad hoc depot battalions, and placed wherever a convenient barracks happened to exist without much regard for the need for regimental supervision. After 1872 the depots had a proper permanent base, and once the newness had worn off they rapidly became regimental homes in a very real sense. Many of the new barracks were complete and occupied by 1877.

As no reserves then existed, the first 18 battalions on the roster for foreign service were kept at a relatively high strength of 820 rank and file, the next 18 being at 620 and the remainder at 520.

The first test of the new system came in 1879 when the Zulu War made necessary the despatch of a number of home battalions. These units, being largely 'feeders' for their overseas links, were in general on the weak side and averaged only about 400 men with over a year's service. The early disasters in Zululand were naturally attributed to the fact that battalions consisted of 'mere boys', and this led to a renewed demand for a return to the 'good old system'. Lord Roberts, a general whose word carried weight, considered that the short-service regiments had similarly 'broken down' in the Afghan war, and thus also advocated a return to the old system; he was closely and warmly supported by the Commander-in-Chief the Duke of Cambridge, an arch reactionary.

There is no doubt that many of the criticisms were justified, for although the garrison battalions in South Africa were strong and efficient, those sent out from home were very much less so. General Sir Bindon Blood (a Captain in the Royal Engineers at the time of the Zulu War) commented in his biography, *Four Score Years and Ten* that:

> The mobilization of the rest of the force, the infantry especially, was not so satisfactory. The battalions all required large drafts to bring them up to war strength and in this case

the drafts were provided by other corps which were already short of trained men and could not spare them. Thus it came about that our battalions landed in Zululand full of incompletely trained men, a great proportion of whom had never fired ball cartridge, while many had never fired a round of blank before they embarked.

The real fact of the matter was that the only well-trained soldiers in England were civilians on the reserve, which could not be called up for small operations. This was basically the system adopted all over Europe, but although it worked well enough for non-colonial powers it never really proved adequate to the demands made on it by Britain's numerous overseas expeditions.

As early as 1876 the inter-regimental friction engendered between the more unpopular links led to the formation of yet another committee to consider the workings of the new infantry system. This committee made the bold, indeed almost revolutionary recommendation, that far from abandoning the system it should be made permanent by converting the linked corps into two-battalion regiments, thus placing almost the whole of the British Infantry on the same footing, and in 1881 this was done.

Thus in nine years the British Infantry had undergone the greatest reorganization in its history and had been placed on a new basis which was to endure (although not without some serious creaking) for the remainder of the period covered by this book. Although Mr Cardwell had been replaced in 1880, he was the principal instigator of the new organization which was always known thereafter as the Cardwell System.

All regiments of the line were given new titles, almost all on a geographical basis as the table on pages 147–9 makes clear, and in theory the old numbers disappeared, although in practice they lingered unofficially for many years. The new groupings became known as regimental districts and there were 67 of these. Two of them, the 60th Rifles and the Rifle Brigade, had four battalions each, 66 had two battalions, and one, that of Cameron Highlanders, had only one, making a total of 141 battalions. The seven battalions of foot Guards, three Grenadier, two Coldstream, and two Scots, already shared a common depot.

The new regimental districts were allotted the old numbers of the senior original regiment; numbers 1 to 35 were consecutive but the 36th Regiment had become a second battalion which left a gap, and this was naturally repeated all through the list of less senior regiments. In seven cases, where it was geographically convenient, two regimental districts were placed together as double depots, which brought the total number of headquarters down to

60. Each depot was commanded by a colonel, usually one who had commanded one of the battalions, although exceptions were made in favour of certain cavalry colonels for whom other employment could not be found.

Once the system was established it worked reasonably well. There had never been any intention of locating home battalions in their own district, the tendency being to group field force units in the vicinity of suitable training areas, for which the earlier wars had shown a great need. The first of these, Aldershot, was established in 1855, Shorncliffe, Colchester and the Curragh being acquired seven years later. This sort of concentration, which had only been made possible by the successful establishment of civilian constabularies, was not only good for training but was also beneficial for health. The existence of large stations also made possible central facilities for libraries and recreation centres, the provision of rations at relatively cheap rates, and other administrative advantages.

The prime function of the British Infantry was to provide garrisons, particularly for India, with the result that home units became part of the training organization for all practical purposes. The annual drafts to be sent overseas averaged 165 if the other battalion was in India, or 145 elsewhere, which imposed a steady but inevitable drain on home battalions. The steady build up of the reserves however tended to counteract this, and when they were called up in 1882 because of the war in Egypt they provided a most welcome reinforcement of mature, steady, experienced men.

The depots themselves consisted of four companies with a major, a captain, and two subalterns. Apart from the officers the companies consisted mainly of non-commissioned officers as instructors, with only a minimum of trained private soldiers (often old or medically unfit) for the essential administrative duties. The volunteers kept very much to themselves but the militia, which were regarded as feeder units for the regular army, were closely integrated; many a young man got his first taste of soldiering in the militia before deciding that it was the life for him and enlisting as a regular soldier. Terms of service at this stage were usually seven years with the colours and five on the reserve, though soldiers in units overseas usually served an extra 12 months, known ruefully as 'the Queen's year'. The Guards, who were not then employed abroad except on active operations, would accept recruits for as little as three years with the colours. This helped them to build a reserve, and as they had no militia regiments to fall back on as feeders this was important.

One of the changes brought about under the new system was the abolition of pay for colonels of regiments. These posts were usually held by distinguished generals, often retired, and were in fact a useful way of rewarding good service. Until 1855 colonels had made what they could through clothing contracts for their regiments, often a profitable although not necessarily a very dignified form of perquisite, but in that year clothing became a Government responsibility and colonels were paid a flat rate of £1,000 a year in lieu. After 1881 the post became strictly an honorary one, other financial arrangements having been made for retired general officers.

Another interesting innovation dating from 1881 was the introduction of warrant rank for certain categories of what had previously been senior non-commissioned officers. Before that date there had been no intermediate level between officers, who held their powers by virtue of a commission from the Monarch, and non-commissioned officers whose authority was derived solely from the rank granted them by their commanding officer. As far as the infantry was concerned the only persons granted this new rank were regimental sergeant-majors and bandmasters, the former of whom relinquished their earlier four chevrons for the more appropriate badge of the royal coat of arms. The grant was by no means universal, since certain categories holding the appointment of sergeant-major, for example those of the regular staff of the militia, continued to be classed as non-commissioned officers. There were then no grades of warrant officer, these only being introduced in 1915, a period outside the scope of this chapter.

Yet another change brought about by Cardwell in this general period was the abolition in 1871 of Purchase, the system under which officers of the cavalry and infantry had bought both their initial commissions and their subsequent promotions for hard cash. The idea was an ancient one, probably originating with the mercenary free companies which were essentially commercial undertakings, and had been in use in the British Army since the Restoration. The system was simple enough in theory. In the mid nineteenth century for example a suitable young man might purchase an ensign's commission in an infantry regiment for £450 and subsequently rise to a lieutenant (£700), captain (£1,800), major (£3,200) and even lieutenant-colonel (£4,540), commissions in the foot Guards costing about twice as much. At each step he could of course sell his earlier commission so that his promotion only cost him the difference between the two.

The rules for the system were clearly laid down in Queen's Regulations, but in practice it inevitably led to all sorts of peculiar financial transactions by and through army agents. In spite of its complete illogicality however there was a good deal of support for it. It ensured that commissioned officers were men of some substance instead of mere adventurers, and it also ensured that they had in due course a modest competence on which to retire at a reasonable age. This was in contrast to the non-purchase corps – these being the artillery and engineers – in which officers hung on grimly and caused fearful promotion blocks in which 40-year-old subalterns waited impatiently for their 60-year-old captains to die.

Inevitably too there had grown up over the years a series of safeguards and sanctions which did at least modify the worst of the inequalities. Certainly by the earliest years of the nineteenth century there were minimum ages for initial promotions and minimum periods in each rank before a further step could be sanctioned, and officers applying to purchase had to be satisfactorily reported on. Commissions and promotions caused by augmentations, i.e. the adding of new companies to a battalion or a new battalion to an existing regiment, were invariably given free, an important consideration in wartime. A steady stream of free commissions was also given to sergeants and gentlemen volunteers who had distinguished themselves in action, as were free promotions to existing holders of commissions. As it was properly held that a commission could not be bequeathed or inherited, any officer dying, whether in battle, by disease, or natural causes, automatically forfeited his, and it then went to the senior qualified officer in the rank below, thus allowing an interesting element of financial speculation to temper the risks of soldiering, and incidentally giving rise to the old army toast of 'A bloody war and a sickly season'.

Nevertheless the system was in essence outmoded, and Cardwell determined to sweep it away. In this he was supported in the Commons but opposed in the Lords, but the latter were quickly overcome. The whole system only existed by virtue of a Royal Warrant and Gladstone, then Prime Minister, soon persuaded Queen Victoria to revoke the Warrant, thus automatically killing it. The Government paid out several million pounds in compensation and Cardwell replaced it with a system of promotion by seniority tempered by selection.

Relatively few organizational changes occurred in the next few years while the Cardwell system was getting under way. In 1887 the establishment for battalions for India increased by 100 rank and file and in 1892 all home battalions were placed on a uniform lower establishment. In the past it had been considered necessary to keep certain home battalions on a higher establishment in case of emergencies, but by 1892 the Army reserve had been built up to the point where this became unnecessary. In 1893 the strength and deployment of line battalions was as follows:

India	52 battalions	1,032 all ranks
Mediterranean and tropical colonies	13 battalions	1,012 all ranks
Temperate colonies	6 battalions	892 all ranks
Home	70 battalions	801 all ranks

These figures were exceptional in that they fell in a period of relative calm. It was generally reckoned that battalions would spend 15 or 16 years overseas and about eight at home; these figures referred to the unit and not to the individuals composing it, who rarely served more than eight years continuously abroad. When battalions finally came home they would of course have a considerable proportion of men with very much less foreign service than this, and these men were often cross-posted to the sister battalion departing on foreign service. This helped to fill the gap between home and foreign establishments.

It sometimes happened that home battalions had to be sent abroad to reinforce a theatre where active operations were in progress. When this happened the size of the depot increased and once or twice it became necessary to form provisional 'holding' battalions to cope with recruits leaving the depots. It was reckoned by the authorities that if it ever became necessary to form a really large expeditionary force, some 50 home battalions could be brought up to strength with reservists and volunteers from the militia and made available for this role. If this ever occurred the plan was then to bring the various depots concerned up to a weak battalion strength so that they too might be available for home defence.

The system of training then in force was thorough, if somewhat unimaginative. Recruits underwent 11 or 12 weeks initial training at the depot; this consisted mainly of musketry (including a recruits range course of 200 rounds), drill and physical training, and at the end of it recruits were considered fit to take their place in the ranks of the home battalion. There they improved their knowledge considerably by taking part in field training and other battalion activities. Their physical training was also continued (the general condition of recruits in the period was poor, and they needed a good deal of 'setting-up') and they had a chance to specialize in signals, pioneers, the transport, or the mounted infantry; school was also compulsory, as was the trained soldiers' annual musketry course of 200 rounds, a proportion of which was devoted to field firing.

It was extremely unlikely that a recruit would be put on a draft with less than a year's service, and in practice the period was usually a good deal longer than this. Soldiers on man-service could

134

not be sent to India until they were 20 years of age, so that those enlisting at 18 served a minimum of two years in the United Kingdom. It will be seen from this that the bulk of private soldiers in a home battalion had less than two years service, while those in the foreign battalion were fairly evenly spread between two and eight, giving an average of five. At this stage private soldiers were not usually permitted to re-engage beyond their initial seven or eight years' colour service unless they happened to be bandsmen, grooms, pioneers, or other particularly useful specialists.

Although the strength of infantry battalions varied according to their location, all were organized on a standard eight company basis, so that drafts moving between battalions were not faced with the problem of learning a new organization; the young soldier joining his foreign battalion for the first time simply found that his company consisted of almost twice as many men as he had been accustomed to. At this stage the company was broken down into two half companies (which on foreign service were each commanded by a subaltern), these half companies being further divided into two sections, each under a sergeant with a corporal to assist him.

In 1889 a considerable step forward in armament was made by the adoption of the Lee-Metford rifle. This was a bolt-action, magazine rifle of 0.303-inch (7.7-millimetre) calibre, sighted to 1,800 yards (1,645 metres) for normal shooting, but also equipped with a special sight designed to allow reasonably effective collective fire to the astounding range of 2,900 yards (2,650 metres). The magazine held eight rounds which had to be loaded singly. When charged, the magazine could be sealed off by a sliding shutter known as a cut-off, which allowed the rifle to be used as a single-shot weapon while still retaining a reserve of rapid fire for emergencies. At first the propellant was compressed black powder but this soon gave place to cordite which, being smokeless, made it very much more difficult to locate troops behind cover than had previously been the case. Although there was always an inevitable delay between authorization and actual issue it is probable that the changeover was complete by 1893. By this time a certain number of the new Maxim machine guns were also in service; the usual system as far as the infantry was concerned was that one battalion in each brigade should have two of these weapons, carried either on pack animals or on wheeled carts and manned by a detachment of one officer, one sergeant and between 11 and 16 rank and file. This detachment was over and above the normal establishment of an infantry battalion.

The increased rate of fire of the new rifles made it essential that a good supply of ammunition should be carried. The scale was 100 rounds on the man, 65 per rifle in the four battalion ammunition carts, and a further 20 rounds per rifle with the baggage echelon. By this stage battalions also had a proper scale of transport, consisting of one cart for picks and shovels, four for ammunition, and four general service wagons, with 30 horses and two mules, the latter being for the purpose of getting ammunition up to the forward companies in action. Battalions overseas had a further seven wagons with an extra mule for the medical panniers, and the whole transport section was under the command of a subaltern officer with a sergeant to assist him. The personnel of the transport were drawn from the rifle companies in peacetime, although on mobilization an increment of a further 35 privates for transport duties was authorized. It will be appreciated that the number of animals listed does not include the chargers for the field officers, the company commanders, and the adjutant, all of whom were mounted.

It was not the custom to post a chaplain permanently to a battalion, although a medical officer was always attached for duty when active operations appeared likely.

Another innovation of the period was the addition of a detachment of mounted infantry to every home battalion. Mounted infantry were simply soldiers who rode to battle but dismounted to fight it, and the possession of a horse (not necessarily a very good one) gave them greatly increased mobility. There were ample precedents in the British Army, dating back to the mounted archers of the French wars, and by the end of the American Civil War the cavalry on both sides were well versed in the role. The various small colonial wars of the nineteenth century, often against mobile savages, had shown an obvious need for mounted infantry in the British service and many such detachments had been hastily improvised locally and often mounted on animals other than horses. Camel corps had been a feature of the operations in Egypt and the Sudan in the period 1882–6, and it was the success of these which finally prompted some slightly more permanent organization.

Detachments of one officer and 32 men attended 10-week courses on the subject. These were held at Aldershot, Shorncliffe, and the Curragh, and the syllabus included riding, stable duties, horse management, mounted infantry tactics, and field firing. At first the necessary horses were borrowed from local cavalry regiments but later a pool of cobs was authorized. There was of course no intention that a mounted infantry detachment should be a permanent feature of every battalion; when courses were complete the detachments returned to their units and resumed their places in the ranks.

If mounted infantry was ever required, it was envisaged that four battalion detachments could be grouped into a mounted infantry company, and sufficient saddlery and equipment for eight of these was kept in store at Aldershot. A system of registering suitable horses for use in national emergency already existed, so that mounts could be found from that source.

The British Infantry were curiously slow to appreciate the effect that the general introduction of the rifle was bound to have on tactics. In the Crimea they had had the huge advantage of being almost completely armed with rifles while the Russians for the most part still had smoothbores, many of them converted flintlocks, and under these circumstances small bodies of British had cheerfully taken on huge Russian columns, confident that their fire would tear the heavy formations to pieces at a range at which the unfortunate Russians could make no effective reply.

The American Civil War of 1861–4 should have pointed the way. The bulk of the infantry on both sides in that terrible conflict were armed with muzzle-loaded percussion rifles of broadly similar capacity to the Enfield, and many in fact *were* Enfields. As we have seen they were by no means perfect. Their high trajectory made careful judgment of range essential, and their rate of fire did not exceed two rounds a minute. Nevertheless they were capable of deadly individual shooting up to 400 or 500 yards (365 to 460 metres) and effective collective fire at twice that distance, which made a frontal attack across open ground an extremely expensive business. Things were made worse from the attackers' point of view by the fact that the natural defence against the bullet was the diligently plied spade, which meant that the defenders were often well-dug in and thus even less affected by the more or less random shooting of their assailants. The days of a quick dash in the face of no more than a single volley had gone. Attacks, given a good field of fire, came under effective fire at about half a mile (0.8 kilometres), and assuming that even a steady advance without pauses would take at least 15 minutes to cover this distance, every defending rifleman could get off 20 or 30 carefully aimed rounds.

The American Civil War however was a remote, far-off conflict and it was events in Europe which finally convinced the British that the time for change had come. The Franco-Prussian War, the first to be fought in which both the opposing infantry forces were armed with breechloading rifles, made it dramatically clear that the tactics which had served Wellington so well were no longer a practical proposition in modern war. The concept of neat lines, or even solid columns, rolling steadily forward behind a screen of skirmishers until a quick volley and a charge decided things was outmoded. Henceforward, so it seemed, attacks were to be conducted by thin, loose, skirmish lines, making their way forward as best they could by the use of ground and covering fire until they were able to dominate their opponents by their sheer volume of fire. In theory this sort of attack could rarely succeed without an overwhelming superiority of numbers, and the fact that it often did so in practice was largely a question of morale. Confident attackers always had a certain moral advantage. The defenders, often young conscripts, tended to become unsteady at the sight; they began to wonder if the flanks were holding; they tended to shoot wildly with their sights still set at 500 or 600 yards (460 or 550 metres), thus sending their bullets high over the heads of their assailants. Having said this however, it must also be emphasized that success was rarely gained without a considerable superiority of numbers at the vital point. This could only be obtained by superior strategy and grand tactics, and once achieved it had to be maintained and even augmented as the decisive moment drew near. Considerable numbers of men had to be pushed forward to replace casualties during the advance, and as these had necessarily to be led forward in small parties, the firing line tended to get into considerable confusion with sections, companies, and even battalions inextricably mixed up. Under these circumstances, which the Prussians (who by virtue of their victories had become the arbiters of all things military) considered as being inevitable, success depended on the efforts of company officers and senior non-commissioned officers who simply caught up as many men as they could and led them forward.

The British Army, while finally accepting the need for extension in the face of modern rifle fire, was nevertheless loath to believe the fact that extreme confusion was inevitable, so they adopted, or perhaps it would be better to say readopted, a method which they hoped would avoid it as far as possible. When applied to an eight-company battalion the idea was that two companies extended in single rank should form the skirmishing line and should advance in alternate rushes, each covering the other by fire. Behind them came a further two companies in support; their function was to thicken the skirmishing line so that the latter might achieve a dominance of fire at about 200 yards (180 metres), preparatory to a successful assault. The rest of the battle remained as a reserve under the commanding officer to reinforce the firing line if necessary, ward off threats from a flank or, at a pinch, cover a repulse. It was realized that companies would become mixed to some extent, but generally hoped that confusion might be restricted to the battalion, where everyone knew everyone else, and soldiers would be ready to fall in on the flank of the nearest formed body; it had, after all happened in the Crimea and it was reasonable to hope that it would happen again.

The concept of a three-line attack was of course by no means new. It had been adopted, although probably not actually invented, by Sir John Moore at Shorncliffe and had been employed frequently by the regiments of the Light Division in the Peninsula.

Although these new tactics became official it is probable that not a great deal of attention was paid to them. The last 30 years or so of the nineteenth century saw the British Army involved in a series of colonial wars, some of them on a large scale, for which special local tactics were required, and it is understandable that commanders of battalions on foreign service should have concentrated on the sort of operations they might be called to carry out at any time, rather than spend too much time in preparation for some hypothetical orthodox European war in the vague future. Home battalions had very much the same outlook; apart from the fact that they were deeply involved in training drafts for their sister battalion, which might well be on active service, they were always hopeful that the current trouble, whatever it might be, would reach the scale where they themselves would be sent to take part. The commanding officers who gained credit and advancement were those who led their battalions successfully on active operations rather than those who concentrated on theory. It was particularly noticeable on field days devoted to the new tactics that many of the more elderly colonels could not or would not realize that things had changed. They had been accustomed to manoeuvring their units in close formations where everyone could hear them, and where the captains of companies played a very minor role, and they were not ready to accept that in future a great deal would have to be left to subordinate commanders. Even when their battalions were extended they insisted on galloping about the field, taking command of companies or sections as the fancy took them, quite regardless of the fact that in a real battle mounted officers in their position would not have lasted 10 minutes.

Although colonial campaigns were very much an irrelevance as far as modern warfare was concerned, the British Infantry spent much of the nineteenth century in this sort of operation so that it may be as well to examine the genus briefly. Although there was a great variety of operations it is possible to identify them under three main headings: warfare in the open plains, warfare in the jungle, and warfare in the mountains.

Operations in the open plains, which includes for this purpose desert or bush, could be conducted to a great extent in the old style. This was partly because visibility was good and movement was easy, but mainly because the enemies encountered had few effective firearms. They were savages more or less, very brave, very active, physically very powerful, and quite prepared to charge to close quarters, which in the absence of firearms was indeed their only means of inflicting casualties. The answer to this was fire power delivered in shoulder-to-shoulder formations of the kind in use in the Napoleonic Wars. As there was no reliable way of securing the flanks against an active enemy, some sort of all-round defence was often essential and this in practice turned out to be a two-deep square, garnished if possible with automatic weapons. Such squares might be on a battalion basis but were quite often formed by much larger bodies. Movement was often made in a type of rather loose, elastic square formation big enough to contain the staff, the transport and other non-combatants. Formations of this type were particularly important where visibility was poor, as for example in broken country or high bush. Forces often harboured for the night in square formation, and if possible constructed thornbush fences or zarebas to disrupt any rush at night-time when rifle fire was less effective. Wagons often proved useful as defences against charging savages; their use had been known to the settlers of North America for many years, and the Boer trekkers invariably employed laagers of this type with great effect.

The battle of Isandhlwana against the Zulus in 1879 was lost largely because of neglecting to use this form of defence, while Rorkes Drift was a decisive victory because the principle was observed. There were indeed no wagons, but hastily erected barricades of sacks of corn and cases of supplies were employed to link up the buildings into a single defensive post. These barriers were frail enough, but they held off the charging Zulus for long enough for the rifle fire to take effect and this was decisive. The final victories of this war were fought in squares which sheltered not only the staff but also the cavalry. As soon as the Zulus had broken themselves in gallant but hopeless charges in the face of rifles and machine guns the cavalry sallied out and completed the victory. It is one of the ironies of war that at a time when tactics and formations were becoming looser as a result of the huge fire power developed by modern breechloaders, the British should have been forced back to close formations by the mass assaults of spearmen with few missile weapons.

Jungle warfare was in many ways the most unpleasant kind of campaigning of all. The climate was hot and humid, visibility poor, and movement difficult. The inhabitants of these regions were not usually as fierce and brave as the plainsmen, but they were cunning and knew the ground well. Being hunters they were often armed with firearms, and although these were relatively primitive they were effective enough at the sort of ranges at which actions occurred; indeed at 20 yards (18 metres) or so a smoothbore flintlock loaded with a handful of rough slugs was likely to be a most formidable and frightening weapon, particularly when discharged from behind a good stout stockade. The answer to a sudden ambush of this type was a quick rush, but troops in single file on a jungle path are very ill-prepared to rush, while the thickness of the vegetation made deployment very slow. The best that could be hoped for, as happened in Ashanti in 1873–4, was that the enemy were sufficiently brave to stand and fight. When this occurred the rapid, disciplined fire power of modern infantry quickly dominated the slower, more scattered fire of the ancient trade guns, and when followed with a bayonet charge it was usually decisive.

Mountain warfare, as far as the British Infantry was concerned, meant the North-West Frontier of British India. Until about 1839 British military operations in the country had been largely confined to the plains, where orthodox tactics could be employed, but from then onwards it became necessary to develop new techniques. When the British first started campaigning in the mountains they tended to keep to the valleys so as to facilitate the movement of the very considerable quantities of transport which were essential to keep the force supplied in a hostile and inhospitable country, but this soon proved to be tactically unacceptable. The hillmen were brave, cunning and active; and above all they were often armed with more accurate weapons than the smooth-bore muskets then in use in the British service. When they occupied the heights they dominated the situation; any attack to dislodge them had to be made up hill, which put the heavily ladened soldiers at a severe disadvantage and led to many casualties, not only from fire but from exhaustion.

It thus soon became apparent that the fundamental tactical rule was to hold the high ground while the column passed or rested, and this was achieved by crowning successive heights on either flank with pickets, parties of infantry about 25 strong. These dominated the high ground and held the hillmen out of effective rifleshot of the column until it had passed, when they were withdrawn. This was by far the most dangerous part of the operation and required careful coordination, for if the hillmen were able to reoccupy the picket position quickly they could inflict heavy casualties on the retiring infantry.

As the century progressed the balance tilted in favour of the British, chiefly because of the great and rapid improvements in firearms. Sheer volume of fire was not enough; the tribesmen were adept at using cover and camouflage, and formal volleys were wasted on them. Slow and careful shooting by selected shots was the answer to small scale sniping, although when a full scale attack was launched volleys were employed as long as possible, after which independent fire was used.

The most difficult operation in the mountains was a withdrawal which the hillmen always followed up closely, always hoping to inflict casualties and, more important, acquire their rifles. As they tortured and mutilated prisoners as a matter of course, it was considered essential to get casualties away at whatever the cost. Four men carrying a wounded comrade offered an excellent target and it often happened that more casualties were inflicted. It was however a point of honour (and also necessary for morale) that every effort should be made, and many of the awards for gallantry made on the North-West Frontier were for saving life.

It often happened that in Afghanistan the enemy employed a proportion of regular troops supported by irregulars and when this was the case they sometimes offered battle. When this happened European-type tactics could be used. Speed was essential, as was good supporting fire, and strong positions could sometimes be won by threatening to cut them off, the prospect of which the tribesman had a natural fear.

One of the changes of the period was the decision that infantry battalions should no longer carry their colours into action. In the days of battles fought in close order they had provided a useful and conspicuous rallying point, but those days had almost gone. The new long-range breechloaders had finally compelled a loosening of tactics in which some degree of concealment was essential, and a colour party had very little place in this new scheme of things. Even in the days of the muzzle-loading musket they had inevitably drawn a great deal of fire, and casualties amongst officers and senior non-commissioned officers had always been heavy. Sergeant William Lawrence of the 40th Regiment, when describing his experiences at Waterloo, wrote that:

> About four o'clock I was ordered to the Colours. This, although I was used to warfare as much as any, was a job I did not at all like; but still I went as boldly to work as I could. There had been before me that day fourteen sergeants already killed and wounded while in charge of those colours, with officers in proportion and the staff and colours were almost cut to pieces.

If casualties on this scale could be inflicted with inaccurate smoothbores is was clear that the losses from breechloading rifles would be unacceptably and quite unnecessarily heavy, and it was felt that the time had come for a change. Isandhlwana was not of course a battle in the modern mould, but the loss of the gallant Melville and Coghill in their attempts to save the colours of the

24th clearly brought things to a head. The custom was not in fact discontinued immediately, for as late as 27 July 1880 the 66th (Berkshire) Regiment lost its colours in an epic battle at Maiwand, in Afghanistan, in which the battalion was practically destroyed after a desperate fight against overwhelming odds.

A War Office letter dated 17 January 1882 eventually laid down that it was no longer considered necessary to take colours on active service, and directed that they should be left at the base, and although the wording apparently left some degree of discretion in the matter to individual commanding officers the practice then finally ended. The last British regiment ever to go into battle with its colours flying was the 58th, later the 2nd Battalion the Northamptonshire Regiment, which did so at the battle of Laings Nek on 28 January 1881, during the First Boer War.

One of the greatest experts of the period in small wars was Garnett Wolseley, who conducted a number of such operations with uniform success. He was a highly competent officer of advanced views, some of which were by no means acceptable to the military hierarchy. In particular he was a great advocate of special forces since he clearly had little faith in the competence of many battalion commanders, or in the capacity of many of their soldiers. In his famous *Soldier's Pocket-Book*, which although primarily a compendium of military knowledge, naturally reflected many of his own views and prejudices, he comments:

> Then again, as the OsC our Regiments obtain their position by living long enough and not by selection, the chances are that many of those in command of the Regiments first on the roster for foreign service would be at best only indifferent leaders . . . my advice is, select all ranks most carefully for these little wars; call for 50, 80 or 100 volunteers from a sufficient number of Regiments until you have your required number, selecting as Troop or Company Officers the best men from each of these regiments, and as COs the very best men of the required rank in the Army. With a battalion of 1000 men so selected you can afford to say 'come on' to your most warlike or most savage enemy.

Earlier in his book he actually goes so far as to propose the use of small corps composed entirely of young officers, on the grounds that our officers cost us nothing. He says, 'There is always a crowd of young gentlemen trying to enter the army, so the nation could afford to lose them, and I wonder what on earth it is in the way of a military enterprise that a battalion of Infantry, or mounted Infantry, composed of English gentlemen could not accomplish.'

One of the more serious deficiencies in the organization of the British Army at the time was the lack of any sort of establishment to formulate and disseminate tactical doctrine. A certain amount was of course done by the Staff College, but this usually dealt with strategic problems concerning armies, and in any case Staff College teaching does not seem to have permeated the Infantry as a whole. The usual result of this was that British battalions often arrived in operational theatres with little idea of what to expect; they simply learnt by experience as the campaign progressed, but their lessons were sometimes expensive ones.

Most of the lower-level schools of instruction then in existence catered for specialists such as signallers, mounted infantry, and even cooks. The only one with any general application to war was the School of Musketry at Hythe, but there the teaching was very narrow, being designed to do no more than turn out competent instructors of musketry. Field Marshal Sir William Robertson who attended a course there as a sergeant in 1881 commented that:

> The curriculum was then about as unpractical and wearisome as it could well be, the greater part of the time – two months – being devoted to acquiring efficiency in repeating parrot-like the instructions laid down in the drill book. Little or no attention was paid to the art of shooting in the field, and the total amount of ball ammunition expended was restricted to the orthodox forty rounds per man.

This attitude was perhaps understandable in its day. The second half of the nineteenth century was a time of British complacency; the Victorians considered themselves as a very superior race whose institutions were so well-nigh perfect that no improvement was possible. As far as the Army was concerned the Duke of Cambridge set the tone. When he first became Commander-in-Chief (a post he was to hold for 39 years) in 1856, he was something of a reformer, but this soon gave place to a thoroughly reactionary attitude to any change. On one occasion, when chairing a lecture on foreign cavalry to the officers of the Aldershot garrison he opened the proceedings by commenting, 'Why should we want to know anything about foreign cavalry when we have better cavalry of our own?' This gives a fair idea of his attitude which was widely, although by no means universally, copied.

Fortunately there were a number of 'thinking' officers in the Army who gave a good deal of consideration to the need to keep abreast of affairs. These individuals gave a great deal of thought to the lessons which had emerged from the American Civil War and the Franco-Prussian War, and from about 1873 onwards considerable private efforts were made to establish some form of tactical doctrine applicable to the changed circumstances brought about by the rifle. As the principal problem involved was to get an assaulting force close to the defences without enormous casualties, it will be appreciated that much of this new doctrine was necessarily concerned with the problems of manoeuvring infantry.

Although relatively little official material was forthcoming, a great many officers wrote books on various aspects of the subject; these were published commercially, often with some degree of official approval, and did much to fill the gap, as did the numerous articles in the various military journals of the period. Possibly the best known of these reformers was Sir Garnett Wolseley, whose *Soldier's Pocket-Book* filled a long-felt want, but there were many others. MacDougall, Hamley, Chesney, Maurice, Callwell and Henderson, to list only the best known, all contributed a great deal of effort, as did the distinguished volunteer writer, Wilkinson. Home and Clery, both officers of the Royal Engineers, produced books on minor tactics which became standard works. As sappers are notoriously intelligent it is not in the least surprising to find one writing books on infantry fire power and its application in war; this was Captain, later Colonel, Mayne whose *Infantry Fire Tactics* appeared in 1889. He, like Robertson, thought little of the School of Musketry as then constituted, and felt that the real need was for,

> A great experimental school, at which officers of all ranks should be assembled to see such experiments of collective fire, inclined fire, indirect fire, etc. as cannot be carried out in every place, and which require experienced officers to conduct them where they can be carried out. Half-yearly reports on any such firing carried out should be sent to all battalions by the School of Musketry. It should be the duty of all officers who had attended the School to impart to their battalions on their return what they have seen and learnt there. The duty of a School of Musketry should be to keep up the instruction of the Army in shooting to modern tactical requirements, and to the ever-improving power of the rifle; it should originate improvements in arms and tactical methods of procedure, and not be content to follow the footsteps of others, – those who follow are always behind.

The truth of this comment is now self-evident but it was not so obvious then. The School of Musketry improved dramatically in the early twentieth century under the stimulus of the South African War and made a notable contribution to the development of infantry fire power in the two World Wars. A proper school of infantry was not however formed until the end of World War 2, and even then it took a further quarter of a century to combine the teaching of fire power and tactics in one location.

In the last few years of the century, increasing colonial commitments made it imperative to augment the Infantry, and 19 new battalions were formed in 1898. The Coldstream and Scots Guards each raised a third battalion, the Camerons at last raised a second battalion and so brought themselves into line with the remainder of the Infantry, while eight regiments, the Royal Warwickshire, the Royal Fusiliers, the Lancashire Fusiliers, the Northumberland Fusiliers, the King's, the Worcesters, the Middlesex and the Manchesters were each allotted two more battalions. This was presumably done in preference to spreading the increase more evenly by adding third battalions only to a greater number of regiments, since this would have upset the careful Cardwell balance, whereas a four-battalion regiment worked on what may be classed as a 'double-Cardwell' system. Third battalions did not of course affect the Guards since they did not serve overseas except in war.

THE CARDWELL AMALGAMATIONS

Number	Pre-1881 [County or other title]	Post-1881
1	Royals	Royal Scots
2	Queen's Royal	Queen's Royal West Surrey
3	East Kent – The Buffs	Buffs, East Kent
4	King's Own	King's Own Royal Lancaster
5	Northumberland	Northumberland Fusiliers (Royal, post-1945)
6	1st Warwickshire	Royal Warwickshire
7	Royal Fusiliers	Royal Fusiliers
8	King's	King's Liverpool
9	East Norfolk	Norfolk (Royal, post-1945)
10	North Lincolnshire	Lincolnshire (Royal, post-1945)
11	North Devonshire	Devonshire
12	East Suffolk	Suffolk
13	1st Somersetshire	Somerset Light Infantry
14	Buckinghamshire	West Yorkshire
15	East Riding	East Yorkshire
16	Bedfordshire	Bedfordshire (and Hertfordshire, post-1921)
17	Leicestershire	Leicestershire (Royal, post-1945)
18	Royal Irish	Royal Irish
19	North Riding	Green Howards
20	East Devonshire	Lancashire Fusiliers
21	Royal North British Fusiliers	Royal Scots Fusiliers
22	Cheshire	Cheshire
23	Royal Welsh Fusiliers	Royal Welsh Fusiliers
24	2nd Warwickshire	South Wales Borderers
25	King's Own Borderers	King's Own Scottish Borderers
26	Cameronian ⎫	
90	Perthshire ⎬	Cameronians (Scottish Rifles)
27	Inniskilling ⎫	
108	Madras Infantry ⎬	Royal Inniskilling Fusiliers
28	North Gloucester ⎫	
61	South Gloucester ⎬	Gloucester
29	Worcestershire ⎫	
36	Herefordshire ⎬	Worcestershire
30	Cambridgeshire ⎫	
	2nd Nottinghamshire ⎬	East Lancashire
31	Huntingdonshire ⎫	
70	Glasgow ⎬	East Surrey
32	Cornwall ⎫	Duke of Cornwall's
46	South Devonshire ⎬	Light Infantry

Number	Pre-1881	Post-1881
33	West Riding ⎫	
76	⎬	Duke of Wellington's
34	Cumberland ⎫	
55	Westmorland ⎬	Border
35	Sussex ⎫	
107	Bengal ⎬	Royal Sussex
37	North Hampshire ⎫	
67	South Hampshire ⎬	Hampshire (Royal, post-1945)
38	1st Staffordshire ⎫	
80	Staffordshire ⎬	South Staffordshire
39	Dorsetshire ⎫	
54	West Norfolk ⎬	Dorset
40	2nd Somersetshire ⎫	
82	Prince of Wales' Volunteers ⎬	South Staffordshire
41	The Welsh ⎫	
69	South Lincolnshire ⎬	Welsh
42	Royal Highland ⎫	
73	Highland ⎬	Black Watch
43	Monmouthshire ⎫	Oxfordshire (and Bucking-
52	Oxfordshire ⎬	hamshire, post-1908) Light Infantry
44	East Essex ⎫	
56	West Essex ⎬	Essex
45	Nottinghamshire ⎫	
95	Derbyshire ⎬	Sherwood Foresters
47	Lancashire ⎫	
81	Loyal Lincoln Volunteers ⎬	Loyal North Lancashire
48	Northamptonshire ⎫	
58	Rutlandshire ⎬	Northamptonshire
49	Hertfordshire ⎫	
66	Berkshire ⎬	Berkshire (Royal, post-1885)
50	West Kent ⎫	
97	Queen's Own ⎬	Royal West Kent
51	2nd West Riding ⎫	
105	⎬	Yorkshire Light Infantry
53	Shropshire ⎫	
85	Bucks Volunteers ⎬	Shropshire Light Infantry
57	West Middlesex ⎫	
77	East Middlesex ⎬	Middlesex
60	Royal American	King's Royal Rifle Corps
62	Wiltshire ⎫	
99	Tipperary ⎬	Wiltshire
63	West Suffolk ⎫	
96	⎬	Manchester
64	2nd Staffordshire ⎫	
98	⎬	North Staffordshire

Number	Pre-1881	Post-1881
65	2nd North Riding ⎫	
84	North and Lancaster ⎬	York and Lancaster
68	Durham ⎫	
106	Bombay Light Infantry ⎬	Durham Light Infantry
71	Highland ⎫	
74	Highland ⎬	Highland Light Infantry
72	Highland ⎫	
78	Highland (Ross-shire) ⎬	Seaforth Highlanders
75	Highland ⎫	
92	Gordon ⎬	Gordon Highlanders
79	Highland (Cameron)	Cameron Highlanders
83	Dublin ⎫	Royal Irish Rifles
86	County Down ⎬	(Royal Ulster Rifles, post-1922)
87	Irish ⎫	Royal Irish Fusiliers
89	⎬	(Disbanded 1922)
88	Connaught ⎫	Connaught Rangers
94	⎬	(Disbanded 1922)
91	Argyllshire ⎫	Argyll and Sutherland
93	Sutherland ⎬	Highlanders
100	Royal Canadian ⎫	
109	Bombay Infantry ⎬	Leinster
101	Irish ⎫	
104	Bengal Fusiliers ⎬	Royal Munster Fusiliers
102	Royal Madras Fusiliers ⎫	
103	Royal Bombay Fusiliers ⎬	Royal Dublin Fusiliers
	The Rifle Brigade	The Rifle Brigade

Note: the first 25 regiments already had two battalions. The post-1881 descriptions are intended for easy identification only and are not necessarily complete. Senior regiments automatically became the first battalions and junior ones became the second battalions.

8 1899–1914 SOUTH AFRICA AND ITS LESSONS

The somewhat complex political causes of the South African War are outside the scope of this book. All that it is necessary to say here is that the situation degenerated so rapidly after the abortive Jameson raid of 1895 that in 1899 Great Britain considered it desirable to reinforce her weak garrison in Natal. This led to an ultimatum by Kruger, president of the Boer Republics, and when this was rejected the war started in October 1899.

At this period the British Army was well-trained – in theory at any rate – in the techniques of modern war against a well-armed European state. Not having been involved in a war of this nature for over 40 years its training had necessarily had to depend on the experience of others, chief amongst these being the American Civil War, the Franco-Prussian War, and to perhaps a lesser degree the Russo-Turkish War. All these campaigns had made abundantly clear the enormous advantages conferred on the defence by the general introduction of rifled weapons, particularly infantry weapons. It had been demonstrated that entrenched infantry with secure flanks, good fields of fire, and adequate artillery support, was virtually invulnerable without an impossibly large superiority on the part of the attackers. This was true in the American Civil War, where the rifles were mainly of the muzzle-loaded Enfield type, and it was more than confirmed in later campaigns involving breechloaders.

The fundamental problem of any attack is for the assailants to be able to pass through the fire zone of the defence sufficiently unscathed (both physically and morally) to be able to make a final successful assault. In the days of the smoothbore the zone had been short and could sometimes be crossed by a rush (although the French had never had much success with it in the Peninsula), but now rifle fire was effective to half a mile (0.8 kilometres), which changed everything.

150

Infantry are not fast movers except for short distances. On campaign it was relatively soon found that the combination of wet and cold, poor food and long marches with heavy loads slowed them down even more. They were certainly never capable of charging for 700 or 800 yards (640 or 730 metres) which even at normal marching speed took eight or ten minutes to cover. In this time even muzzle-loaders might fire 20 rounds at them, while with breechloaders the number could well be in three figures.

Prussia had won a decisive victory over the French in 1870 and her doctrines were therefore accepted, but her victory had been purchased at considerable cost, particularly as far as her infantry were concerned. Her technique was to advance a strong skirmishing line to a point where it gained fire superiority over the defence, and this could only be done by a continuous build up of the line from reserves in the rear. As these reserves could not be moved in close formation under fire, they had tended to press forward into the firing line so as to get to close contact as quickly as possible, and although this gave the attack considerable momentum it also meant that the assault was made in some confusion, with a whole jumble of units and subunits pressing on together under the nearest officers they could find. Although this method proved reasonably effective, if costly, it made pursuit difficult without a major reorganization, while quick counterattacks were always likely to be dangerous. One considerable advantage had been the fact that black powder smoke made it easy to locate the enemy positions with great accuracy and thus greatly helped the effectiveness of both the rifle and the artillery fire of the attackers.

The British teaching was based fairly closely on the Prussian. It was accepted that battles would open at longer ranges than before, and that great dispersion was required; when a frontal attack became necessary maximum use was to be made of supporting fire, including long-range rifle fire, to subdue the defence. Battalion attacks were conducted in three lines. In front was the skirmishing or firing line, usually of two companies, extended in single rank and advancing in alternate rushes, each covered by the fire of the other. Behind them came the supports, their distance from the firing line and their formation being varied according to the ground. Their business was to replace casualties in the line in front and thicken it up for the final effort at about 200 yards (180 metres) or less, preparatory to a charge. The remainder of the battalion was held in reserve under the commanding officer, ready to intervene as the situation required.

Perhaps inevitably the practice was somewhat less satisfactory. Home-based battalions were invariably understrength – a weakness of the Cardwell system which had been based largely on a

concept of small colonial wars fought by the troops on the spot –
and spent much of their time and effort on training drafts. Even
when commanding officers had the time and the men to carry out
tactical training, facilities were almost non-existent. The best that
could be hoped for was a barrack square, plus possibly a few acres
of local common, and this was not much good for any form of
realistic training. The bulk of the soldiers in the infantry were
townsmen, unused to open spaces and uneasy in the dark, and they
needed intensive effort to eradicate these failings; this however
they rarely got. Drafts really only began to learn much more than
the rudiments of their business when they joined their overseas
battalions, and in the nature of things the instruction they got
tended to be based on local conditions. Long years of colonial
warfare had meant close formations and steady volleys, valuable
against charging savages but the very antithesis of modern
warfare.

Only in India, where battalions were strong and mature, was
there any serious attempt at tactical training. This, it is true, was
based on the requirements of that best of battle training areas, the
North-West Frontier, but even so, as it turned out, much of it was
relevant to the needs of South Africa. Unfortunately Indian ideas
rather tended to upset the home authorities and, although much of
the teaching might have filtered back in time, there was, in this
particular instance, no time available.

Battalions in the United Kingdom were therefore limited not
only in fighting strength but in ability. They were on the whole
well drilled (and it must be borne in mind that much barrack-
square drill was then applicable to the battlefield) and well-
trained in mainly mechanical musketry. This latter had been
proved beyond question by the appalling casualties inflicted on the
Dervishes in the recent campaigns in the Sudan, the bulk of which,
in spite of counter-claims by machine guns and artillery, were
probably inflicted by rifle fire. The most gallantly pressed charges
were shattered at 600 or 800 yards (550 or 730 metres), although
oddly enough no one seems to have given any serious thought to
the possibility that such fire might also stop British soldiers.

As for the rest, battalions had had some marching (always from
barracks back to barracks), but on the whole they had had but little
experience of outpost duties, scouting, or patrolling. Nor were they
really able to fend for themselves in bivouacs, having been
conditioned to regular meals prepared by someone else and eaten
in the relative comfort of a barrack room.

The only form of dress in home stations was scarlet, with frocks
of poor quality material for rough work and tunics of somewhat
better stuff for more formal occasions. Battalions going overseas to

tropical stations were however fitted out with khaki drill and this was the case with units for South Africa; the stories one hears of British soldiers in action in scarlet in that war are without foundation.

It may now be as well to consider the structure of a British battalion on the outbreak of the South African War. It consisted of a battalion headquarters and eight companies, each of a nominal strength of three officers and about 110 men. Companies were divided into two half companies under subalterns, these being again divided into two sections under sergeants.

It is difficult to identify a truly typical battalion, but two clear types could be discerned. Overseas battalions were kept up to strength and had in their ranks, mature well-seasoned soldiers. Home battalions on the contrary were always weak, and particularly so after a draft had just been despatched. Some indication of this may be given by the fact that of the various infantry battalions sent from England to the seat of the war, those of the Guards averaged about 40 per cent reservists and those of the line 65 per cent; these figures do not necessarily indicate deficiencies in actual bodies because a considerable number of serving soldiers were too young and immature for overseas service. It is an indication of the problem of sending battalions overseas in a strong state that when the 2nd Battalion the Royal Berkshire Regiment sailed for South Africa on a routine, peacetime posting in 1898, its overall strength of 812 included over 400 men of less than one year's service. Having quoted this particular battalion as an example it is but fair to say that it gave gallant and efficient service in the war which followed.

The Army reservists of the Infantry, of whom no less than 98 per cent responded promptly to their recall to the colours, were good men, but several years of civilian life had left many of them in a relatively poor state of physical fitness for active operations. Nor did they get much chance of preliminary hardening, for in most cases several weeks on a troopship, followed by several more in a train, were the only prelude to arduous marching and fighting. In spite of this they did remarkably well; one example was 15 Brigade which having come straight from England with over 50 per cent reservists, marched 31 miles (50 kilometres) in 23 hours in pursuit of General Cronje with remarkably few stragglers. The six and a half original garrison battalions in South Africa were of course strong and in good shape, as were the various units which arrived hastily from Mauritius, the Mediterranean, and India.

The Boers, whom these soldiers were off to fight, were a formidable body of at least 60,000 strong. They were not soldiers in the accepted sense but a form of militia, armed with the latest

153

Mauser rifles and mounted on tough country ponies. They were organized in a loose formation of commandos under elected leaders, many of whom were experienced veterans of the numerous native wars, and were supported by some excellent modern artillery, much of it manned by European volunteers.

Many of the earliest in the field were back-veldt hunters and farmers, tough as leather, good shots, and blessed with excellent eyesight, but there were also a number from the more settled parts who were originally less well equipped as combatants. Inevitably, as the war progressed, many of the original fighting men were killed or captured, and quite often their places were taken by replacements of lesser quality.

After their first advances their tactics were based on mobility combined with a somewhat passive defence, for which their vast, empty country was well suited. It abounded with good defensive positions offering wide fields of fire, good observation and ample cover to hide wagons and horses, and when possible the Boers also made use of river lines or of the wire stock fences which were surprisingly common.

At first they sited themselves on the tops of kopjes, the small, rocky hills which rise abruptly out of the veldt, but later they dug their deep, narrow trenches at the foot of these so that their flat trajectory rifles might sweep the ground in front of them. The combination of good camouflage and smokeless powder made their positions hard to locate, and this of course was the root of the problem, for artillery preparation was often wasted on undefended kopjes, the summits of which had an irresistable attraction to British gunners.

The Boer guns were usually widely dispersed in well prepared positions, and unlike the British batteries, which tended to fight in gallant but exposed lines, were often impossible to locate. When shelling came close the Boer gunners would often explode small charges of black powder well away from their real position to distract the British observers.

The first small battles turned out well enough for the British; the Boers, outnumbered, at first held the hilltops as they had done against the native enemies, but this made their positions relatively easy to locate and dominate by fire. Even the mechanical section volleys, though they did little material damage, kept the Boers' heads down during the advance and allowed the final classic rush with the bayonet, but as battles got larger the enemy learnt faster than the British.

Many of the early attacks were very slap-dash affairs; infantry scouts hardly existed and the British cavalry showed no great ability in the reconnaissance role, with the result that detailed planning was hardly possible. The initial tendency was to fan out and advance like beaters on a grouse moor, but as the Boers sat tight and shot unpleasantly straight, the results were disastrous. Early casualties led to undue caution and over-extension, the usual formation of a battalion being three companies up, in single rank and extended from five to fifteen paces, with a second similar rank a couple of hundred yards back. Initially attempts were made to retain a reserve in close order, but experience soon showed this to be impracticable, and later a third but weaker line took its place. This over-extension made the line weak at all points and had an adverse effect on control. Reconnaissance was sometimes by fire, a process known in West African campaigns as clearing volleys, i.e. shots fired into woods, brush and other cover in the hope of eliciting a reply.

The general technique was to advance extended to about 500 yards (460 metres) which was usually possible without undue casualties. Progress was then by short rushes of 30 or 40 yards (27 or 36 metres), one section moving while the other fired, and sometimes it was necessary to resort to crawling. All this however, although sound enough in theory, proved very difficult in practice. The infantry were often exhausted by heat, long marches, and inadequate food and water even before the action started, and once down it was difficult to get them up; as any move at close range often brought one or more bullets this was understandable, yet the inaction was often a serious matter in itself. Men suffered agonies from heat and thirst, and even if they were fortunate to be behind a friendly rock they still hardly dared move, while the wounded often had to be left untreated. Fire control in such circumstances was impossible, with the result that the exasperated soldiers very soon blazed off their 100 rounds, often without ever seeing a Boer, and since replenishment was impossible in daylight they ceased thereafter to be of any fighting value whatsoever.

Supporting fire was difficult to arrange. The gunners had no means of indirect fire and thus often came into close action in the open where they suffered heavily from rifle fire. The machine guns were in the same position, for their high, wheeled carriages made them far too conspicuous; one of the sad features of the war was the frequency with which both field and machine guns fell silent with their gallant detachments dead around them.

The really dangerous zone was surprisingly narrow. As we have seen, it was often possible to get within 500 yards (460 metres); and at 300 yards (275 metres) the Boer positions could often be identified and swept with fire sufficiently accurate to keep their heads down. It was in that vital 200 yards (180 metres) that the bulk of the casualties occurred and from first to last the problem of crossing it was never satisfactorily solved.

The real answer was to attack the flanks, for the Boers were always very apprehensive if their line of retreat was menaced. When their position was threatened they liked to slip off to their horses and ride quietly away, and the prospect of meeting opposition then did not appeal to them. The main problem on the British side was lack of mobility, for visibility was usually good and any attempt to use infantry to outflank could generally be countered by the swift movement of mounted Boer riflemen to meet the new threat.

The type of troops best suited for this sort of work was undoubtedly mounted infantry, but these could not be manufactured or improvised in days or weeks. In the War of the Spanish Succession in Spain in the early eighteenth century, Lord Peterborough had converted a battalion of infantry into mounted infantry by leading them to waiting horses and bidding them mount, but this was hardly a good precedent. Horses had to be obtained, and men taught to ride them properly, otherwise casualties to both riders and mounts were enormous, particularly to the latter. Forage was a constant difficulty and it was found that without it English troop horses lost condition very quickly. A fairly scratch collection of horses – British, Australian, Argentinian and country-breds to name the most common – was eventually assembled and men taught to ride them. Every battalion was required to provide a company and these were reinforced by locally enlisted regiments of mounted rifles, British settlers for the most part with scores to pay off against the Boers. The regular cavalry too, deprived of its traditional feats with the *arme blanche*, handed in its carbines, drew rifles in lieu, and settled down to the distasteful but essential business of learning to fight on foot.

A second alternative to overcome the defence was to operate by night. The veldt was often open, and on a clear night it should have been possible to get close to the Boers with a view to a rush at first light. Night operations need good prior training however, and this did not exist. The presence of hundreds of unskilled soldiers blundering round in the dark would have been obvious to the Boers, who would probably have slipped away, to stand again further back. On the one major occasion when the Highland Brigade essayed a night attack at Magersfontein the results were disastrous. Four battalions advanced in mass of quarter columns, presumably with the intention of deploying in good time. In the event there was some miscalculation, for the leading troops struck a wire fence festooned with jangling tins and in a few seconds the Boers were pouring fire into the close-packed ranks, one bullet often striking down two or three men. There was no lack of gallantry; many officers dashed forward with the few men they could collect, and some died on the very parapets of the Boer trenches; others hung on, within 200 yards (180 metres) of the enemy, for the whole day when lack of water and cartridges drove them back. It was an experiment not tried again.

Major B.F.S. Baden-Powell, who saw a good deal of service in South Africa as a regimental officer in the Scots Guards, said in his book *War in Practice* that setting fire to undergrowth sometimes produced a good smokescreen if the wind was right. He also discussed the possibilities of smoke-shells, although it was to be a dozen years before they finally materialized for use in a much greater war.

The first phase of the war was won fairly quickly, in spite of everything, by superior numbers and intelligent strategy, but the second phase took a great deal more time and trouble to bring to a satisfactory conclusion. The Boers were natural guerillas, operating in a vast, empty land where the few inhabitants were friends – always ready to provide food or exchange a lame pony for a second one. A vast network of wire fences and block houses was constructed over much of the country and the areas enclosed were driven systematically by mobile forces. The evacuation of women and children into camps and the destruction of farms was a sad but very necessary part of this operation.

The official German account of the war, produced by the Historical Section of the General Staff, is worth reading. It was compiled primarily for the instruction of the German army and contains a good deal of information from Boer sources not then available to the British. Although often sharply critical it was not written as propaganda and its strictures, though sometimes severe, are not biased. One interesting, if perhaps obvious suggestion, was that the British were not conditioned to casualties on the European scale, and were thus not prepared to push their attacks to the limit. They quote the defeat at Colenso where the six battalions principally engaged lost about 15 per cent of their troops in killed, wounded and missing, which the Germans, with memories of the slaughter of 1870, clearly and understandably regarded as ludicrously small. It is clear however that they had seriously underestimated the problems raised by the smokeless powder in a flat and often featureless land. Nor do they appear to have considered the results of pressing a thick skirmishing line forward across half a mile (0.8 kilometres) of ground swept by fire of an effectiveness far superior to anything they had ever experienced. It was a lesson they were to learn expensively a little more than 12 years later, from expert riflemen who had themselves taken a leaf from the book of their former foes.

The South African War threw an enormous strain on the British Army, which was in no real sense geared to undertake operations on the scale required. The Cardwell system had envisaged overseas garrisons strong enough to cope with what may well be classed as imperial policing, while units in England consisted of little more than basic training and drafting organizations. No such large-scale intervention, in or out of Europe, had been envisaged, and although home defence was of course considered it was felt, perhaps rightly, that skeleton home battalions, quickly reinforced by reservists and supported by militia and volunteers, could have dealt with this, always bearing in mind that the attackers had first to cross the seas in the face of a large and efficient fleet. Some indication of the problem is given by the fact that whereas in the early months of 1899 there were 71 battalions in the British Isles, by February 1900 there remained but nine, three of Guards and six of the line, all of which were full of immature soldiers.

One of the first steps taken was to raise garrison battalions from retired officers and soldiers who had passed the reserve limit, and in the first few months of 1900 thousands of copies of a personal letter from the Queen went out to people in this category. They were offered one year engagements with a £12 bounty on engagement and a further £10 on discharge, and by the end of the war there were four such battalions, one in Malta, one in Gibraltar, one in Canada and one at home. At first they were known as Royal Reserve battalions, but subsequently became the Royal Garrison Regiment. They did a good job on the whole although, as perhaps was to be expected, discipline tended to be rather lax. They were also more expensive to maintain than normal battalions since they contained a very high proportion of married men. They had all gone by 1906.

Recourse was also had to the militia; at first this was done by sending individual companies to their own regular battalions, but by the end of the war 68 complete battalions had gone overseas, the bulk to South Africa where they were chiefly employed on the lines of communication, but some to Mediterranean garrisons and one at least to St. Helena.

The volunteers, who although keen had been neglected and rather derided for years, were also anxious to help, and by January 1900 carefully selected companies were on the way to join their county regiments, where they did well. The London Volunteers were particularly enthusiastic; they mostly comprised young men of middle class, and as their units were less scattered than those in country districts they tended to be better trained. Soon there had come into existence a regiment known as the City Imperial Volunteers, raised, clothed, and well-equipped by the City of

London, which consisted of an infantry battalion and one of mounted infantry, and gave good service.

In the long term the City Imperial Volunteers proved much more popular than the attached companies. The latter, being integrated with regular troops, had virtually no chance of promotion, whereas the former had good chances, not only of promotion but occasionally of a commission. They also wore a more dashing uniform and received the munificent sum of 5s. per day, so that they tended to recruit at the expense of the regular army.

No very severe strain appears to have been placed on the economy, so that extra arms, ammunition and equipment of all kinds were produced without much trouble. One unusual requirement was to equip all soldiers with khaki field service uniform. At first drill was provided, but later this was changed to the more familiar khaki serge which subsequently became the standard dress. Boots were also a problem. Soldiers in those days were expected to maintain their footgear at their own expense, so footgear with cheap clumped soles was provided. This was a ridiculously shortsighted policy, particularly for the infantry which relied on its feet. As early as the Abyssinian campaign of 1868 it had been necessary to hurry good boots off to the theatre, and G.W. Stevens, a newspaper correspondent in the Sudan in 1898, speaks of three battalions marching into Berber with 'hundreds of men all but barefoot; the soles peeled off, and instead of a solid double sole, revealed a layer of shoddy packing sandwiched between two thin slices of leather'. If thousands of pairs of good stitched boots had not been hastily purchased for South Africa, half the army there would have been barefoot too.

The war ended and its many lessons were remembered, a fact which had not always been the case in previous wars. The committee which sat to consider it came to the conclusion in its report that many of the lessons were also applicable to modern European warfare, and on this basis the whole scope and system of training the British Army came under close scrutiny. Before an army can be trained efficiently however it has to exist, and as was usual at the end of a war the British Army had shrunk alarmingly in size. In the past this had of course happened as a matter of official policy, but this time it gave rise to a lot of official forebodings. Volunteers, militia, reservists, and time-expired regulars all streamed out, the garrison battalions were disbanded, and as recruiting was bad the Army found itself seriously overstretched.

Various expedients were tried. Some savings were made by reorganizing overseas garrisons, but these were necessarily small. A system of limited engagement was tried, men being allowed to engage for three years with the colours and nine on the reserve in place of the more usual seven and five. Men on the latter engagement received an extra 6d. per day, but few came forward. The short engagement, moreover, made drafting to India almost impossible, since many men only served a year there, and it was soon abandoned except for the Guards, for whom the problem did not exist. It may be said here that the Brigade of Guards had received an accession of strength by the formation of the Irish Guards in 1900, Lord Roberts being their first colonel.

At one time there was a proposal to have two types of infantry, one for general service and the other, a kind of fencible, for home service only, but this was not proceeded with. Yet another proposal was to abolish the Cardwell system and so have fewer but stronger battalions at home, while recruits were fully trained at large central depots and drafted thence to overseas battalions directly, but this too was abandoned. In 1906 it became necessary to disband 10 battalions raised eight years before, these being the 3rd battalions of the Coldstream and Scots Guards, and the 3rd and 4th battalions of the Northumberland Fusiliers, the Warwicks, the Lancashire Fusiliers, and the Manchesters, all of which were so weak as to be non-effective. That year there were 52 battalions in India, 32 in the colonies, and 72 in the United Kingdom, but the latter were mostly so weak as to be incapable of any form of operational duties. They could just about manage their own domestic affairs and that was all.

Fortunately things improved thereafter. The situation in Europe and Britain's alliance with France against Germany made it obvious that there was a threat, a very real threat, close to home. There was also a slight recession with increased unemployment, and slowly the battalions began to fill. In view of the troubles looming ahead it was not a moment too soon.

One basic requirement for giving soldiers tactical instruction is land on which to do it, and in England this had always posed a problem. Most of the land was privately owned and under cultivation, and although the occasional patriotic landowner could be found who would tolerate manoeuvres being held over his land they were few and far between. The standard cry, (then as now) was, 'of course we realize that soldiers must be trained; all we ask is that it should be done somewhere else'. The only answer was for the War Department to start purchasing its own land on Salisbury Plain and elsewhere; this had in fact started in 1897 and was well advanced by 1902, although it was not finally completed for another 30 years.

There was clearly a need for improvements in musketry. Volley firing, although old-fashioned, had proved surprisingly effective at long range. The weakness of the British Infantry had been in its close-range shooting at up to 300 or 400 yards (280 or 380 metres), and a high standard of shooting at this range was considered vital because it was at about this distance that a strong, final attack might start. Long-range shooting was all very well in South Africa but fields of fire of even 800 yards (730 metres) were relatively rare in Europe, which was considered likely to be the next theatre of operations. The fundamental musketry training given was sound enough, but it required updating and enthusiasm and interest, both things which commanding officers with South African experience were only too happy to give to it.

One of the leading lights in this field was Lieutenant-Colonel N.R. McMahon D.S.O., of the Royal Fusiliers, who very fortunately for the British Infantry, and indeed for the British people, was at that time Chief Instructor at the School of Musketry at Hythe in Kent. He was an enthusiast on machine guns, which although they had not proved very valuable in South Africa had performed prodigies in the Russo-Japanese war of 1904–5. In 1907 he gave a lecture on fire power, primarily that of machine guns, to the Aldershot Military Society which was considered so important that the British Army's Field Service Regulations were rewritten to include his teachings. It is said that much of what he preached was also included in various training manuals produced by the German General Staff. In spite of this the scale of machine guns in the British Infantry battalion was only two, and remained at this figure until after the outbreak of war in 1914. The only difference was that the older Maxim had been replaced after some delays by the Vickers gun, a weapon of very similar type, but lighter and mechanically more reliable.

McMahon, despairing of ever seeing any increase in the scale of automatic weapons, which he considered vital, turned his attention to speeding up the rate of fire, even at some sacrifice to pin-point accuracy, of the individual rifleman as a substitute. Like many of the younger officers of his day he was a realist who was concerned with fighting the next war, which it was by then fairly clear would be against Germany. German infantry tactics were known to favour a steady advance by men in fairly close order and McMahon well understood that with targets of this type it was chiefly important to hit them quickly without bothering too much whether the bullet hit the head, the body, or the ankle of the man aimed at – or even, for that matter, the man behind him. What was required was the 'browning' of a mass, rather than careful snap shooting at the glimpse of a head behind a rock. In this he had the support of his superiors at the School of Musketry and was perhaps particularly lucky that his Commandant was Colonel Charles

161

Monro, an officer who was to reach high rank in the war then looming.

He was also fortunate that as a result of experience in South Africa the old long Lee-Enfield had been replaced by the short magazine Lee-Enfield, a handy rifle loaded by charger and having a breech mechanism ideally suited to rapid manipulation. Although it initially drew much scornful criticism from gunsmiths and target riflemen of the old school, the next few years were to demonstrate that it was probably the finest weapon of its type ever to be placed in the hands of the British soldier.

It was in fact largely a matter of luck that the British Army went to war in 1914 armed with this excellent service weapon, because by 1913 a new rifle had been developed. Apart from a reduced calibre of 0.276 inches (7 millimetres), which gave it a very flat trajectory, it had a Mauser-type bolt with forward-locking lugs for increased strength. At first it showed promise but trials soon showed that the breech overheated to such an extent that after comparatively few rounds a cartridge placed in the chamber fired itself, a condition known colloquially to soldiers as a cook-off.

This experimental Pattern '13 was therefore abandoned as a general issue, although a later version with a 0.303-inch (7.7-millimetre) calibre saw limited service as the Pattern '14. It was very accurate, but being quite unsuitable for any form of rapid fire it was chiefly used as a sniping rifle in both World Wars. It was also adopted by the United States who called it the Enfield '17, and in 1940 the wheel turned full circle when some thousands of these by then venerable weapons were leased back to the United Kingdom and issued to the Home Guard.

It is also likely that it was the uncertainty over a possible change of calibre which caused the delay, already referred to, in the changeover to the new Vickers machine gun, since it was clearly highly desirable that both types of weapon should fire the same cartridge.

The infantry soldier, after having undergone a thorough and painstaking recruits' course to establish his basic skills, thereafter fired an annual trained-soldiers' course, usually referred to as 'Table B'. Apart from preliminary grouping at 100 yards (91 metres) this course consisted of slow, snap and rapid practices at ranges up to 600 yards (550 metres), the most impressive being the rapid practice at 300 yards (275 metres). One minute was allowed for 15 rounds and there were very few infantrymen who could not put all their shots into a two-foot (61-centimetre) circle in that time; many indeed could almost double this rate of fire with no appreciable loss of accuracy. The course, which allowed a total of 250 rounds per man annually, included field firing under conditions as nearly approaching those of actual war as the need for safety would permit, so that altogether a good deal of shooting was done, apart from extra ammunition fired in competitions. Fire control was important, this being a subject which could be practiced 'dry' or even indoors on landscape targets. A proportion of the unit's pool of ammunition was laid aside for instructional shooting at ranges up to 1,000 yards (910 metres), the object of this being to give officers and non-commissioned officers practice at marking the strike of bullets at long ranges.

Apart from the actual firing, a good deal of time was devoted to manipulation of the rifle with drill rounds, which could be done on the square or in barrack rooms. Many walls in barracks were adorned with painted targets; alternatively men fired at an eye-disc held by an instructor or comrade so that the accuracy of their aim could be checked. All this inevitably involved a good deal of repetition, a thing frowned on now because soldiers get bored. It is very probable that the soldiers of pre-1914 got bored; but they also became very proficient.

It is given to few men of relatively low rank to have an important influence on the training of a whole army, so that McMahon was exceptional. He served with his regiment in France in the early days of 1914 and the horrid heaps of German dead in front of the British positions must have given him a certain sober satisfaction, if only because they vindicated his professional judgment in the clearest possible way. In the autumn of 1914 he was promoted to Brigadier-General but was killed by a stray shell before he could take over his new command.

Vast improvements were also made in tactical training. As early as 1902 Colonel Henderson, well-known as a military writer and theorist, was rewriting *Infantry Training* and a provisional manual appeared that same year; after his premature death the task was finished by an Aldershot committee under General Stopford. The work was completed and issued under the title of *Combined Training* in 1904, the more specialized *Infantry Training* following in 1905, and the training of the infantry element of the British Expeditionary Force may be said to have been based on these two books.

At the end of 1913 an important reorganization took place within infantry battalions, as a result of which the number of companies, previously eight, was reduced to four. This was achieved by making them twice the size, the so called double-company system. Most of the major armies of Europe had worked on this system for some years but the British had stuck to their eight small companies, although whether this was from natural conservatism or tactical desirability it is now difficult to say. The small company had certain advantages in the old close-order days in that it could be manoeuvred by one man and also fitted tidily into column formations, but by 1913 it was finally accepted that a larger company, but with more subunits, was a more flexible organization when dispersion was required.

The new battalion headquarters consisted of a commanding officer, second-in-command, adjutant, quartermaster, transport officer, machine gun officer and an attached medical officer, together with 93 other ranks, these being mainly the band, the horse transport, and the machine gunners. A great many more men were required for headquarters duties (usually about 80 though it varied slightly from battalion to battalion), but in the absence of any headquarter company organization these men were carried on the posted strength of rifle companies and detached for their various specialist functions.

The fighting troops were organized on a four-square basis, i.e. four rifle companies each of four platoons each of four sections. The nominal strength of a company was six officers and 221 other ranks, though for reasons already explained the latter strength was reduced to about 200. The company headquarters consisted of two captains (commander and second-in-command), a company sergeant-major, a colour-sergeant (whose business was now primarily concerned with stores, supplies, and other 'Q' matters) and 10 soldiers, leaving four platoons each of a subaltern and 47 men. Platoons in their turn were broken down into a headquarters of the officer, a sergeant, a batman and a runner, and four sections each of a corporal and 10 men.

The rank of company sergeant-major was by no means a completely new one as far as the Army as a whole was concerned. The 95th Regiment (Rifles) from the time of its formation had customarily appointed the senior sergeant of each company to act in that capacity and apparently under that title, although it seems to have been a purely regimental arrangement without official sanction and not involving any extra pay for the incumbent.

The rank is also shown in the official establishment table of a mounted infantry company in 1889, while the appointment of company sergeant-major instructor was also held by certain grades of the Corps of Instructors at the School of Musketry in the earliest years of the twentieth century. In spite of these precedents however, the rank was a new one as far as the ordinary infantry battalion was concerned. Soldiers holding the rank were at first classed as non-commissioned-officers, and it was not until 1915 that they were upgraded to warrant officer class II; when this occurred the original holders of warrant rank were all upgraded to class I.

The new organization was based on the clear need for dispersion. In the close-order days of the eighteenth and nineteenth centuries the company had been the basic fighting subunit, although half companies had occasionally been employed on pickets, outposts, and the like. Wolseley, in his various colonial wars, had regarded the section as the basic unit and had often applied for special service officers so that each might be commanded by an officer; here of course we must bear in mind the vagaries of British military nomenclature by remembering that the section was in those days a quarter company, probably of an average strength of 20 men and usually commanded by a sergeant. In South Africa, even this had often been found to be too big for effective control.

The new section was probably the most interesting aspect of the reorganization. There has always appeared to be an accepted, if not very clearly defined, upper limit to the number of men who can be effectively controlled in one group, and 11 seems to be a fair average. Perhaps it goes back as far as the family group, say a patriarch, two or three sons, and a number of grandsons old enough to hunt. In the eighteenth century, when battalions were weak, it probably represented an actual section; in Sir John Moore's brigade it was a convenient size for a mess; and if we consider civilian organizations we find boards of directors, gangs of workmen, together of course with football and cricket teams, all hovering at that oddly critical figure.

Apart from the two Vickers machine guns (and excluding swords and pistols which can hardly be taken seriously) the real weapon of a battalion consisted of the rifle and bayonet which was carried by virtually every soldier below commissioned rank with the exception of the regimental sergeant-major and the number ones on the machine guns. The active scale of small-arms ammunition was 120 rounds on the man with a further 100 in battalion reserve; these latter were packed in 50-round cloth bandoliers which could be slung round the shoulders over the other equipment if required. The machine guns had a total of 11,500 rounds available, these being packed in the standard 250-round belt.

Having regard to the clear need to dig, a surprisingly generous scale of tools was available. Apart from the entrenching tools carried by all soldiers, two waggons of the first line transport carried between them 76 picks, 110 shovels, 40 billhooks, eight crowbars and a handsaw. The machine-gun section, which might on occasions have to work detached, also had its own scale of digging tools, a further supply also being carried in brigade reserve.

Communications, although still fairly basic, were better than ever before, consisting of flag, lamp, and heliograph for mobile operations, with field telephones for use in defence. In addition the officers of battalion headquarters were always mounted, as were company commanders, so that gaps in communication facilities could often be bridged by personal contact. It was of course accepted that a mounted officer could not survive in the actual firing line, so that company commanders often had to function on foot.

Infantry battalions of 1914 had reached a high standard of tactical training. Inevitably it was based on musketry (an ancient term which nevertheless produced modern results) and marching which gave them the basic skills to produce a large volume of accurate fire, together with the ability to deliver it at the right place and at the right time, but within this framework it was modern and practical. Anyone reading *Infantry Training, 1914*, the last of the prewar series, must be impressed by the scope and essential soundness of its teachings.

Very properly the attack was held to be the decisive operation of war and a good deal of time was devoted to it. The old and well-tried system of a firing line in single rank, reinforced as necessary by a second line of supports and followed by a reserve, was adhered to. In order to reduce confusion, companies were in depth; the proportions of the various parts naturally varied according to the ground, the scale of the attack, and the strength of the enemy, but assuming that there was the equivalent of one company in the firing line, one in support, and two in reserve, some attempt was made to dispose the companies in depth. Thus the firing line might consist of the two forward platoons of two companies with the remainder forming the supports. This had the advantage that when supports were pushed forward they usually went to their own company which at least localized confusion.

The need for careful preparation and reconnaissance had become obvious, so that commanding officers always went forward to examine the ground from some vantage point, accompanied by the machine-gun officer and the company commanders. In the early stages of an attack, i.e. out of small-arms range, the battalion moved extended in small platoon groups, but once under effective rifle and machine-gun fire a firing line was formed. Attacks were supported by the battalion machine guns and by fire groups from local reserves, which fired overhead or from a flank according to the ground. It goes without saying that attacks were also always supported by artillery fire. The Royal Artillery had improved its techniques very much since 1902. Proper arrangements now existed for indirect fire which could be controlled by observers moving with the leading infantry, and the system, although by no means perfect, was to prove a sound basis for later developments.

The main objects of an attack were to maintain momentum and to establish superiority of fire as quickly as possible. As the attack progressed the supports were pushed up, preferably by sections, to thicken the firing line and replace casualties. Advances under effective fire were by short rushes, alternate subunits moving under the covering fire of their neighbours. As many casualties tended to occur in the critical period when men were scrambling to their feet to make another rush, the ideal situation would perhaps have been for the whole operation to be conducted in one smooth sweep, but this would have been testing soldiers very highly. Brigadier-General Haking in his book *Company Training* comments that, 'The logical conclusion is that we ought never to halt to fire, but logic has not much place in battle, where human nature dominates most things, from the general to the proverbial drummer-boy with a bullet through his bugle'.

It was considered that the impulse for the final assault must often come from the firing line, being the best people to detect the critical moment when the enemy fire was slackening. When this time came any commander who considered that the time was ripe had a duty to charge, and those on his flanks had a similar duty to rise and charge with him. In view of the limited distance which a tired and heavily ladened soldier could cover in one rush, the line should not generally be more than 100 yards (90 metres) from the enemy when the final assault was ordered.

It was realized that even a successful assault would result in considerable confusion and this was generally accepted as being the inevitable accompaniment of any modern attack. It was hoped that sections at least might remain as entities; otherwise officers and senior non-commissioned officers were simply to reorganize as quickly as possible, taking under command all soldiers in their vicinity irrespective of their original subunit or even unit, since only in this way could a pursuit be organized or a counterattack dealt with. In view of the inevitable reaction of the enemy's artillery it was generally considered desirable to reorganize well forward of the captured positions.

Defence was dealt with on equally thorough lines, and depth was considered essential, as were good fields of fire. Trenches should be dug so that the fire of their occupants swept the ground as thoroughly as possible, and should be sited away from conspicuous features likely to attract artillery fire, a lesson very clearly learnt from the Boers. Cover, camouflage and intercommunication were all dealt with in detail; the general rule was that the firing line and supports required a maximum of one rifle per yard of front, while local reserves, preferably not less than 50 per cent of the total force, should be placed so as to be able to reinforce the firing line, beat off a counterattack from a flank, or otherwise act as the situation required. Positions were sited so as to be mutually supporting and crossfire was carefully coordinated. It was appreciated that gaps which could be covered by fire in daylight would need filling at night, usually by standing patrols from the reserve companies supported by machine guns and artillery defensive fire. Fire control was vital and this was primarily a matter for section commanders. The common *aide-mémoire*, which remained in use for many years, was the word DRINK, for the following sequence:

D   Designation
R   Range
I   Indication of target
N   Number of rounds
K   Kind of fire

Encounter battles were dealt with, as were withdrawals; the latter were to be strictly controlled and carried out by bounds, one subunit supporting its neighbour when it moved back. Rearguard positions needed good fields of fire and good covered lines of withdrawal; the role of machine guns was vital, and it was accepted that detachments might have to sacrifice themselves in order to cover the rifle companies' backs. The important question of fighting in woods, close country, and villages, was also practised, so that all in all it may be said that the British Infantry had reached a stage of tactical training higher than ever before, and, as it turned out, much superior to that of either its allies or its enemies. The main trouble, inseparable from the Cardwell system, was that as the Expeditionary Force would necessarily have to be found from home battalions, many of the reservists necessary to make up their fighting strengths would have little or no experience of the new methods. Nevertheless a sound basis existed, and in the event there was a sufficient framework of experienced non-commissioned officers to ensure that the newly recalled members of the battalion made no mistakes.

In March 1907 the Haldane reforms were put into effect, and although they had little immediate impact on the regular infantry their long term effect was to be considerable. The regular army at home was properly organized into a striking force of six infantry and one cavalry division, complete with proper staffs and full administrative backing. On mobilization being ordered, this force had only to absorb its reservists before it was ready to be despatched overseas as an expeditionary force if required. Its place in the home defence was to be taken by a new territorial army, formed by the amalgamation of the yeomanry and the volunteers and organized into 14 infantry divisions and 14 cavalry brigades. In the event, this home defence role was to be considerably extended a few years later. Under the new organization the old militia became a special reserve, primarily to provide reinforcements for the regular army, which had after all been its principal role for many years.

9 1914–1918 MACHINE GUN AND SHOVEL

The British Expeditionary Force which went to France in August 1914 lived up to its promise, for it fought superbly, and if it did not win the war it at least ensured that it was not irretrievably lost in those first few vital months of fighting. In view of the huge disparity of numbers this could not be achieved without heavy losses. The German infantry, although by no means as well trained as the British, were strong in numbers and extremely brave, and being supported by numerous machine guns and an efficient and well-handled artillery they inevitably took a heavy toll. Apart from battle casualties in the narrow sense of the word, a considerable number of men were lost from exhaustion, for the weak home battalions had necessarily been filled with reservists and these, although they fought as well as the regulars, were often unfit, having in many cases been called back to service, after several years in civil life, only a few days before going into action. This was a weakness of Cardwell's system, although it is only fair to say that when it was introduced there had been little prospect of any British intervention in Europe – at least not by land forces.

Thus after a very few days of combat the British Infantry had dwindled alarmingly. Lieutenant-Colonel Hutchinson later wrote that, 'Thursday 27th August 1914 presented battalions reduced from a thousand rifles to not more than two hundred. The superb riflemen, so assiduously trained and nurtured, had begun to disappear.' There were in fact a good many more available in units in overseas garrisons, stronger and often better trained than the original ones of the Expeditionary Force, but it took time to relieve them with territorial units and get them to France. Even so their numbers were small when compared with the scale of the war.

The overall expansion of the British Infantry at this period was of course huge, the bulk of it being achieved by the formation of hundreds of 'New Army' or service battalions. These ignored the existing framework of the territorial associations and were raised from scratch by Kitchener from amongst the vast numbers of volunteers who rushed to join the Army. They were at first somewhat sketchily staffed by a mixture of retired officers and pensioned warrant and non-commissioned officers, and as many of these were very much out of date in their knowledge, much of the initial training was outmoded. The problems of equipping these new units were also formidable but they were eventually overcome so that by 1915 the service battalions were fighting in France where they worthily upheld the traditions of their regiments. Some indication of the scale of the operation is given by the fact that by 1918 some regiments had raised over 50 battalions, while none, even those based in the more sparsely populated rural counties, had less than a dozen.

As it turned out, the open phase of the war was a short one, for both sides, balked of a really decisive result by battle, simply extended their flanks until they rested on unturnable obstacles, the North Sea at one end and Switzerland at the other, after which static trench warfare became the order of the day. The initial positions were often simple; fortuitous ditches hastily deepened, sunken cart tracks, and the like, and although they were of little tactical value in themselves they established the main fronts on which the armies were to fight and were gradually improved thereafter. Some reference has already been made to siege warfare in the eighteenth and nineteenth centuries and it will therefore be clear that the war on the Western Front soon settled down, perhaps degenerated, into a vast two-sided siege. Unlike similar operations of earlier days however, both sides had unlimited space for defence in depth and neither could be menaced by a relieving army. In earlier times the opening of a practicable breach had usually ensured the fall of a fortress but those days had gone. Any form of penetration was hard to achieve and even quite deep ones could be eventually sealed off by reserves hurried up from the rear. The low-lying terrain, with all its age-old drainage systems wrecked by shell fire, soon degenerated into near impassable quagmire, while the machine gun, protected by steel and concrete and supported by artillery concentrations of a size and power never previously envisaged, quickly halted every offensive with appalling casualties.

The general conditions of trench warfare in the Great War of 1914–18 are well known. There exists a vast literature on every aspect of the war, ranging from formal histories of armies, corps, divisions, brigades and battalions, through diaries and books of reminiscence, to a huge quantity of fiction, often written by men with first-hand experience. This being so, there is little point in trying to recapitulate their contents here; instead this chapter is mainly devoted to the mechanics of the business, the establishment, organization, and tactical handling of infantry units of the period. In spite of the huge volume of literature already referred to, these are detailed facts often not readily obtainable yet they are essential to any serious student of the military history of those times.

The pattern of trench warfare had been very clearly established by 1916–17 and it may therefore be of interest to consider a British infantry battalion as it existed in 1917. Although broadly similar in numbers and general organization to that of 1914 it had become vastly more complex internally and was full of specialists made necessary by the unique conditions imposed by three years of static warfare.

As fire power was still the prime consideration it may be as well to consider that first. The basic infantry weapon remained the familiar bolt-action magazine rifle equipped with a bayonet, although proficiency in its use had declined considerably. The skilled riflemen of 1914 had gone and there had been no time to replace them, so that in the huge and hastily trained new armies a soldier who could load his rifle and discharge it in the general direction of the enemy was deemed to be trained. The old Vickers guns had gone too, having been transferred to the new Machine

BATTALION HEADQUARTERS

Fighting portion	*Administratve portion*
1 commanding officer	1 assistant adjutant
1 second in command	1 quartermaster
1 adjutant	1 transport officer
1 Lewis gun officer	1 quartermaster sergeant
1 signalling officer	2 quartermaster storemen
1 bombing officer	1 company quartermaster-sergeant
1 sergeant-major	7 storemen
1 orderly room clerk	45 transport and grooms
2 gas orderlies	3 shoemakers
13 signallers	3 tailors
4 stretcher bearers	2 butchers
9 runners	1 postman
11 pioneers	2 cooks
2 cooks	3 batmen
6 batmen	
55 Total	73 Total

Gun Corps which will be discussed later, but a substitute of a sort had appeared in 1915 in the shape of the Lewis gun. This was a light machine gun capable of being carried and fired by one man; it proved extremely useful and added greatly to the fire power of an infantry battalion, but it was not a medium machine gun and its tactical handling bore little relation to that of the Vickers. They were issued initially on a scale of four per battalion but by 1917 this number had risen to 16.

The hand grenade had regained importance after a lapse of almost 200 years, and after some initial experiment and local improvisation had settled down to the familiar Number 36 grenade, then perhaps better known as the Mills bomb and still in service with the British Army 60 years later. Similar weapons had also been adapted so that they could be discharged from the normal service rifle; the earliest had a rod which fitted down the bore of the rifle, but later a cup was introduced to screw on to the muzzle; smoke grenades of various types had also made their appearance.

The official organization of a standard infantry battalion on the Western Front was laid down in G.H.Q. letter OB/1919 dated 2 February 1917 and is shown in the table.

There was still no headquarter company organization so that, as in the 1914 battalion, extra men were detached from companies at the commanding officer's discretion, the suggested figures being:

Fighting portion	Administrative portion
21 – made up of extra stretcher-bearers, runners, regimental police or scouts	10 – as required

Somewhat inexplicably this establishment makes no allowance for an intelligence officer (also supervising snipers and scouts), although every battalion had one as a matter of necessity. The omission of the medical officer and padre is explained by the fact that they were only attached to the battalion, as was the R.A.O.C. armourer.

The number of rifle companies remained at four and these each consisted of a company headquarters and four platoons of four sections made up as:

COMPANY HEADQUARTERS

1 company commander (captain)
1 second in command (captain)

1 company sergeant-major
1 company quartermaster-sergeant
4 signallers
4 runners (including batmen)
1 cook

---

17 Total

These numbers could be supplemented by extra stretcher-bearers, runners, scouts, etc. at the company commander's discretion, the total not normally to exceed four.

PLATOON HEADQUARTERS

---

1 platoon commander
1 platoon sergeant
1 signaller
1 batman
1 runner

Lewis gun Section	Bomber Section	Rifle Section	Rifle Section
1 N.C.O.	1 N.C.O.	1 N.C.O.	1 N.C.O.
9 Ptes	9 Ptes	9 Ptes	9 Ptes

The specialized section had been devised to suit the requirements of trench warfare. All members of all sections (with the exception of number one on the Lewis gun) carried rifles and bayonets, and the personnel of the rifle sections included a proportion of rifle bombers.

It was of course quite usual for the strength of a battalion to fall very considerably below establishment because manpower difficulties in the United Kingdom often made it difficult to replace casualties. At company level it was generally accepted that the minimum number for a viable section was six, and when numbers dropped below this the custom was to disband a platoon. Efforts were also then made to call back extra-regimentally employed soldiers, which even by G.H.Q's admission averaged an astounding 3,500 per division. The administrative portion of battalion headquarters, which normally did no regular duty in the line, could also sometimes be combed out, although there were obvious limits to this.

When a battalion went into the line to take part in an attack, as opposed to a normal tour, it became necessary to leave behind a proportion of warrant officers, non-commissioned officers and various specialists. Their grim function was to act as a framework on which to reform the battalion when it returned shattered (as it often did) and as a cadre to train the raw drafts posted in to replace casualties. The scale 'left out of battle' was:

EACH BATTALION	EACH COMPANY
	1 sergeant
2 company sergeant majors	1 corporal
10 signallers ⎱ provided that these	1 lance corporal
13 runners ⎰ were up to strength	4 rifle bombers
1 gas instructor	4 scouts/snipers
1 bombing instructor	8 Lewis gunners
2 Lewis gun instructors	
3 other specialist instructors at	
commanding officer's discretion	
32 Total	19 Total

The tactical handling of a battalion under the peculiar conditions of trench warfare was a highly specialized branch of the art which had been evolved by hard experience since the end of 1914, and the best way to describe it is to go through the whole routine of the various operations involved, primarily from the point of view of the battalion commander.

When a battalion at rest was ordered to take over a sector of the front line in a routine relief (which for obvious reasons took place after dark) its commander usually went forward on a reconnaissance on the morning of the previous day, taking with him his adjutant, transport officer, company commanders, bombing officer, signalling officer, Lewis gun officer and intelligence officer, together with a proportion of specialist non-commissioned officers and orderlies. His first port of call was the brigade headquarters of the battalion he was relieving (his battalion might of course be from another brigade) where he was briefed by the brigade commander, while his adjutant was similarly put in the picture by the brigade major. The whole party were then led forward by guides sent back by the battalion in the line, and usually planned to reach battalion headquarters by mid-morning, thus allowing as long as possible a period of daylight for the visit. The party was reduced at this stage by the departure of the transport officer who had only come to reconnoitre the route forward.

At battalion headquarters the two commanding officers first discussed general matters while the remainder of the group were led off by their counterparts. The lieutenant-colonels then went off for their own tour of the position, discussing points of interest on the way; if the two were friends the thing was much simplified; if strangers, the incoming commanding officer naturally hoped that the unit he was relieving was a good one, since then the trenches would be drained and signed, the area clean, and everything in as near apple-pie order as circumstances would allow. If things fell much below his own standards he was expected to point that out, tactfully or otherwise according to his nature and relative seniority.

In the front line the incoming commander looked at the wire, any shell craters likely to be used by the enemy, any difficult salients, and a host of other things based on his previous experience. He checked the distance to the enemy front line, and if possible had a word with one or two officers and non-commissioned in the forward companies, particularly regarding the activity (or supineness as the case might be) of the enemy unit opposite.

The course notes of the Senior Officers' School at Aldershot, which were published in book form in October 1917, make it abundantly clear that no heroics were expected at this stage. Infantry commanding officers were valuable people and were not expected to take unnecessary risks, which is apparent from the following extract from the exercise devoted to taking over a sector. The problem posed on the incoming officer is:

> On approaching a part of the line you find that the enemy are trench-mortaring and shelling it – not very badly but sufficient to make the trench unhealthy. You are anxious to see that part of the line but you don't want to get knocked out. Colonel WHITE (the outgoing commanding officer) says 'Oh! we will go on; it is ten to one against their getting us'. What will you do?

The eminently sensible School solution (which would presumably have involved white feathers all round in the brave days of 1914) was:

> I tell Colonel WHITE that if he likes to go on and get his head blown off by a shell he can do so; I am not going to follow his example. I therefore wait until the shelling stops and then go on.

The tour completed, the two commanding officers (still, one hopes, on speaking terms) returned to battalion headquarters where the remainder of the reconnaissance group should have already assembled, and after a brief final discussion the visitors departed, reporting in again to brigade headquarters on the way. Back with his battalion, the commanding officer called an orders group and gave out details for the move forward the next day.

Once the relief had actually started he reported his arrival to the brigade headquarters in effective command of the sector, discussed any last minute matters with his opposite number, gave him dinner and bade him farewell on his way rearward as soon as the completion of the takeover had been reported. As was customary, the intelligence officer of the outgoing unit usually stayed on for twenty-four hours for the sake of continuity.

As the new commanding officer was very sensibly expected to remain within reach of a telephone on his first night in the line he usually sent his second-in-command round the position during the hours of darkness, and went himself at stand-to next morning, partly to reassure himself that all was well and partly for purposes of morale. This done he had breakfast, discussed fire plans with his gunner officer, probably had a brief discussion with the engineer officer resident in his sector, and then settled down to deal with the inevitable and sometimes ridiculous correspondence which had followed him into the line. Essentials were noted for his first trench conference which he probably held in the afternoon, all else being left for the next billet conference out of the line.

The Senior Officers' School narrative checks briefly at this stage while the commanding officer has a brush with his adjutant. The young man, who had been brought up as 'a clerk', and not 'a fighting adjutant' by the previous commander, is told to go round the line, demurs briefly on the excuse of pressing correspondence, is given a swift flea in his ear, and duly departs. He went again next morning still mildly protesting, and it is difficult to believe that the hard-bitten ex-battalion commander preparing the exercise did not have some particular individual in mind as he wrote.

The same evening the commanding officer dealt with his quartermaster and transport officer who had presumably come up with the rations, the mail, and other essentials, and also went into the requirements of the Royal Engineers for working parties. Once he was settled in he naturally concentrated on tactical matters as much as possible, checking the positions of machine guns and trench mortars, signal companies, tunnelling companies, gas companies, and other likely residents of the sector, not always actually under his command but in practice very much his responsibility. He also regularly toured the line and kept a sharp eye on the reports of snipers, patrols, and listening posts regarding enemy activity. Then on the seventh day a new battalion came up in its turn (perhaps the very one commanded by the redoubtable

Colonel White who scorned trench-mortar bombs) and he himself went back with his own unit to rest and train, thankful for a reasonably quiet and uneventful week.

The actual deployment of a battalion in a trench system naturally varied according to the nature of the ground, the complexity of the system, and the degree of activity of the enemy, so that it is impossible to be too specific. As a general guide however it may be said that assuming the battalion frontage to be about 700 yards (640 metres), the usual form was to have two companies up in the actual front line. Close behind them, often not more than 20 yards (18 metres) back was the close support line and there would be situated the two company headquarters concerned, sometimes, though not usually, with a platoon each in reserve.

Two or three hundred yards (180 or 275 metres) back was the support line, held by one fairly widely deployed company and about the same distance further back again was the reserve line, which was occupied by the fighting portion of battalion head-quarters and by the fourth company, in reserve. Quite often there were other almost equally complete systems behind the main one, these being held by reserve formations and units.

By 1917 the defensive system had become very different from the odd trenches, ditches, and breastworks which had marked the front line in 1914, and had reached a stage of considerable depth, permanence, and complexity. Trenches were deep, as well-drained as their situation would allow, and properly revetted, that is the sides were shored up and prevented from crumbling by means of sandbags, sheet iron, hurdles, and fascines (long bundles of sticks) all held in place by posts, pickets, and wire. The usual trace of a trench was in the form of what may perhaps best be described as a square zigzag. The forward parts, usually from 15 to 30 feet (5 to 9 metres) long were fire bays and were equipped with firesteps so that the men could fire over the parapet. The solid rectangles of earth left between these bays were known as traverses and were designed to offer shelter from flanking fire which might otherwise have swept a trench from end to end.

Strongpoints, often of steel and reinforced concrete, were provided at intervals for machine guns, as were posts for snipers and observers, while the ground below was honeycombed with deep dugouts, often interconnected underground. These were constructed with their entrances on the front side of the trench so as to reduce the chance of stray shells dropping into them. All the main trenches were connected by communication trenches, constructed in broad zig-zags to give some protection from frontal fire and wide enough if possible to accommodate two-way traffic including reliefs, stretcher bearers, carrying parties, and prisoners. If these trenches faced a dangerous flank they too were often provided with a fire step on the proper side. The whole front of the position was of course covered by one or more wide belts of barbed wire entanglements.

A G.H.Q. memorandum of 14 December 1917 laid down the broad principles upon which a defence was to be conducted. After explaining that the situation on the Russian and Italian fronts might make it possible for the enemy to move strong reinforcements to the Western Front, it laid down that as far as possible the defence was to be actively conducted by means of local offensives, raids, and the use of gas to harrass the enemy. Defences were to be sited in depth and counterattacks were to be planned in detail. The main battle zone was to be between 2,000 and 3,000 yards (1,830 to 2,750 metres) deep in successive lines, and switch systems were to be included so that in the event of a breakthrough the enemy could be prevented from turning outwards and rolling up the line from the flank. The first line of defence was to be an outpost line, based on machine guns and sited as far as possible to give good fields of fire, and wire was to be sited so as to conform to the machine gun plan and not vice-versa. The memorandum explained that the situation was made worse by a reduction in the strength of infantry in the theatre. In January 1917 there had been 735,681; in January 1918 this number had fallen to 665,747, the drop of some 70,000 being well in excess of the entire infantry strength of the British Expeditionary Force of 1914.

The primary object of this chapter is to deal with the mechanics of warfare of the Western Front, and it will, it is hoped, be appreciated that the foregoing description is necessarily a somewhat idealized one of what a good system should have looked like in fine weather and during a period of minimum enemy activity, although this was a combination rarely achieved. Even routine shelling and trench mortaring, aided and abetted by rain, made it a constant effort to keep the system barely habitable, while the hours or even days of intense artillery preparation which preceded an attack on any scale naturally had a disastrous effect. Whole systems were quickly reduced to mere networks of shallow crumbling, muddy ditches in which men nevertheless lived miserably, fought desperately, and not infrequently died unpleasantly.

Battalions were relieved as regularly as possible and then went back a few miles behind the battle zone to rest; this period varied according to the situation but was usually a minimum of one week. The term 'rest' was of course relative, since much of the time was taken up in training and short refresher courses; there were few soldiers, officers or other ranks alike, who were so well trained by the middle of the war that they would not benefit from even a few days extra instruction, and it was thus the commanding officer's business to make the most of the time available. If things were reasonably quiet during his spell in the line he could usually have a programme ready, at least in outline, before relief, relying on his quartermaster, transport officer, and padre, to reconnoitre and improvise training or welfare facilities on his behalf.

The prime need was to ensure as far as was possible the comfort and welfare of all ranks of the unit, so that the first day out was usually devoted to hot baths, clean clothes, the issue of pay, and generally settling in to the most comfortable billets which the wiles of the quartermaster had been able to obtain. Arrangements would also have been made for beer and other canteen facilities, concert parties and bands, church services, visits to local towns (bearing in mind that many, only a few miles behind the line, were relatively untouched by the war) and some longer leave if possible for at least a proportion of the battalion. The commanding officer would also usually interview all new arrivals and ensure that they were posted according to their particular skills; the bulk would be relatively ill-trained recruits but there would be the occasional older soldier, perhaps recovered from wounds, and these were always eagerly sought.

The programme for the next few days was necessarily simple; the officers and non-commissioned officers were put through short refresher courses on drill and tactics, while the remainder were left in the hands of the various specialist instructors for lessons in Lewis gun, gas, grenades, the duties of scouts and snipers, order and messages, and other useful military subjects, many of which would hardly have been touched on during initial training. A simple ceremonial parade and one or two elementary tactical exercises were also performed, the latter being based on the need to retain some capacity for open warfare when the great day of the final breakthrough eventually came. There was also some sport, physical training, soccer matches and other games, all designed to keep the soldiers fit and interested.

The main emphasis however seems to have been on musketry, for since 1914 the standard of rifle shooting had dropped deplorably. Training facilities for the new armies were short, there were few expert instructors, few available weapons, and little time, for what there was had to be carefully apportioned so as to give the new soldier at least a bare introduction to many new weapons and many new skills. An experienced ex-battalion commander, addressing the students at the Senior Officers' School on the subject, told his listeners to: 'Remind them of the efficiency of the old Regular Army and of the results. They knew if a Boche appeared 300 yards away they could put into him three shots quick. If these men (i.e. of the new armies) saw a German 300 yards away they would throw a bomb at him.' This was a bitter enough comment but demonstrably true, although considerable, if often unavailing, efforts were constantly being made to improve the situation. Not even the most optimistic hoped to return to the shattering musketry of 1914 or anything like it; the best that could be hoped for was that the soldier should shoot reasonably straight at fairly short ranges, and that he should shoot where he was ordered. Aiming rests, eye-discs, targets, even ranges, were hastily improvised; nevertheless the standard remained low.

Although lip service was still paid to the broad principles of the attack in open country as laid down in *Infantry Training* of August 1914, they bore in fact so little relevance to the requirements of a normal trench to trench assault that a whole new system had had to be devised for the latter, which was by far the most common form of offensive action seen on the Western Front.

This type of attack was practically never delivered by a single battalion but by whole divisions, corps, and armies on fronts of several miles, and supported by massed artillery firing preparative programmes which often lasted for days and involved the expenditure of millions of shells. Lack of good communications however usually meant that the major attack consisted in practice of a series of more or less unconnected efforts by individual battalions. It is the action of one of these which it is now proposed to consider.

The broad principle was that a battalion attacked on a front of 200 or 300 yards (180 or 275 metres) with two companies up. Each company had two platoons up and each of these platoons formed up in two lines, with bombers in the second. Men were two or three yards (1.8 or 2.8 metres) apart, and the distance between lines rarely exceeded 20 yards (18 metres). The two rear platoons of the forward companies also formed up in similar fashion about 50 yards (45 metres) further back, the whole effort of these two companies being classed as a wave.

The rear two companies also formed in the same way about 100 yards (90 metres) further back, and these constituted the second wave. If the objective was very deep it was of course necessary to post other battalions behind the leading ones, but as this is somewhat outside our present consideration it will not be discussed further here.

Each wave was allotted a linear objective, i.e. a trench line, which was usually further broken down into company objectives. The leading wave might either rush straight through the first objective and assault the second one further back, or waves might leapfrog through each other as seemed best. As the ground to be attacked was often a featureless sea of mud, careful reconnaissance was essential, and in the later stages much use was made of aerial photography to supplement this.

One serious problem was where to assemble the attacking troops. This could either be done in the front line itself, often in the close support line which was rarely strongly held, or in shell holes in front of it, or if really necessary, by digging a new trench for that specific purpose. Forming up was even more difficult, since it usually had to be done in the open, on the enemy side of the wire. The enemy positions were of course under heavy artillery fire at the time but even so it was a hair-raising operation, especially when the opposing trench lines were close together. Speed and careful timing were essential, since the object was to reach the enemy's trench as quickly as possible after the barrage had either stopped or lifted. This had two distinct advantages: in the first place the enemy troops might be caught either in their dugouts or just emerging from them; in the second place the rear wave might be out of its assembly area, formed up, and moving forward before the inevitable enemy artillery response arrived on the British front line.

The leading wave moved as close to the barrage as it dared, 100 yards (90 metres) being the interval laid down. The infantry, heavily laden, were to march to within 80 yards (73 metres) of their objective, then break into a slow double before a rush over the last few yards. If the barrage was slow in lifting the lines halted in the open, and in theory at any rate were forbidden to lie down because of the very real risk of loss of control. This meant in fact that the very natural reluctance of men to get up once they are down might adversely affect the whole advance.

As soon as the assault had been launched, control of the battle virtually passed out of the hands of the commanding officer who, having no reliable communications, remained as a matter of necessity in the assembly area until the attack was successful – or otherwise as the case might be. The battle was thus fought initially by the company, platoon, and section commanders.

If all went well the objective was taken, trenches (and particularly dugouts) were cleared, and order of a sort established. Contact was established with flanking units, if in fact they had been successful; when the trenches on one or both sides were still held by the enemy, bombers and Lewis gunners had to man blocks to protect the flanks from the almost inevitable local counterattack. Company commanders coordinated the immediate defence as best they could and sent back regular messages, timed and signed, to battalion headquarters. As these went by runner, their arrival was by no means certain; the casualty rate amongst runners was high, and their general devotion to duty was proverbial.

As soon as the commanding officer received notification of success he informed his brigade headquarters and at once went forward to coordinate the defence of his sector and prepare for the next phase, which was to hold the ground he had gained in the face of almost certain heavy artillery fire followed by a large-scale counterattack. The official manuals of the period tended to dislike the use of the term consolidation to describe this process because they insisted with much truth that the true consolidation of a trench line taken by assault after days of heavy shelling might well take a week.

The only real element of surprise obtainable in an attack of this nature was one obtained by careful timing. The enemy knew well enough that an attack was coming but he could not know exactly when, so that a really swift, coordinated rush behind the barrage might just possibly catch him unawares, stunned by days of shelling and never quite sure that this pause was the critical one. In practice this happened very rarely; the machine guns, the very soul of any defence, were often situated in such vast permanent works that some of them were reasonably certain to survive the barrage and be ready to open fire when the assault came in. Later in the war, smoke screens were often used to shield the attackers and confuse the machine guns, but as the latter could be laid on fixed lines it was only necessary for them to maintain a sustained fire in order to be reasonably certain of getting results.

Speed was perhaps even more important in the second phase, because it might well be half an hour or more before the enemy artillery received firm news of the loss of the position and began to shell it. Before this happened however there was also the risk of a local counterattack by bombing parties down the communication trenches and this also had to be guarded against. The really vital thing was to dig fast, for the captured trench would probably not offer much protection after its battering; but men also had to be placed in position, sentries posted, grenades and Lewis guns made ready, extra ammunition issued and order generally restored after the inevitable confusion of a successful attack. Even if the trench was not seriously damaged there was much to be done. Existing firesteps, for example, were on the wrong side and although in theory they could be used from the other side, in practice it was better to resite them. Surviving dugouts could be made use of, although they too faced the wrong way. A direct hit might do little more than block the entrance, so as long as the new occupants had picks and shovels they could usually extricate themselves.

If the enemy was unusually slow in reacting it was sometimes possible to bring up vital stores, water, ammunition, wire, and food, by means of carrying parties and this naturally increased the prospects of holding the position successfully. Although many attacks were planned for dawn so as to allow the maximum possible daylight, many practical soldiers preferred the afternoon; this not only ensured the assaulting troops a reasonable ration of sleep the night before, but often meant that success was achieved at last light, thus allowing vital stores to be brought forward and vital work done during the hours of darkness. The maintenance of morale was of paramount importance and commanding officers were required to give this their constant personal attention. If they considered that their units were unable or unlikely to be able to hold a captured position they were at once to say so, although it would perhaps have taken a very dedicated officer to go so far.

We must now consider the more mundane subject of the sort of equipment and stores which made this type of attack possible, bearing in mind the virtually complete reliance on carrying parties as the only means of transport within the forward zone. Individual soldiers went into action in battle order, that is to say in normal equipment less the big pack, in place of which the haversack was carried on the back with the waterbottle below it and the ground sheet attached to the belt. Every man also had an entrenching tool plus three sandbags, and if it was considered that communications were going to be particularly difficult he also carried a pick or a shovel. The scale of rifle ammunition was 120 rounds in the pouches with a further one or two bandoliers of 50 rounds, and every rifleman carried two grenades. Lewis gun magazines were carried in special containers on men's backs since the characteristic bucket type, carried in the hand, tended to attract sniper fire. Officers wore private soldiers' uniform and equipment for the same good reason.

Resupply was from previously established dumps which were positioned as far forward as possible on a company basis. The quantities of stores envisaged were huge, as witness the official recommended scale for one battalion:

```
5,000  Mills bombs
   10  boxes small-arms ammunition
  100  shovels ⎫ If ground was hard the proportion
   30  picks   ⎭ of picks was increased
2,000  sandbags
    5  coils french (i.e. Dannert) wire
   20  pickets
 some 'P' bombs (red phosphorous)
 extra rifle grenades
```

The quantity of grenades is so huge that one may at first suspect that an extra nought has crept into the total, but by comparison with several other sources it appears to be correct. The whole problem of resupply, upon which the eventual success of the operation might depend, was so great that on occasions one platoon per company had to be detailed purely for carrying purposes, a sad but apparently inevitable diminution of fighting strength.

The special roles of various individuals in the attack had become fairly clearly defined by 1917. Subaltern officers, on whom the bulk of the fighting leadership actually fell, were bidden to be discreet, wear private soldier's clothes in the attack and not charge wildly ahead of their first line. The official doctrine on the subject was clear: 'no one impugns the standard of courage amongst British Officers, and it is their duty to get as many Germans killed as possible with as few casualties as possible.'

Before any attack was launched, snipers were to work their way forward to within 60 yards (55 metres) or so of the enemy front line and take up camouflaged positions in shell holes or other suitable cover, from where it was their duty to try to deal with the opposing machine guns or snipers. A somewhat lower grade of good rifleman, generally referred to as company sharpshooters, were similarly to take up covering positions in the enemy trench as soon as it was captured so as to deter counterattacks, at least for the first half-hour or so, after which time enemy shelling would probably compel them to take cover.

Lewis gunners were to move on the flanks of the second line so as to engage opportunity targets, support their bombers, and possibly establish crossfire with their opposite numbers in neighbouring subunits. In long advances they were to be pushed forward boldly to support the main advance, one important role being to try to stalk and destroy machine guns. The regimental bombers were experts who supplemented the ordinary bombing capacity of the rifle companies. They moved as lightly equipped as possible, often carrying up to 20 bombs in special waistcoat type carriers, but otherwise armed only with revolvers or even coshes, and were often accompanied by other soldiers carrying reserve grenades for them. Their primary function after a successful attack was to establish quick blocks in trenches offering likely lines of approach to a counterattack.

The wave system of trench to trench attack could, it was felt, be adapted fairly easily to the requirements of open warfare, for in spite of occasional references back to the teaching of 1914 it was clear that the old concept of a reinforced firing line closing steadily on a defensive position, and then subduing it by sheer volume of fire as a preliminary to a successful assault, had gone. The official

185

view as taught at the Senior Officers' School stated that:

    (a) The assault no longer depends upon rifle fire, supported by artillery fire, but upon the artillery solely, with very slight support from selected snipers and company sharpshooters

    (b) The decisive feature in every attack is the bayonet.

Almost all the infantry attacks launched across open country took place in the Middle East. In Palestine they seem to have been conducted on the wave principle, with an assembly area and start line, and supported by a considerable weight of artillery. This was made possible by the fact that there was ample space available, and that trench systems were nowhere as sophisticated as those in the West. At that time too the Turks, although still fighting well, had nothing like the resources of heavy artillery available to their German allies. Finally of course the presence of a huge body of good cavalry, operating over suitable terrain, made outflanking movements relatively simple.

In Mesopotamia the older system of advances by alternate rushes seems to have held sway longer, although it was by no means always successful. The flat open desert offered splendid fields of fire for well-sited machine guns in defence, while the mirage made it very difficult for artillery to deal with them. This theatre was always somewhat neglected, so that lack of good cavalry, or even adequate numbers of guns, made offensive operations expensive to the infantry taking part.

The advent of the tank in 1916 at first offered some hope of a swift and decisive breakthrough, but in the event this did not materialize. The tactical system evolved was for the tanks to precede the infantry, moving as closely behind their own barrage as was possible. Their role became largely that of mobile machine-gun posts, which it was hoped might be able to dominate the fire of the defending machine guns and shoot their own infantry onto the objective. The German answer to this was to use field guns well forward in an anti-tank role; these guns then became the principle target both for artillery concentrations and for local infantry attacks.

In the event however things still bogged down, for much of the battle area was low lying and the shelling had wrecked the ancient drainage systems and caused the country to revert to its original swamp. Movement on any serious scale became virtually impossible so that, provided the flanks of a penetration held, the Germans were always able to bring up reserves to seal it off faster than their attackers could exploit the situation. Thus the most likely result was that the original penetration became a salient, subject to fire from both flanks and therefore difficult and expensive to hold. Even in the high chalk country, where there was good natural drainage, the same limitations existed, although to a lesser degree. A vast mass of really efficient armoured vehicles might have done the business, but could never be assembled in the necessary strength. The first really successful penetration occurred at Amiens in August 1918, but this came at a time when the enemy was almost played out.

Although there seems to have been little overall effort to prepare the infantry for a return to a more open type of warfare, many of the more forward looking Divisional Commanders had done a good deal in this direction. The concept of attacking loosely linked German strongpoints, instead of a continuous line, had shown the need for small infantry/tank battle groups rather than the concept of waves following a barrage, and this doctrine had begun to spread. It is easy to forget that the last few months of 1918 saw a resumption of open warfare, and it is greatly to the credit of the erstwhile trenchbound infantry that they did so well at it.

Another and lesser form of offensive operation was the trench raid. The main object of this type of local, small-scale attack was to obtain prisoners, for which headquarters of all levels appear to have had a voracious appetite in 1914–18, but there was also the important, if secondary, object of keeping the war going. After years of static warfare both sides had become weary, and at times opposing units showed a distinct tendency to conduct their war on a 'live and let live' basis. This however, though comfortable for the participants, was anathema to the more fire-eating of the generals, who thus regarded raids as an excellent way of blooding new arrivals and keeping all concerned on their toes.

They were usually company operations, conducted in the dark, and needed to be carefully planned if excessive casualties were to be avoided. The general technique was to seal off the objective with heavy artillery concentrations on its flanks and rear so as to isolate it completely, and then attack suddenly through gaps previously cut in the attackers' own wire. Paths could be blown in the enemy wire by means of Bangalore torpedoes, lengths of drainpipe packed with high explosives and fitted with a simple fuse and detonator. These could be thrust through the enemy wire, and with luck would clear a lane through it. The attackers, lightly armed for the most part with daggers, bludgeons, and grenades, and with faces blackened, moved as fast as possible, snatched their prisoners, and retired before the inevitable enemy artillery response descended on them.

An even more specialized form of attack was the occupation of a crater. When the ground was suitable, Royal Engineer tunnelling companies might burrow forward under the enemy lines and there establish mines charged with tons of high explosive which could be blown in accordance with a prepared plan. It was difficult to make detailed arrangements because no one could ever predict with absolute accuracy quite how the landscape would be changed by the explosion. The general principle was to use lightly equipped troops initially, with a very high proportion of bombers who could seal off surviving enemy trenches to the flanks and rear. Every man engaged on such operations usually carried five grenades while the specialist bombers went into action carrying 20 or more, being closely followed by carrying parties ladened with as many more as they could reasonably carry. The numbers of this type of weapon used – or at least made available – were astounding. On a relatively small, two-battalion operation of this type launched in 1916 a special forward *reserve* of 15,000 grenades was established. This figure was in addition to those carried by the assault forces; nor did it include the normal battalion and brigade reserve of 10,500.

As soon as trench warfare started it became very clear that the machine gun was going to be the vital infantry weapon, and in December 1914 a Machine Gun School was set up at St. Omer to train men in the weapon. The small machine gun sections of the original Expeditionary Force had suffered huge casualties so that replacements were urgently required. Although before the war it had been considered that it took two years to train a really competent machine gunner, the wartime soldiers had to learn the rudiments of the business in six crowded weeks; thereafter they became more expert by hard practical experience, a wasteful and expensive method, but one to which there appeared to be no real alternative.

The need to group guns so as to make the best and most economical tactical use of them over a wide front had long been appreciated, and from the time that trench warfare started brigades had been grouping their four machine-gun sections into extemporized companies under the brigade machine-gun officer. These proved successful, but it soon became apparent that even more centralization was required, so by a Royal Warrant of 22 October 1915 a new Machine Gun Corps came into being, all the existing brigade companies being transferred to it and allotted corps serial numbers.

The problems of finding both men and equipment were formidable, for although the 100 or so guns of the original Expeditionary Force had increased to something over 1,000 by June 1915, this number was still found to be inadequate, bearing in mind that the

German Army had entered the war with some 5,000 Maxim guns already in service. Eventually however Great Britain's enormous manufacturing potential was fully developed, while the new armies made available almost unlimited numbers of men, inexperienced indeed but of a quality rarely seen before in any British army, so that the work went forward better than might have been expected. By mid-1916 the Corps had risen to a strength of some 4,000 officers and over 80,000 men and was functioning well, the work of individual companies being supervised and coordinated by corps and divisional machine-gun officers.

Doctrine was still elementary, but enthusiasm and unlimited opportunities for experiment in the field itself soon produced vast improvements in the deployment and handling of weapons. Guns were employed in batteries of four or eight for barrage, flanking, or overhead fire. In the attack guns were handled boldly, a good deal being left to the initiative of the officer commanding them within the general framework of orders. In defence they were sited in depth, mutually supporting, and as far as possible defiladed, i.e. protected from the front, since flanking fire against attacking lines was clearly the most effective possible. Low wire entanglements were often constructed to hold attackers briefly, and so offer opportunities for devastating fire against stationary targets. Machine guns were often sited in powerful steel and concrete bunkers which were proof against all but the heaviest artillery shells. Although artillery almost certainly caused more casualties overall, it is arguable that the machine gun was the more important defensive weapon because of its swifter reaction. In those days before wireless, telephone lines back to the guns were often cut, thus causing delays in the firing of S.O.S. tasks. These delays were usually short, but where opposing lines were close together even a few minutes could be vital and it was in this respect that the machine gun scored, because it was always there and always ready to bridge any gap. Its value was further enhanced by new systems of indirect laying and other techniques devised by a number of enthusiastic scientists-turned-soldiers, all of which combined to make the Vickers gun even more deadly. Personnel were always of the highest quality and morale was high; on one occasion at least, when a surprise attack involved the assault force lying in no-man's-land within 80 yards (73 metres) of the enemy front line before rushing it at first light, the machine gunners in support left their own guns, rushed the German posts, and quickly turned the captured Maxims against the enemy's trenches.

Machine guns were considered ideal for S.O.S. tasks, since they combined central control with flexibility and their response to calls for fire was very fast. Given good crews and adequate supplies they were capable of incredibly long periods of sustained fire; one famous case, often quoted, occurred at High Wood on 22 August 1916 when 10 guns of the 100th Company fired 999,750 rounds over a period of 12 hours with little more breaks than were necessary to clean, oil, and reload their guns, change barrels, and top up water-jackets. Two companies of infantry acted as carrying parties for ammunition and water, and when supplies of the latter ran out the contents of every urine tub for a long distance round were requisitioned and used in lieu. German reports and statements by prisoners later confirmed that the results had been annihilating, with vital reserve pinned down and whole counter-attacks shattered by the remorseless fire.

By early 1918 divisional machine-gun battalions had come into existence; each consisted of four companies of 16 guns and by the middle of the year there were on the Western Front 57 such battalions of the British Army, plus those of the Canadian, Australian and New Zealand armies, together with a number of independent squadrons. The new corps thus ended the war on a high note, but after that everything was anticlimax; there were the familiar cries of 'No more war', and the equally familiar demands for economy, and in 1922 the Machine Gun Corps ceased to exist, the weapons reverting to infantry battalions in a similar fashion to 1914, although on a more generous scale.

Another new infantry unit which came into being in the winter of 1914–15 was the Trench Mortar battery. The mortar is a very ancient weapon, as old as gunpowder itself, and had been in the service of the British Army for many years as an artillery weapon. The early ones were heavy, clumsy, and relatively immobile, and although they had been used extensively in siege operations they had dropped out of use soon after the Crimea War. By the winter of 1914–15 the war on the Western Front had developed into a vast two-sided siege and a number of weapons previously considered obsolete were hastily brought back into service, among them being the mortar. The earliest ones used were either ancient pieces borrowed from French museums or cast locally by the Royal Engineers from melted down cartridge cases, but by the end of the year a number of factory-made pieces had begun to reach the front.

The first of these was almost certainly the two-inch trench howitzer, which fired a toffee-apple shaped bomb weighing 51 pounds (23 kilogrammes) to a range of 500 yards (460 metres). The second was the four-inch trench howitzer, the barrels of which were hastily made by the ingenious conversion of naval armour-piercing shells. These incidentally were rifled with three grooves and fired a studded projectile of a type previously long obsolete;

they were the only rifled mortars ever used in the British service, which gives them a modest place in the history of firearms. The projectiles they fired weighed about 11½ pounds (5.2 kilogrammes) and had a maximum range of 430 yards (390 metres). The third was the 3.7-inch trench howitzer, very similar to the four-inch model but of much lighter construction; it fired a 4½-pound (2-kilogramme) bomb to a range of 340 yards (310 metres).

The propellant used in all these consisted of shredded gun cotton yarn, the firing mechanism being the breech mechanism of a Lee-Enfield rifle screwed into the bore so that the discharge of a blank cartridge loaded with pistol powder ignited the charge. The two-inch howitzer bomb had a normal 31A artillery fuse, but as the complexities of the manufacture of fuses of all types soon caused a serious bottleneck in ammunition procedure, the projectiles of the other models were simply equipped with lengths of safety fuse, cut to the length required according to a range-table provided, and ignited by the flash of the propellant.

Early in 1916 there appeared the Stokes three-inch mortar, a more sophisticated weapon not materially different (except as regards range) from the type in use today. The base of the bomb had a built-in cap and a firing pin was incorporated in the bottom of the barrel, so that to fire the piece it was only necessary to put a bomb in the muzzle and release it; its own weight then took it down with sufficient force to fire the cap and blow it straight out again.

There were also other and heavier mortars in use at the same time, but as these were the responsibility of the Royal Artillery they need not concern us. The two-inch howitzer was also soon found to be far too heavy for a mobile role, so that it too soon passed out of the hands of the infantry leaving them with the various pieces classed as 'light', i.e. the four-inch, the 3.7-inch and the Stokes. By the early months of 1918 the Stokes had become the principal infantry weapon of its type, although at least a few of the others seem to have remained in service until the end of the war.

An infantry trench-mortar battery, one of which formed part of the establishment of an infantry brigade, usually consisted of four guns, although by 1918 there were also a few eight-gun batteries in existence. The four-gun batteries were broken down, artillery fashion, into two sections each of two subsections of one gun; the establishment varied slightly, but by 1916 had settled down to two officers with a small headquarters and four detachments, each of a non-commissioned officer (the number one) and five others. Numbers one, two and three actually handled the weapon, the others being ammunition numbers, although they were all trained to operate the mortar if required.

Although technically portable, the Stokes mortar constituted a fair load for three men, the barrel weighing 44 pounds (20 kilogrammes), the bipod 18 (8 kilogrammes) and the baseplate 29 pounds (13 kilogrammes). The carriage of bombs was an even greater problem, and the unfortunate ammunition numbers were on occasion transformed into mere beasts of burden. Each carried four bombs in a special waistcoat-type carrier, two front and two back, with a further three rounds carried in a container by hand, and as the bombs weighed almost 11 pounds (5 kilogrammes) each, seven of these constituted a considerable load, particularly since all numbers carried normal equipment and rifles. On special occasions number three also carried four bombs in a waistcoat and number one carried three in a box, these loads being in addition to the baseplate and bipod respectively. Number two, having the barrel to cope with, was excused, which is probably just as well. Even so, 28 rounds could be fired away in two or three minutes so that considerable reserves were necessary, these being established in the reserve line. When a major attack was imminent, up to 500 rounds per gun might have to be stacked, which inevitably meant the employment of carrying parties from some unfortunate infantry battalion.

The relatively short range of all these types of mortar made them essentially close support weapons. In defence, when an attack was expected, they registered on the enemy's likely forming up positions, since their quick response to calls for fire made them very suitable to deal with the sudden appearance of massed targets. In the attack they were often massed to produce heavy concentrations on a few selected points, although some were usually kept mobile so as to be able to deal with groups of the enemy retiring across the open.

Although useful accessories when things were active, trench mortars were not always popular with the front-line infantry in quiet periods. As occurred with trench raids, belligerent brigade commanders would send forward their mortar batteries to make a nuisance of themselves to the enemy when things were quiet, but as communications on both sides were slow, they had often finished their shoot and retired before the inevitable enemy response arrived, to the discomfort of the more permanent occupants of the sector. When the war ended the trench mortar disappeared completely until a new and improved version of the Stokes mortar was issued to infantry battalions in the 1930s.

In summing up the results of the Great War of 1914–18 it may be said at once that it produced few positive and enduring tactical lessons of any real value. The restricted theatre and the total absence of flanks made frontal attack inevitable, but given the development in modern fire power, such attacks could only hope to succeed by sheer weight of men and material. Millions of shells were followed by hundreds of thousands of men floundering hopelessly but bloodily in bottomless mud under the relentless fire of massed machine guns. It was in many ways the very nadir of tactics which did little but cause a vast spilling of the best blood of the nation.

The senior officers of the British Army in the post-war years were gallant veterans, but not always of high intellectual calibre. The shattering of half a generation had left dreadful gaps in every aspect of national life and it was hardly to be expected that the Army would escape this. As far as most generals were concerned the war, which in any case they regarded as something of an aberration, was over. They could forget tanks, forget aircraft, forget the internal combustion engine; in fact they could forget progress and get back to proper soldiering, a hazy and idealized concept in which jingling cavalry squadrons wheeled in the Long Valley with all the panoply of war, while rows of khaki-helmeted infantry stormed distant heights in the face of a dropping fire from a handful of Pathans. It was noble stuff indeed, but hardly a good basis on which to train a twentieth century army for future use.

Happily there were also a good many survivors of real calibre, but for years the stagnation of all things military kept them in subordinate positions, where at least they could think and plan, even if they could not put their ideas into immediate effect. Fortunately the bulk of these had the patience to endure, with the most beneficial results for the country, and perhaps the world, a quarter of a century later.

10 1919–1945 WORLD WAR 2

November 1918 brought to a victorious conclusion the 'war to end all wars,' and with it the huge British armies melted rapidly away. Within a year demobilization was almost completed and all that remained was a somewhat nominal regular army smaller than it had been in 1914. The constitution of the Infantry remained practically unchanged, the only permanent addition to its strength being the Welsh Guards, which had been raised in 1915.

Although the war was over there was plenty of work for the few soldiers available, for apart from its usual role of imperial policing there were certain international committments which had to be fulfilled. In the few years following 1918 the British Army was actively employed in Russia, Afghanistan, Waziristan, North-West Persia, Burma, Mesopotamia, Chanak (Turkey), Cyprus, Shanghai, Egypt, Palestine and India, to say nothing of the pressing problem of Ireland and the need to maintain an army of occupation on the Rhine.

Much of the committment was inevitably for infantry and the Infantry were in no real state to cope with it, though in the event they did very much better than anyone had a right to expect. There were very few of the prewar 'old hands' left and not many of the experienced wartime soldiers could be persuaded to sign on, so for the most part battalions were full of raw young soldiers who, although keen and anxious to emulate the great deeds of their elders, needed a great deal of training before they could really be considered fit for the arduous and varied duties required of them. Somehow or other the small remaining cadre of officers, warrant and non-commissioned officers not only very soon succeeded in teaching them to be soldiers but had also done a good deal to get back to prewar standards of drill, discipline, and behaviour.

The bulk of battalions of the line were organized on the very suitably titled 'Small Wars' establishment of 1920, which allowed

194

for a battalion headquarters of nine officers and 129 soldiers and four rifle companies of six officers and 209 soldiers. The internal breakdown of companies into platoons and sections remained essentially as it had been in 1914 with the difference that platoons now consisted of two Lewis gun sections and two rifle sections. The battalion at that stage had no medium machine guns because the Machine Gun Corps was still in being. The old and clumsy system of drawing soldiers from rifle companies to strengthen battalion headquarters was initially still in existence, but in 1921 an additional headquarter wing was introduced. This new and useful subunit commanded and administered all the soldiers employed in battalion headquarters, thus relieving the rifle companies of considerable dead wood.

In 1922 the Machine Gun Corps was disbanded. In view of its distinguished services and obvious utility it had been hoped to retain it as a permanent unit of the British Army, but the usual need for utmost economy made this impossible. On its demise, infantry battalions were each allotted eight machine guns which became part of the headquarter wing. Some battalions also had mortar platoons for a brief period, but these were soon withdrawn in favour of a close support regiment which was added to the divisional artillery.

In the same year the infantry suffered a further loss by the disbandment of five Southern Irish regiments, a decision made necessary by the grant of Home Rule. The regiments concerned were the Royal Irish (originally 18th), the Connaught Rangers (originally 88th and 94th), the Leinsters (originally 100th and 109th), the Munster Fusiliers (originally 101st and 104th), and the Royal Dublin Fusiliers, (originally 102nd and 103rd). The last three had been taken onto the British establishment from the East India Company's army when the Crown assumed responsibility for India in 1860, and all had fine records.

Although in view of the state of Ireland there was naturally a certain amount of disaffection in these regiments, many individuals transferred to other units, so that the net loss in soldiers was less than might have been expected. The situation, sad though it was, was further lightened by an act of great generosity. The original list for disbandment had included the Royal Irish Fusiliers on the grounds that although it recruited all over the island the bulk of its recruits came from the South. This would have reduced the Irish line regiments to two, the Royal Inniskilling Fusiliers and the Royal Irish Rifles (who changed their title to the Royal Ulster Rifles). The former regiment however offered its second battalion for disbandment in order to keep its fellow fusiliers in existence, and in March 1922 this offer was accepted, so saving a third regiment. The two regiments then worked as a corps until, as we shall see in due course, their second battalions were restored to them.

As if these losses were not enough, a further 10 regular infantry units were swept away; these were the third and fourth battalions of the Royal Fusiliers, the Worcesters, the Middlesex, the 60th Rifles and the Rifle Brigade. The first three of these had had two extra battalions since 1898, the latter since 1860.

In 1928 the machine gun platoon was detached from the headquarters wing and became a company in its own right, its eight guns being increased to 12 and organized in three platoons of four, with the promise of a fourth platoon on mobilization. As manpower was still very short, this alteration could only be made at the expense of one of the rifle companies. At the same time battalions were given three Carden-Lloyd carriers, small tracked vehicles armed with Hotchkiss light machine guns and used primarily for reconnaissance.

By the mid 1930s the threat from a revived Germany had become very clear and it was decided to undertake a major reorganization. There was unfortunately no question of achieving this by the wave of a magic wand, for it is one thing to order, quite another to implement. Men were short, money was short, and as British industry was in no way geared to defence needs, arms and equipment of all kinds were short too. The maintenance of the Indian garrison at reasonable strength was still of paramount importance, so that many home battalions shrank to mere cadres. Almost everything of importance began to be represented by flags, so that battalion exercises tended to have a somewhat inappropriate air of carnival. There was already in existence a system under which sections carried red and blue screens, about one yard (0.9 metres) wide and half a yard (0.45 metres) high; these were an umpiring device under which sections showing red screens were regarded as being pinned down while those showing blue ones could only advance by fire and movement. Added to these were platoons (large yellow flags) and anti-tank guns (green flags with white diagonals) so that the general effect was gay but unwarlike. Things were indeed moving, but very slowly, and the initial steps, although in the right direction, were short and infrequent.

In 1936 battalion support companies (the post-1935 title of the old machine gun company) were strengthened by the addition of two three-inch mortars. These were an improved version of the Stokes gun and fired 10-pound (4.5-kilogramme) bombs, both high explosive and smoke, to a range of 1,600 yards (1,460 metres). At about the same time there was considered (though never actually introduced) a concept of making infantry brigades consist of three light battalions with rifles, light machine guns and mortars, and one support battalion with machine guns, anti-tank guns, and a reconnaissance element, but this was soon changed. The idea of having support battalions on a brigade basis was abandoned, being replaced by machine gun battalions in the role of divisional or corps troops, which it was felt would give great flexibility within the order of battle.

A number of infantry units were earmarked for conversion to machine gunners, the original ones being two battalions of Guards and the first and second battalions of 13 line regiments. These numbers were eventually reduced, the final list consisting of the Northumberland Fusiliers, the Cheshire Regiment, the Middlesex Regiment, and the Manchester Regiment, including some, but by no means all of their territorial battalions. All the regiments concerned appear to have completed their conversion by 1937, while many others on the original list had also finished retraining for their new role before the order was received to revert to the normal infantry role.

Some indications of the problems facing infantry commanders in those days is given by the fact that no sooner had the 1st Battalion of the Manchester Regiment completed its conversion than it had to revert briefly to its original role for internal security duties in Palestine.

The years immediately preceding World War 2 led to some belated increases in the strength of the Infantry. At first it had been planned to add no less than 14 new battalions to the establishment, but in the event this was reduced to four. The Royal Inniskilling Fusiliers and the Royal Irish Fusiliers both had their second battalions restored to them in 1937, and two years later the Irish and Welsh Guards both formed second battalions.

The new establishment for the standard infantry battalion was approved in 1937 but for reasons already explained it must not be assumed that conversion to it was completed immediately; it is significant that *Infantry Training 1937* makes provision for the handling of both types of unit, although the emphasis is naturally on the newer one.

The new battalion organization had the usual battalion headquarters but the old headquarter wing had been renamed headquarter company and consisted of a signal platoon with lamp, flag, heliograph and line, an anti-aircraft platoon with light machine guns on special mountings in 15-hundredweight trucks, and often manned by the Corps of Drums, a mortar platoon with two three-inch mortars, and a self-explanatory administrative platoon. Further additions were envisaged in the shape of a carrier platoon and a pioneer platoon, but in most cases these did not materialize until 1938 or 1939.

The fourth rifle company had been restored, and each company still had four platoons but the number of sections in each platoon had been reduced to three, each of which had one of the new and efficient Bren light machine guns which gave the company considerable fire power. Each platoon also had a bulky if not very efficient Boys anti-tank rifle, and a light two-inch mortar, the latter a handy little weapon capable of throwing high explosive or smoke bombs to a range of about 500 yards (460 metres).

A new innovation at this time was the introduction of platoon sergeant-majors, a new grade of third-class warrant officers introduced to make up the chronic shortage of subalterns; they commanded a proportion of the platoons, including one or two of the support platoons.

By this time the horse had virtually gone and the old transport platoon with its horsy subaltern, village blacksmith type sergeant, and drivers and grooms, had given place to a new breed of technician in oily overalls. The motor transport of a battalion had by then reached a total of 57 vehicles ranging from Austin pick-ups to three-ton trucks.

One of the minor but interesting results of the new three-section system was an alteration in the style of drill. In earlier days the basic formation for movement had been fours; the subunits had formed in the traditional two ranks, doubled them, turned to a flank, and moved off on a frontage well calculated for movement on a normal road. On exercises or actual service each rank of the platoon in fours had consisted of a section, so that deployment outwards was quick and simple; but now, with the reductions, the standard formation for movement became threes.

Infantry Training 1937 went some way towards modernizing tactics in the light of recent experience. As was to be expected at a period of major change, the doctrine was kept fairly general, and left more to the discretion and common sense of formation and unit commanders than had previously been the case. There were some references to 'the barrage', and the infantry/tank cooperation smacked rather of 1918; nevertheless, taking it all round, there was a distinct loosening of tactics. Attacks were made on wide fronts, and companies had to be prepared to fight their own way forward by fire and manoeuvre, making use of all the supporting fire available. Attacks on prepared positions were to be reconnoitred and planned in detail, with properly coordinated fire plans.

Defence was to be in depth, having due regard to the need for concealment and mutual support, and ample reserves were to be kept available for counterattack, while maximum use was to be made of mortars, machine guns and artillery for defensive fire tasks. A good deal of space was also devoted to anti-tank defence, anti-aircraft precautions, and the means of obtaining protection from gas, while battle procedure, that is the art of coordinating all preliminary activities so as to save time, was well covered. As it transpired, the early battles of the war were planned as far as possible on this doctrine, although in the event practical circumstances often differed materially from those envisaged.

The Mobilization of 1939 went fairly smoothly, and generally speaking the supply of personal arms and equipment for the returning reservists was adequate, although more specialized items were still inevitably in short supply. Infantry battalions on the home establishment were, as ever, mere cadres, and although it is impossible to give absolutely accurate figures it seems probable that most of the battalions which departed with the Expeditionary Force were composed of about 60 per cent regulars and 40 per cent reservists. Perhaps fortunately, the main change in rifle company weapons in the previous few years had been the substitution of the Bren gun for the Lewis, but as the new gun was simple and reliable it did not take long for the reservists to master it. The first batch of new militiamen called up for compulsory service only reported to their depots in July 1939 so they did not reach their units until later.

It may be as well at this stage to consider the establishment on which infantry battalions mobilized in 1939, since it was only subject to one really major change during the whole course of the war. Battalion headquarters consisted of four officers and 42 other ranks, the bulk of these being, oddly enough, the band, who acted as stretcher bearers. Headquarters company had six platoons, details of which were:

No. 1 Signals	1 officer and 33 other ranks with 3 motorcycles
No. 2 Anti-aircraft	1 P.S.M. and 15 other ranks with 4 15-cwt. trucks
No. 3 Mortars	1 P.S.M. and 14 other ranks, 2 mortars and 2 15-cwt. trucks
No. 4 Carriers	1 officer and 29 other ranks with 10 carriers, 1 for platoon headquarters and 3 sections of 3. (Carriers were light, tracked vehicles armoured against small-arms fire and with good cross-country performance. Each had a Bren light machine gun. They were used for reconnaissance and outpost duties.)

No. 5 Pioneers   1 P.S.M. and 19 other ranks
No. 6 Adminis-   Quartermaster, transport officer and
    trative   various cooks, storemen, clerks and
                     similar categories. It also included the
                     medical officer, the chaplain, the arm-
                     ourer and certain R.A.S.C. drivers, all
                     classed as 'attached'.

There were the usual four rifle companies, each consisting of a company headquarters of two captains, company sergeant-major, company quartermaster-sergeant, and six soldiers, but the number of platoons had been reduced from four to three, due to lack of manpower. Only one platoon was commanded by an officer, the others by P.S.M.s, and their total strengths were 30 in the case of the officer's platoon and 29 in the other two, the reason for this being that the officers got a batman. Each platoon had three sections of a corporal, two Bren numbers, and five riflemen, and each platoon headquarters had a Boys anti-tank rifle and a two-inch mortar. It is an interesting fact that the strength of this company was three officers and 97 other ranks, almost exactly what it had been in the old eight-company days, although its fire power was of course very much greater.

The transport for a battalion was considerable, consisting of 14 motorcycles, eight-hundredweight trucks, 33 15-hundredweight trucks, two water carts, an office vehicle, 12 30-hundredweight trucks and two attached R.A.S.C. three-ton trucks for rations. Rifle companies each had four 15-hundredweight trucks, one for H.Q. and one for each platoon. Battalion H.Q. and the headquarters company could lift themselves at a pinch but the rifle companies still marched.

The period immediately after Dunkirk was one of considerable confusion, so that although the official establishment remained unchanged, large deficiencies of equipment made modification and improvisation essential. The threat of invasion also gave rise to reconnaissance platoons, tank-hunting platoons, and other more or less irregular specialists, some raised with official blessing, others the brain children of various originally-minded commanding officers. Communications were still slightly sketchy, although the situation was improved by the introduction of the manpacked Number 18 wireless set in 1941; this (with luck) provided moderately reliable communications from battalion H.Q. down to company H.Q.s, and was a great convenience on mobile operations.

The next year or two saw a steady build up in equipment, particularly in support weapons. This caused the headquarters company to become large and unwieldy, and the unfortunate officer commanding it often had difficulty in combining his dual role of administration and support. This situation was resolved in 1943 by the introduction of a separate support company, a rather overdue reorganization which a few commanding officers appear to have anticipated unofficially.

Under the new organization the support company comprised the mortar platoon, now increased to six mortars and transported in carriers, the carrier platoon with an extra section of three carriers and under the command of a captain, and a new anti-tank platoon, consisting of six six-pounder guns each towed by a carrier and with another for ammunition, this also being a captain's command. The pioneers became the assault pioneers, their chief responsibility being mines, explosives, and the construction of field works.

Rifle company organization changed little. Company commanders became majors to bring them into line with their brethren of the Royal Artillery, and two snipers were allotted to company headquarters. This however was a temporary expedient and they were eventually concentrated in a sniper section at battalion headquarters. Sections were increased at the same time by two men and now consisted of a commander, a Bren group of a lance-corporal and two men, and a rifle group of six. One notable change was the disappearance of the P.S.M. since ample supplies of officers were being turned out from the various officer cadet training units. The fate of the existing holders of the rank varied; one or two dropped quietly out, others went on to become regimental sergeant-majors, and not a few were commissioned to end the war as company or battalion commanders.

Rifle company armament remained largely unchanged. The anti-tank rifle departed unlamented in 1943, to be replaced by the projector infantry anti-tank, usually shortened to PIAT; this was a fearsome weapon with a huge spring, which required a special knack to compress, and which was reputed to have been a not infrequent cause of rupture amongst newcomers to it; but it also destroyed a considerable number of German tanks, which was its principal object. A new rifle, the Number 4, was introduced in place of the old and well-tried short magazine Lee-Enfield, but the handling and performance of the new weapon were virtually identical to the old, so that no further comment is necessary. A new range of grenades also appeared, although the reliable Number 36, the Mills bomb of an earlier war, continued to be the principal weapon of its type. The sub-machine-gun, previously the chosen weapon of the Chicago gangster, came into use in 1940; first the American Thompson, heavy, clumsy, but reliable, and then the Sten. This was a wartime weapon hastily knocked up in small engineering works, back-street garages, and the like. Few people loved it, although in fairness it should be said that it improved in quality and reliability as the war progressed. Further improvements in communications were provided by the Number 38 wireless set, which worked from company headquarters to platoons.

There were also extensive changes in the scale and distribution of motor vehicles, although it hardly seems necessary to go into these in great detail. One terrifying addition to the support company in 1944 was a section of Wasp flamethrowers mounted in carriers.

The British Army in India was not immediately involved in the war at first, and therefore did not mobilize until Japan entered the war in 1941. Even after this had happened priority for new weapons, vehicles and equipment of all kinds still went to other theatres so that it was some time before battalions even began to approximate to their opposite numbers in North Africa. In view of the peculiar circumstances of jungle warfare British battalions in India remained on the 1939 mobilization establishment throughout and did not form support companies; because of the apparent lack of any threat of armour, the battalion's support weapons consisted of six three-inch mortars only. Companies had Number 18 wireless sets to connect them to battalions, and battalions usually had the heavier Number 22 to communicate with the brigade. There were no wireless links to platoons, and the nature of the country often made the Numbers 18 and 22 sets unreliable.

Tactics naturally varied from theatre to theatre, and even within theatres as the terrain changed. In reasonably flat, open country, as in much of north-west Europe, the North African desert, and the coastal plain of Italy, the Infantry was able to employ what one may class as 'normal' tactics. Attacks were conducted in reasonably open order and well supported by artillery and armour. The preliminaries varied a little according to circumstances, but where possible the idea was to establish the battalion in a secure assembly area where it could make its final administrative arrangements including a hot meal. The battalion then moved forward to a forming-up point, where ideally it remained only long enough to shake out into its attack formation. A clearly defined 'start line', preferably at right angles to the line of advance, would already have been selected as close to the forming-up point as possible, and the battalion crossed this at the time laid down. This was referred to as 'H' hour and all timings were worked on a plus or minus basis from it.

It was considered desirable that the infantry and armour should marry up reasonably early, preferably in the assembly area, so as to coordinate signals and plans, and net wireless sets. This was not always possible and it was not unknown for the coordination to take place hurriedly just behind the start line.

The basic concept at battalion level was to attack with two companies forward and two in reserve, each company having one or two platoons forward according to the situation. As objectives were often in depth, it was usual for the leading companies to seize the first ones and the rear companies to pass through. When defences were in great depth it became necessary to pass fresh battalions through to maintain the impetus of the attack. The great improvement in communications made the artillery very flexible, and a difficult battalion attack might on occasion be supported by the whole of the divisional or even corps artillery. The techniques of infantry/tank cooperation were also much improved, this again largely being made possible by improved communications. The tanks selected their own lines of advance and were often able to 'shoot the infantry in' from a flank. Once the attack had succeeded the usual form was for the tanks to remain on the objective to deal with the enemy armour supporting the almost inevitable counterattack until such time as the various infantry support weapons could be brought forward.

One interesting and significant innovation in 1944 was the introduction of armoured personnel carriers for infantry. These were old Canadian Ram tanks with their turrets removed, and as they were capable of lifting a section they added appreciably to the speed and flexibility of a combined infantry/armoured attack and were particularly useful in the latter stages of the war when the principal type of operation on the Allied side was the pursuit. All modern armies now have vehicles of this type. Transport was usually divided into three echelons. There was the F (fighting) echelon of the most essential vehicles for communications, ammunition and support weapons, and A and B echelons with reserve ammunition, stores, cooks and other less immediately necessary items; these A and B echelons were often handled under brigade arrangements and kept well back. Food was naturally cooked there and brought forward in insulated containers by the quartermaster during the hours of darkness.

Fighting in mountainous areas, as in much of Italy, made certain obvious modifications necessary. Everything took longer and was slower, and there were considerable limitations on the use of armour, while artillery could not often be concentrated as much as it was in the plains. Road communications were necessarily limited, and some sort of intermediate transport had to be improvised to get ammunition, food, and stores of all kinds forward. Mules were used extensively in Italy but in the last resort, as usual, the reliance was on manpower, with the result

203

that reserve companies were often called upon to provide carrying parties, an exhausting and often dangerous business.

Italy is a country of rivers, many of them flowing swiftly in deep valleys so that river crossings were frequent. The basic technique was to select a likely spot from information from air photographs, patrols, and other sources, and to push infantry over in assault boats to seize a bridgehead; this was almost always done in darkness with considerable artillery support available. The bridgehead was then expanded while the engineers threw bridges across the river so that fighting echelons, artillery, and armour, could be brought over. Warfare in Europe necessarily involved fighting in towns, which apart from being communication centres, and therefore strategically important, offered many opportunities for prolonged defence. Preliminary bombing had usually reduced them to rubble before the infantry attacked and this rubble, often concealing networks of cellars, took a great deal of clearing with bayonet, grenade and machine gun.

Jungle fighting brought serious problems of its own and many modifications had to be made to the 'normal' tactics already described. Movement was often on foot, usually in single file, and deployment was very slow, if indeed it was possible at all. Attacks had to be launched as best they could, and as visibility was bad and communications basic, commanding officers and even company commanders could often do little to control or influence the battle. In some ways the fighting resembled street fighting in Europe; the Japanese dug very extensively and made much use of overhead cover. They often defended positions literally to the last man, so that clearing an objective was a slow, dangerous and exhausting business involving hand-to-hand fighting and extensive use of grenades. Much of the country was completely unsuitable for tanks but when these could be got forward a troop, or on occasion even a single tank, was of great use in blasting the solid enemy bunkers.

Supporting fire tended to be rudimentary. Concentration of guns was difficult and observation often impossible, while transport problems imposed restrictions on the amount of ammunition available. Ideally the infantry liked to be only a few yards behind their supporting fire but poor observation often made this dangerous. The little 3.7-inch mountain guns were sufficiently accurate for this purpose although their shells were not highly lethal. The infantry three-inch mortar was a useful weapon in the jungle, but as it had a large beaten zone it was not possible to keep very close behind its bombs.

Flamethrowers were used on occasion, but the little manpack models had obvious fuel limitations. The type mounted on a universal carrier was the best, always provided that the vehicle could be got forward.

Defensive positions were usually close because the thick undergrowth made infiltration easy. Platoons, companies and battalions went into tight 'boxes' and all-round defence was the rule. Digging was limited to two-man slit trenches in overnight positions but if a more extensive stay was envisaged these were often connected up with crawl trenches. As there was relatively little risk of tank attack, mines were not employed; wire was usually too heavy to be transported, but positions were often garnished with belts of panjis, bamboo stakes about two feet (0.6 metres) long, split, sharpened and driven into the ground at an angle of 45 degrees towards the enemy. These were quick to make and put out, and a five-foot (1.5-metre) belt of them, perhaps reinforced with trip-wires made from creepers, would hold up the most determined charge at least long enough for the Bren guns, which formed the essential framework of any infantry defence, to take their toll.

The infantryman under attack had to be self-contained. His slit trench contained his food, his water, and his ammunition; it was his home, his castle, on occasion his latrine, and not infrequently his grave.

Transport was necessarily limited by the almost complete lack of anything except narrow game paths, so that reliance had to be placed on mules – and inevitably men's backs – and adequate supplies of all essentials had to be dumped forward if time permitted. As the basic defensive rule in Burma was to hold the high ground, and as the basic natural rule was that streams should be in the valleys, even water became a serious problem; at Kohima the ration at times was one pint (0.6 litres) a day for all purposes, not an over-generous allowance on which to fight in a hot climate. Very fortunately the technique of air supply had been well developed by then, and given a degree of air superiority it was possible to replenish beleagued troops on an extensive scale. Map reading was not easy and occasionally air drops went astray; when that happened it sometimes became necessary for the unfortunate infantry to have to fight a battle for their vital supplies of ammunition and food. A familiar feature of most defensive positions in Burma were the hundreds of parachutes festooning the trees.

It will be appreciated that these brief, bald descriptions of basic tactical developments are all that can be included in a book of this type, and the reader will well understand that they hardly do justice to the difficulties and dangers of the various operations mentioned.

So far this chapter has dealt with what may be classed as

'normal' battalions. There were however a number of variations on these caused by the need for certain specialist infantry units and these must now be considered.

Brief reference has already been made to the conversion of certain regiments to be machine gun battalions. Most of these had completed the changeover by 1938 and were organized on a basis of three machine gun companies, each of three platoons of four Vickers guns, and one anti-tank company of four platoons, each of four of the new two-pounder anti-tank guns which were just coming into production.

In 1942 the establishment was altered to include a company of the new 4.2-inch mortars, organized on a basis of four platoons of four mortars each, and when this occurred the title of this type of unit was changed to infantry support battalion. A platoon of Oerlikon 20-millimetre anti-aircraft guns was also added, but soon withdrawn. The battalion was largely an administrative organization for the next two years, the tactical subunit becoming the brigade support company of 12 Vickers guns and a platoon of 4.2-inch mortars, together with a proportion of the Oerlikons as long as they remained on the establishment; divisional support companies were also formed, consisting of 24 guns. In 1944 the battalion organization was reinstated, although even then the machine gun companies were usually detached to brigades. Soon after the end of the war the system was abandoned, and by 1946–7 all regular machine gun battalions had reverted to the normal infantry role.

The concept of armoured formations moving on different axes from infantry formations, and also often a considerable distance apart, soon made it clear that some integral close-support infantry would be required to seize and hold vital ground where tanks could not operate unsupported, to hold anti-tank obstacles, to provide local protection, to carry out close reconnaissance, and such other purely infantry tasks as might become necessary. Certain infantry battalions, most of them either of the Rifle Brigade or the 60th Rifles, were therefore converted to motor battalions, the first of them being the 1st Battalion The Rifle Brigade in 1937.

As mobility was of extreme importance, all ranks of a motor battalion were mounted in light vehicles, wheeled or tracked, with a reasonable cross-country performance. An armoured brigade consisted of three armoured regiments, and the structure of a motor battalion was designed to provide one motor company to each. In 1943 the establishment consisted of a battalion headquarters, a small H.Q. company with administrative personnel, signals and pioneers, three motor companies and a support company. A motor company had a headquarters, a scout platoon of

10 carriers, and three motor platoons, each with a headquarters and three sections of one non-commissioned officer and six men carried in a 15-hundredweight truck. The support element consisted of two platoons each of four six-pounder anti-tank guns, two platoons each of four medium machine guns, a mortar platoon with six three-inch mortars, and a motor platoon. The latter had the usual 15-hundredweight trucks but the remainder were all mounted in carriers. The total strength was 37 officers and 782 other ranks. As the war progressed some changes were naturally made, particularly as regards transport; by 1945 the motor companies were equipped with wheeled scout cars for the sections and two half-tracks for company headquarters. The scout cars were by then driven by Royal Army Service Corps drivers.

As companies often had to work independently they were as self-contained as possible and included their own administrative element; as they were intended to work dispersed, good communications were essential and wireless sets were provided down to section level. The large proportion of drivers and wireless operators meant that the actual assault strength of a company was quite small, so that care had to be taken not to give it tasks beyond its strength. An armoured division included an infantry brigade carried in troop-carrying vehicles in order to provide an immediate infantry back up on occasions when the size of the operation necessary looked like being outside the capacity of the motor company or battalion to handle.

In the early months of 1940 a number of independent infantry companies were formed to carry out seaborne raids on the coast of Europe and by June 1940 these had been grouped into larger units known as commandos. The original commandos were the irregular corps of Boer mounted riflemen who had fought the British in South Africa some 40 years earlier, and the new units adopted the title because they too were to be mobile raiding forces. It is possible that Mr. Churchill, himself a veteran of the Boer War, had some say in the matter.

The function of the commandos, all of whose members were selected volunteers, was to make seaborne raids on military targets on the European littoral. A surprise arrival, a short sharp battle, and a swift withdrawal was their usual method of operating, and because of this they had no need for any permanent administrative tail. The units consisted of little more than their personnel, their arms, and certain specialist equipment; in England all ranks even found their own private accommodation, and such transport and other items as they might need was improvised or borrowed as necessary. When, as later happened, units were sent abroad to the Mediterranean or the Far East some more permanent administrative arrangements naturally had to be made, but even so no commando ever encumbered itself more than was absolutely necessary.

The establishment of a commando was fairly simple. There was a commanding officer, a second-in-command, an adjutant, an intelligence officer, a signals officer and an administrative officer at commando headquarters, together with an R.S.M. and R.Q.M.S., a signal section, a small administrative section and a basic motor transport section, a total of six officers and 66 other ranks.

The fighting element consisted of five troops of three officers and 45 other ranks, each troop being broken down into two sections of an officer and 20 other ranks. These were armed and equipped basically as infantry but with a higher proportion of automatic weapons. In addition there was a heavy weapons troop with four medium machine guns, four three-inch mortars and a demolition squad, a total of three officers and 50 others. At various times in the war commando units were called upon to take their place in the line as ordinary infantry units. When this occurred they found that their administrative backing was insufficient, a problem which was solved by increasing their establishment, usually on a brigade basis. On these occasions they also found it necessary to ask for anti-tank guns and a proportion of jeeps and other light vehicles.

The commandos had some claim to have started airborne forces in the British Army, since in July 1940 Number 2 Commando were trained as parachutists and after a brief period under the title of Number 11 Special Air Service Battalion, eventually became the 1st Parachute Battalion in 1941. By the end, the total number of army commandos had risen to 10; these were all disbanded soon afterwards, although others, which had been formed by the Royal Marines, remained in permanent existence in what became in fact the prime function of that corps in the post-war period.

The Germans and the Russians both started experiments with parachute troops in the mid 1930s and by the outbreak of World War 2 had made good progress. The German troops of this type were so successful in the campaign in France and Flanders in 1940 that in June 1940 the British Prime Minister demanded a similar force 5,000 strong for offensive operations. Training started immediately, the first troops to undergo it being a commando, as already mentioned; a little over a year later a parachute brigade was in existence and more units were being trained. By the end of the war there were four parachute brigades, organized into two divisions.

Parachutists were all volunteers and in view of the very high standards demanded, the rejection rate was high. Battalions were organized on a similar establishment to that of a normal infantry battalion before 1942, i.e. four rifle companies (sometimes reduced to three), and a headquarters company which incorporated support weapons. Companies consisted of a headquarters of two officers and 12 others, and three platoons each of an officer and 36 others, platoons being similarly subdivided into three sections. Weapons were of normal infantry type and included a platoon of medium machine guns and one of three-inch mortars. In view of the problems which then existed over the dropping of heavier weapons, parachute troops were not normally intended to fight prolonged battles against normal land forces. The situation regarding support weapons was later eased by the development of gliders capable of carrying jeeps, artillery, and even light, tracked weapons. At this time there was no regular cadre of paratroops, all ranks being seconded. It was not until eight years after the end of the war, and therefore strictly outside the period covered by this book, that direct enlistment into the Parachute Regiment became possible, while all officers continued to be seconded until 1958.

A force which had close connections with the Parachute Regiment was the Special Air Service which was the brainchild of Lieutenant David Stirling of the Scots Guards. Stirling arrived in the Middle East with a commando in 1941 and seeing the vast size of the theatre of operations soon conceived the idea of raiding deep behind the enemy lines; instead of concentrating his force however, he considered it better to employ small parties dispersed. Their first parachute operation was a failure due to circumstances beyond their control. After that they changed their technique and were carried to their destination by units of the Long Range Desert Group until they had organized transport of their own.

Early in 1943 a complete regiment was formed, and by the end of the year this had risen to a brigade of three, which saw a great deal of service in Italy, France, Holland and Belgium. Its functions were to harrass rear areas, disrupt enemy troop movements, encourage and as far as possible guide partisan activities, and provide intelligence to the main armies. Unlike many of the somewhat unorthodox special forces formed during the war, the Special Air Service became a part of the regular army, two regular regiments remaining in service.

Although parachute troops were well suited for an initial assault they usually required a fairly quick back up, so in 1941 it was decided to convert certain infantry battalions to air landing battalions which could be flown in gliders to reinforce an initial attack by parachutists. The earliest gliders available were the Hotspurs which could only carry eight passengers, meaning that a force of any size was largely split up into penny packets. In 1942 however the new Horsa came into production; this was a very much larger craft which could carry up to 30 men or a jeep and an anti-tank gun, and once these became available it was possible to split a unit into reasonable loads based on a more or less normal fighting establishment. By the early months of 1943 the establishment was reasonably settled, with a battalion headquarters, four rifle companies each of four platoons, and a support company with signals, a platoon of four three-inch mortars, a reconnaissance platoon mounted on motorcycles or jeeps, and the pioneer platoon; in order to avoid an extra headquarter company the battalion administrative element was also included with it. In addition there was an anti-aircraft and anti-tank company comprising two platoons each of six six-pounder anti-tank guns and two equipped with Hispano guns. The four rifle companies were on a four platoon establishment and each company had two three-inch mortars of its own. Except for non-operational administrative purposes, the transport consisted entirely of jeeps and motorcycles and there were no carriers. This was substantially the establishment for the D-Day landings in June 1944.

Some organizational changes were made early in 1945 as a result of actual operational experiences. Rifle companies were reduced to three platoons each of an officer, a sergeant, and 28 others, and in addition to their normal arms and equipment each platoon had a light handcart. In the support company the anti-tank guns had been reduced to eight in two platoons and a medium machine gun platoon of four Vickers guns had been added. The mortars originally dispersed to companies had been centralized and formed into three platoons each of four. This organization was in operation at the time of the Rhine crossing in 1945 and remained substantially unchanged until the air landing battalions reverted to the normal infantry role at the end of the war.

In all there were two air-landing brigades formed, each of three battalions. Although they worked in close conjunction with the parachute forces their role was not confined to support, since they often carried out independent missions, landing their gliders near bridges and other vital points and capturing them independently. Unlike the Parachute Regiment, men of the air-portable battalions were not volunteers but normal battalions converted *en bloc*.

Some use was made of glider-borne troops by Wingate on his second expedition into Burma in 1944, the equivalent of a division being flown in to establish strongholds across the Japanese lines of communication. These not only acted as bases for offensive operations but also drew fierce and prolonged attacks, in which the Japanese sustained heavy casualties to no advantage.

Infantry battalions were also occasionally employed in other roles, notably as beach groups and anti-tank regiments, and certain Guards battalions even converted themselves into armoured regiments. As however they then, temporarily at any rate, ceased to be infantry in the true sense of the word, their role is strictly outside the scope of this book.

The complex needs of modern war made it essential that the soldier should be properly trained. Apart from the basic requirements of discipline, drill, and physical fitness he had to be able to handle a variety of weapons, motor vehicles, wireless sets and other complex items of equipment against a proper background of tactical knowledge. The old, easy days, when a recruit was taught basic drill and manual exercise and then pushed into the rear rank of a company to learn from his comrades as best he could had gone. Nor was there any time for the thorough, leisurely bringing on of the peacetime recruit.

One innovation of World War 2 was the introduction of battle drill. This was a laudable attempt to teach simple tactics on the parade ground with a view to training the soldier to react quickly and correctly when actually under fire. Basic drills were devised to cover the more common tactical situations likely to arise; once these were understood the instructor simply called out the situation, for example 'leading section under fire', upon which the soldiers under instruction carried out the appropriate movements, although inevitably in a somewhat stylized form, shouting out the details of what they were doing (in this case 'down, crawl, observe, aim, fire') as they did so.

It was never really of great value, mainly because inexperienced junior commanders tended to regard it as an end in itself, a panacea for all ills, regardless of the ground or the other numerous factors which necessarily influence minor tactics in battle. This is of course a personal view, based on the writer's own experience, but in his recollection he was by no means alone in holding it.

Infantry depots became infantry training centres on the outbreak of war in 1939 but they quickly proved to be too small. They often lacked adequate accommodation, range and training facilities for the numbers pressed on them, so that in 1941 they were grouped, usually in pairs but sometimes more, which economized on administrative staff and offered better facilities for specialized training.

In 1942 they became organizations for the basic instruction of recruits of all arms, who underwent eight weeks at them before going on to specialist training units. Special wings gave prospective infantrymen a further eight weeks of special-to-arm training before passing them on to a home-based battalion where they might gain more experience before being posted overseas.

At the outbreak of war there were already in existence a number of specialist training establishments which catered primarily for the Infantry. The oldest of these was the original School of Musketry, mention of which has been made earlier. This continued to function throughout under different titles, being known at the end of the war as the Hythe Wing of the Small Arms School. There was also a school at Netheravon, originally to instruct in the medium machine gun, but later expanded to cover all infantry support weapons and redesignated the Infantry Heavy Weapons School. Finally there came into existence in 1941 a general headquarters battle school, which was located at Barnard Castle with the object of teaching infantry tactics under realistically simulated war conditions; there was also a non-commissioned-officers' tactical wing at Warminster.

At the end of the war all these establishments were grouped together under the new title of the School of Infantry with its headquarters and tactical wings at Warminster. Barnard Castle was abandoned, and the Hythe Wing, which had been moved to Bisley as a wartime necessity, returned to its traditional home. The wing at Netheravon stayed where it was. The establishment of a School of Infantry was a welcomed and long overdue step forward, although the new arrangement was not wholly satisfactory from the geographical point of view.

The importance of the infantry in modern war was also recognized in 1943 by the establishment of a Director of Infantry. Until then infantry training had been supervised by the Director of Military Training, who was often not even an infantryman, so that this was another important and long overdue innovation.

Although this book is primarily concerned with the Infantry as a fighting arm, it may be as well to say a little about the different types of battalion as they existed in the early days of the war. In the first place there were the regular battalions; those overseas consisted almost entirely of serving soldiers, while those at home had been made up by regular reservists, sometimes as many as 50 per cent. Then there were the Territorial Army battalions of volunteer part-time soldiers with no more than a small training cadre of regulars. Lastly, as the war progressed, there were a variety of wartime units consisting chiefly of conscripts, who under the title of national servicemen were called up systematically in batches. In the nature of things there was a good deal of cross-posting between the various categories of battalion within a regiment so that in a surprisingly short time the distinctions were blurred. Regular battalions, especially those in the Far East which saw little fighting until half-way through the war, did perhaps retain a certain distinctive regular outlook, but in terms of operational capacity they were indistinguishable. There were other battalions too. In 1939 certain national defence companies were grouped in home defence battalions and affiliated to county regiments. They originally consisted of older men, unfit men, and young soldiers and as the need for home defence receded they tended to be phased out. Young soldiers' battalions were also formed; they consisted of prenational service volunteers, and as these reached maturity they were usually drafted on to an active battalion. Infantry holding battalions were also formed; their primary function was continuation training but they also dealt with a variety of soldiers, those medically unfit, returning from abroad, awaiting postings and other movements. In the early days some of them became service battalions, but by 1943 one had been linked to each infantry training centre and allotted the same number.

EPILOGUE

It is probable that by 1945 the British Infantry had passed its peak efficiency. The manpower shortage was being felt by the whole Army, and indeed by the whole country, for although casualties had not been nearly as high as those of 1914–18 they had certainly not been negligible. The Army alone had suffered well over half a million in killed and wounded and in the nature of things a disproportionately high percentage of these had fallen on the Infantry, who thus found themselves deprived of a great many leaders or at least potential leaders. The whole Army was suffering from war weariness, one of its manifestations being an unusually high desertion rate (notably in Italy) and again the Infantry, by virtue of its arduous role, had proved most susceptible to this offence. The few surviving prewar regular soldiers, many of them overpromoted, had been for too long overseas so that they, together indeed with the experienced wartime soldiers, were anxious only to get back to Britain and their families.

The new post-war National Service Army was originally planned to be a little over 300,000, but in the event a further 100,000 had to be made available in order to cope with numerous unforeseen tasks. Although the Infantry remained by far the most important arm its relative strength had declined considerably; at the outbreak of the war in 1939 it had numbered over half the total strength of the Army, but seven years later it had dropped to barely a fifth due to the enormously increased demand for other arms, and in particular technical services of all kinds.

The Cardwell system was by then virtually defunct. It had proved unequal to the demands and strains of major and prolonged wars (for which it had never been designed) but previously it had always been revived in peacetime. Although it had played a useful role in the past it was clearly too rigid a system for the post-war calls upon it, for the requirements were not for regular routine garrison duties but for extremely flexible reserves which could be moved around the world as necessity arose. In particular its chief *raison d'etre*, the need to find battalions for India, had almost gone, for the whole great subcontinent was about to find itself in the throes of a somewhat sudden (and hideously bloody) independence.

In October 1946 therefore the whole system was abandoned, the great bulk of infantry regiments being reduced to single battalions; as far as possible it was second battalions that went but this was largely a question of strategic availability. The term used for this process was not disbandment but suspended animation, with more than a hopeful hint of resuscitation in due course, but few regular infantrymen believed this. A few second battalions were in fact reraised briefly to meet the needs of the Korean war, but this was a strictly temporary arrangement.

In order to improve flexibility, the surviving regiments were grouped, usually in sixes, on either a geographical basis or by categories, e.g. light infantry, one battalion being detailed to relinquish its field force role and carry out the duties of a training centre. These groups (which soon changed their title to brigades) remained in existence, albeit with some readjustments, until 1967. The system of group training centres was done away with in 1951–2 in favour of the old system of regimental depots, a reversion which gave many infantrymen a brief (and wholly erroneous) hope, that things were going to revert to what they had been.

The severe reduction in the total number of battalions did not lead to redundancy at that stage. As far as officers were concerned, large numbers were required for extra-regimental employment on the staff or with colonial forces; even so there were times when major was the most common regular commissioned rank in a battalion; adjutants, company seconds-in-command and other appointments customarily held by captains were filled by field officers which made the promotion pyramid very odd and gave middle-piece officers little hopes for their future.

Further reductions were announced in 1957. National Service was to be abolished and the new all-regular Army would have to be reduced to its approximate recruiting potential. Over the next few years almost all the old infantry regiments disappeared from the Army List. Many were amalgamated in pairs to form new single-battalion regiments; in other cases the old brigades became 'large' regiments, usually shedding at least one battalion in the process, while the Cameronians, an awkward mixture of Scotsmen and riflemen, opted for disbandment with the same independence which had marked the regiment in a long and distinguished career since its formation in the seventeenth century.

These reductions, together with the rapid disappearance of the old colonial forces as colony after colony achieved inevitable (if premature) independence, led to a very considerable surplus of experienced middle-piece officers, warrant and non-commissioned officers, all of whom were retired prematurely with a modified pension and a modest capital sum usually referred to somewhat cynically as the 'golden bowler'. Perhaps fortunately the economic situation was then buoyant and most of these found suitable employment in the civilian market, which seems to have appreciated – perhaps rather to its own surprise – the previously unsuspected value of sound military training.

Regimental depots, those old cornerstones of the regimental system, were also swept away. They were of course uneconomical, but they had nevertheless given peripatetic battalions at least some semblance of a firm base.

By 1967 it had become clear that the old 'brigades' had become too small, and regiments were then grouped into 'divisions', usually of eight or nine battalions, which reinforced the dark suspicions of many infantrymen that the anonymous 'they', the tidy-minded planners who controlled their destinies, were moving inexorably towards the final goal of a corps of infantry. This was, and still is, an emotive subject, but it must be admitted that, sentiment apart, there are a good many cogent reasons for advocating such a new and revolutionary change, although the brief epilogue to an account of 300-odd years of the regimental system is hardly the place to enumerate them. Nevertheless there are infantrymen – sound regimental soldiers – who would argue that had the British Infantry resigned itself to such a change in 1946 (when the second battalions went) or in 1957 (when the butchery of the old Cardwell regiments began), it would have been a stronger and more cohesive arm than it now is.

The withdrawal from Aden in 1967 marked the end of a 22-year period in the role of what might properly be described as an imperial rearguard, in which the British Army had seen active service in Malaya, Korea, Egypt, Kenya, Cyprus, Arabia and Borneo, together with other bloodless, though not less arduous, services round the world. In spite of constant reductions and reorganizations the infantry, on whom the great brunt of the work fell, carried it out supremely well.

There was not however to be much respite even then, for the British Army was almost immediately deeply involved in internal security duties in Ulster, a role which they are still fulfilling with no apparent end in sight. Anyone who had suggested in 1963 that the next few years would see the British Army, and again principally the British Infantry, in action *in the United Kingdom* would have been laughed out of court. Yet it has happened uncomfortably close to home and may come closer yet. All that can be hoped is that successive governments may be brought to see the value of retaining a body of good infantry to meet unforseen requirements, as typified by the Falkland Islands campaign of 1982, rather than let the arm run down as a form of false economy. It is fatally easy to disband good infantry, but remarkably difficult to reraise it.

As this book has shown, the British Infantry is a flexible organization with an almost infinite capacity for survival against fearful odds. Nevertheless it must be nearing the lower limits of viability, and it would be sad indeed if the end finally came, not by annihilation in battle but at the stroke of some politician's pen.

BIBLIOGRAPHY

In order to write this book it has been necessary to read, or at least consult, a very large number of earlier works dealing with the subject so that a full bibliography would be a long one. On consideration however there appeared to be but little advantage in listing hundreds of books when the bulk of them would be for all practical purposes inaccessible to the general reader for whom this book is primarily intended. This being so it seemed best to compromise by including a selected list of books which have proved useful, and which are in the main sufficiently modern and general to be reasonably easily obtained. There are separate sections for handbooks and pamphlets, and regimental histories.

Aldington, R. *Wellington*, (London, 1946)
Baden-Powell, B.F.S. *War in practice*, (London, 1903)
Baker, E. *Remarks on the rifle*, 11th edn. (London, 1835)
Balck (translated by Kreuger, W.H.) *Infantry Tactics*, vol I (London, 1911)
Bell, G. *Rough notes by an old soldier*, (London, 1867)
Biddulph, K. *Lord Cardwell at the war office*, (London, 1904)
Blackmore, H. *British military firearms* (London, 1961)
Blood, B. *Four score years and ten*, (London, 1933)
Boguslawski, A.V. (translated by Graham) *Tactical deductions for the war of 1870–71*, (London, 1872)
Bond, B. *The Victorian army and the staff college*, (London, 1972)
Bunbury, H. *Passages in the Great War with France*, (London, 1927)
Burne, A.H. and Young, P. *The Great Civil War*, (London, 1959)
Callwell, C.E. *Small wars; their principle and practice*, (London, 1899)
Callwell, C.E. *Tactics of today*, (Edinburgh, 1900)

Chandler, D. *The art of warfare in the age of Marlborough*, (London, 1976)

Clery, C. *Minor tactics*, (London, 1880)

Clifford, H. *Letters and sketches from the Crimea*, (London, 1956)

Cole, D.H. and Priestley, E.C. *An outline of British military history*, (London, 1937)

Colville, H.E. *History of the Sudan campaign*, (London, 1889)

Costello, E. *Adventures of a soldier*, (London, 1852)

Craster, J.M. (ed.) *Fifteen rounds a minute*, (London, 1976)

Cruikshank, C.G. *Elizabeth's army*, (London, 1946)

Doyle, A. Conan *The Great Boer War*, (London, 1903)

Dunlop, J.K. *The development of the British Army 1889–1914*, (London, 1938)

Earle, E.M. (ed.) *The makers of modern strategy*, (Princeton, 1952)

Edmonds, J.E. *History of the Great War*, (London, 1920–21)

Firth, C.H. *Cromwell's army*, (London, 1902)

Fortescue, J. *History of the British Army*, (London, 1910–30)

Fortescue, J. *Wellington*, (London, 1925)

Freemantle, T.F. *The book of the rifle*, (London, 1901)

Fuller, J.F.C. *Armament and history*, (London, 1946)

Fuller, J.F.C. *The conduct of war*, (London, 1962)

Fuller, J.F.C. *British light infantry in the eighteenth century*, (London, n.d. (c. 1926))

Fuller, J.F.C. *Grant and Lee*, (London, 1933)

Fuller, J.F.C. *Sir John Moore's System of Training*, (London, n.d. (c. 1925))

Furneaux, R. *The Zulu War*, (London, 1963)

Glover, M. *Wellington's army*, (Newton Abbot, 1977)

Goodenough, W.H. and Dalton, J.C. *The army book for the British Empire*, (London, 1893)

Gwynn, C.W. *Imperial policing*, (London, 1934)

Hobart, F. *Pictorial history of the machine gun*, (London, 1971)

Horne, R. *A precis of modern tactics*, (London, 1882)

Hutchinson, G.S. *Machine guns*, (London, 1938)

Hamer, W.S. *The British Army 1885–1905*, (Oxford, 1970)

Harris (ed. Curling), *Recollections of Rifleman Harris*, (London, 1848)

Hay, I. *The British infantryman*, (Harmondsworth, 1942)

Henderson, G.F.R. *The science of war*, (London, 1919)

Heneker, W.C.G. *Bush warfare*, (London, 1907)

Hine, H.W.L. *Stray military papers*, (London, 1897)

James, C. *Military dictionary*, 3rd edn. (London, 1810)

James, D. *Lord Roberts*, (London, 1954)

Johnstone, H.M. *A history of tactics*, (London, 1906)

Kane, R. *The campaigns of King William and Queen Anne*, (London, 1745)

Kincaid, J. *Adventures in the Rifle Brigade*, (London, 1830)

Kraft, Prince Zu H.I. *Letters on infantry*, translation 2nd edn. (London, 1892)

Laffin, J. *Tommy Atkins*, (London, 1966)

Lawrence, W. (ed. Banks) *Autobiography of Sgt William Lawrence*, (London, 1886)

Liddell Hart, B.H. *History of the Second World War*, (London, 1970)

Liddell Hart, B.H. *Sherman*, (London, 1933)

Lloyd, E.M. *A review of the history of infantry*, (London, 1908)

Longford, E. *Wellington, the years of the sword*, (London, 1969)

Longstaff, F.V. and Atteridge, A.H. *The book of the machine gun*, (London, 1917)

Luvaas, J. *The education of an army*, (Chicago, 1964)

Macdougall, P.L. *The theory of war*, 3rd edn. (London, 1862)

MacMunn, G. *The Indian Mutiny in perspective*, (London, 1931)

Mahan, A.J. *The influence of sea power upon history*, (London, 1890)

Malleson, G.B. *The Indian Mutiny of 1857*, (London, 1891)

Maude, F.N. *Notes on the evolution of infantry tactics*, (London, 1905)

Maurice, F. and Arthur, G. *The life of Lord Wolseley*, (London, 1924)

Maurice, F. *War*, (London, 1891)

Maurice, J.F. *The diary of Sir John Moore*, (London, 1904)

Marbot, Baron de *Memoirs of Baron de Marbot*, (London, 1907)

Mayne, C.B. *Infantry fire tactics*, (London, n.d. (c. 1889))

Mayne, C.B. *The infantry weapon and its use in war*, (London, 1903)

McElwee, W. *The art of war; Waterloo to Mons*, (London, 1974)

McGuffie, T.H. (compiler) *Rank and file*, (London, 1964)

Montgomery of Alamein *A history of warfare*, (London, 1968)

Myatt, F. *The Soldier's trade*, (London, 1974)

Myatt, F. *Nineteenth century firearms*, (London, 1979)

Napier, W. *The Peninsular War*, (London, 1834–40)

Oman, C. *A history of the art of war; the Middle Ages*, (London, 1898)

Oman, C. *A history of the art of war in the XVI century*, (London, 1937)

Oman, C. *A history of the Peninsular War*, (London, 1902–31)

Oman, C. *Wellington's army*, (London, 1912)

Parker, R. *Memories of the most memorable military transactions*, (Dublin, 1746)

Parkman, *Montcalm and Wolfe*, (London, 1884)
Pridham, C.H.B. *Superiority of fire*, (London, 1945)
Reitz, D. *Commando*, (London, 1929)
Reynolds, E.G.B. *The Lee Enfield rifle*, (London, 1960)
Richards, S.F. *Old soldiers never die*, (London, 1933)
Roads, C.H. *The British soldier's firearm*, (London, 1964)
Roberts of Kandahar *Forty-one years in India*, (London, 1897)
Rogers, H.C.B. *The British Army of the eighteenth century*, (London, 1977)
Russell, W.H. *My Indian Mutiny diary*, (London, 1966)
Russell, W.H. (ed. Bentley) *Despatches from the Crimea*, (London, 1957)
Sheppard, E.W. *A short history of the British Army*, (London, 1926)
Shipp, J. *Memoirs of the military career of John Shipp*, (London, 1829)
Slim, W. *Defeat into victory*, (London, 1956)
Smith, H. *Autobiography of Sir Harry Smith*, (London, 1901)
Sommer, D. *Haldane of Cloan*, (London, 1960)
Steevens, C.W. *With Kitchener to Khartoum*, (London, n.d.)
Surtees, W. *Twenty-five years in the Rifle Brigade*, (London, 1833)
Swinson, A. *Kohima* (London, 1966)
Turner, E.S. *Gallant gentlemen*, (London, 1956)
Turner, J. *Pallas Armata*, (London, 1670)
Wagner, A.L. *Organisation and tactics*, 4th edn. (Kansas City, 1901)
Waters, W.H.H. (translater) *German official account of the war in South Africa*, (London, 1904)
Weller, J. *Weapons and tactics*, (London, 1966)
Weller, J. *Wellington in the Peninsula*, (London, 1962)

Handbooks and Pamphlets

These are arranged alphabetically by titles, since authors names are rarely given in official publications. They are included here in the case of semi-official publications only.

Artillery Notes No 6 (Trench Mortars) March 1916
Artillery Notes No 6 (Trench Mortars) June 1916
Classbook for the School of Musketry, Wilford, E.C. (Hythe, 1861)
Combined training 1902
Company training, Haking, R.C.B. (London, 1913)
Eight lectures on musketry, Watson, K. (Hythe, 1862)
Elements of war, Hood, N. (London, 1803)
Field exercise 1824 (Torrens)
Field exercise 1862, 1870, 1877, 1884

Field service manual 1914 (Infantry Battalion Expeditionary Force)
Field service pocket book 1914
Field service regulations 1909
Field service regulations 1935
Handbook for Hythe, Busk, H. (London, 1860)
Handbook for the 3.7-inch trench howitzer 1916
Handbook for the Stokes trench mortar 1916
Infantry drill, 1889, 1892, 1893, 1896
Infantry manual 1857
Infantry training 1902
Infantry training vol. 1, 1922
Infantry training (training for war) 1937
Instruction of musketry 1856
Knowledge for war, Lake, B.C. (London, n.d. (c. 1916))
Light infantry officer, The, Cooper, T.H. (London, 1806) (there is a facsimile reproduction of 1970)
Manual and platoon exercise 1923
Military Training Pamphlet No 23 1941 (The infantry battalion and the attack)
Musketry exercises (provisional) 1904
Musketry regulations part 1 1909
Musketry regulations part II 1910
Notes for commanding officers, Students at the Senior Officer's School (Aldershot, 1917)
Principles of military movements, Dundas, D. (1788)
Regulations for conducting the musketry instruction of the army 1867
Regulations for conducting the musketry instruction of the army 1870
Regulations for the Rifle Corps, Coote-Manningham (1800)
Rifle exercise and musketry instruction 1874
Rifle exercise and musketry instruction 1891
Rifle and how to use it, The, Busk, H. (London, 1860)
Rules and regulations for the formation, field exercises and movement of His Majesty's Forces, Dundas, D. (London, 1792)
Soldier's pocket-book, The, 5th edn. Wolseley, G. (London, 1886)
Small arms training 1924, vol. I
Small arms training 1931, vols. I, II, III
Treatise on military discipline, 2nd edn. Bland, H. (London, 1727)

Regimental Histories

Although practically all infantry regimental histories have been consulted, only those of particular interest have been listed.

Buffs, Historical records of the, 5 vols. Knight, K.H. and others (London, 1923–51)

Cap of honour (Gloucester Regiment), Daniell, D.S. (London, 1951)

Grenadier Guards, History of, 2 vols. Hamilton, F.W. (London, 1874)

Kings Own, The, 3 vols. Cooper, L.I. (London, 1939)

Lancashire Fusiliers, History of the XX Regiment, Smyth, B. (London, 1889)

Life of a regiment, (Gordon Highlanders) 5 vols. Greenhill Gardyne, C. (London, 1929)

Northamptonshire Regiment, Gurney, R. (Aldershot, 1935)

Queen's, History of the Second, 7 vols. Davis, J. (1887 onwards)

Royal Inniskilling Fusiliers, Regimental History Committee (London, 1934)

Royal Scots, Regimental records of the, Leask, J.C. and McCance, H.M. (Dublin, 1915)

Welch Regiment part 1, The, Whitehorn, A.C. (Cardiff, 1931)

Worcestershire Regiment, XXIX, Everard, A. (Worcester, 1891)

INDEX

Certain recurring subjects are indexed under the four main headings of Battalions, Regiments, Tactics, and Weapons. Battles and campaigns which have provided useful lessons are in many cases indexed under Tactics.

224